Life Lived, Reading the Word

Daily Teachable Moments

Paula Bramlett

Copyright © 2018 by Paula Bramlett

All rights reserved

Published by Christian Book Press

ISBN-10: 1-948153-02-5

ISBN-13: 978-1-948153-02-7

All rights reserved. This book or any portion thereof may not be reproduced or used in any manner whatsoever without the express written permission of the publisher except for the use of brief quotations in a book review.

PREFACE

Legacy. This word has been in the back of my mind for several years. I looked it up in the dictionary to get the real and whole meaning of the word: *Something handed down from an ancestor or predecessor from the past.* An explanation given was: a legacy of religious freedom. This was the great gift from God to America, since its foundation.

It was God's Spirit within me that inspired me to leave 'my legacy,' here and now - a '365 devotional;' for my children, grandchildren, and even great grandchildren. They are all gifts from God, to my husband and me.

This is not about me but what God has allowed me to remember how He has guided and sustained me all of my life with His love, mercy and grace. He is with me always.

For any reader, it is my desire that one would meditate on God's Word given and written out each day. I believe this is so important to read His Word daily and not just skip over a Scripture reference like I have done so many times when reading devotionals.

If you read anything in this book, read the Scriptures. They are straight from the heart of God to you – from His Holy Word.

CONTENTS

JANUARY 6

FEBRUARY 38

MARCH 72

APRIL 106

MAY 142

JUNE 178

JULY 210

AUGUST 242

SEPTEMBER 276

OCTOBER 308

NOVEMBER 340

DECEMBER 374

JANUARY

FLOWERS IN THE WEEDS

<u>I Peter 1:24, 25</u>
For, All flesh is as grass, And all the glory thereof as the flower of grass. The grass withereth, and the flower falleth: But the Word of the Lord abideth forever.

JANUARY 1

HAPPY, HAPPY NEW YEAR

Have you heard the **Good News**?
God is not dead!
God is the same; yesterday, today and forever! God promises never to leave us or forsake us. God is a Friend that sticks closer than a brother Proverbs 18:24 (how a brother should be). And there is so much more!

Our Journey Together Begins

Exodus 33:14
My presence shall go with thee, and I will give thee rest.

Hebrews 13: 8
Jesus Christ the same yesterday, and today, and forever.

Isaiah 57:15
For thus saith the high and lofty One that inhabiteth eternity, Whose Name is Holy; I dwell in the high and holy place, With Him also that is of a contrite and humble spirit, to revive the spirit of the humble, and to revive the heart of the contrite ones.

John 17:3
And this is life eternal, that they might know Thee the only true God, and Jesus Christ, Whom Thou hast sent.

Jeremiah 10:10
But the Lord is the true God, He is the living God, and an everlasting King: at His wrath the earth shall tremble, and the nations shall not be able to abide His indignation.

Psalms 90:2
Before the mountains were brought forth, or ever Thou hadst formed the earth and the world, even from everlasting to everlasting, Thou art God.

JANUARY 2

GOD'S DEAR CHILDREN

What a wonderful PICTURE of a TRUTH!

We can become a child of God – the very God of Creation! A child of the Heavenly Father – Abba Father.

Galatians 4:6
And because ye are sons, God hath sent forth the Spirit of His Son into your hearts, crying, Abba, Father.

Even as a very young child, I understood God's love for me through His Son, Jesus. From there God taught me through His Holy Spirit what I needed to know as I grew up into maturity, Spiritually. We all can know Him, no matter the age, what He has done for us through our own will to desire to know Him. Just like physical food, we need God's "food," His Word, to help us grow, day by day. God knows all about us, even our weaknesses and yet He loves us so, God gave Himself for us.

Matthew 18:3
And said, Verily I say unto you, Except ye be converted, and become as little children, ye shall not enter into the kingdom of heaven.

Romans 8:15
For ye have not received the spirit of bondage again to fear; but ye have received the Spirit of adoption, whereby we cry, Abba, Father.

Galatians 3:26
For ye are all the children of God by faith in Christ Jesus.

Ephesians 5:1
Be ye therefore followers of God, as dear children.

I Thessalonians 5:5
Ye are all the children of light, and the children of the day: we are not of the night, nor of darkness.

JANUARY 3

SEEK and FIND

Remember back to childhood and recall all the times you enjoyed playing "Hide and Seek." There were times when you could not find the "hider!" But you kept on seeking anyway. Here, God is not hiding, but He asks us to "seek" Him and promises us that we will "find" Him. God even provides us with help – His Holy Spirit! A desire on our part to seek God is proof that you believe there is a God and you want to know Him. He will not disappoint you!

Job 23:3
Oh that I knew where I might find Him!

Isaiah 26:9
With my soul have I desired Thee in the night; yea, with my spirit within me will I seek Thee early:

Isaiah 34:16
Seek ye out of the book of the Lord, and read:

Matthew 6:33
But seek ye first the Kingdom of God, and His righteousness; and all these things shall be added unto you.

Luke 11:9
And I (Jesus) say unto you, Ask, and it shall be given you; seek, and ye shall find; knock, and it shall be opened unto you.

Proverbs 8:17
I love them that love Me; and those that seek Me early shall find Me. And ye shall seek Me, and find Me, when ye shall search for Me with all your heart.

Isaiah 58:2
Yet they seek Me daily, and delight to know My ways

JANUARY 4

BE STILL and KNOW

Do you find it hard to just sit still and do nothing in quietness? With all the noise in the world, it is almost impossible to shut it all out. We are taught at school and home, from an early age, that we are wasting time or being lazy if we are not busy doing something. Laziness may be true sometimes, but usually we are so busy with work, family, friends, entertainment, listening to loud music, iPhones, emails, Twitter, YouTube, etc.; that we don't know how to: "**_Be still_, and _know_** that I am God" (Psalms 46:10).

There is no better way to know Him!

Jeremiah 24:7
And I will give them an heart to know Me, that I am the Lord: and they shall be My people, and I will be their God: for they shall return unto Me with their whole heart.

Psalms 23:2
He maketh me to lie down in green pastures: He leadeth me beside the still waters.

Psalms 143:8
Cause me to hear Thy loving kindness in the morning; for in Thee do I trust: cause me to know the way wherein I should walk; for I lift up my soul unto Thee.

Ecclesiastes 7:25
I applied mine heart to know, and to search, and to seek out wisdom, and the reason of things, and to know the wickedness of folly, even of foolishness and madness:

Proverbs 1:2
To know wisdom and instruction; to perceive the words of understanding;

JANUARY 5

FAITH GROWS

When we look at any new shoot on a plant or tree, we have faith that it is naturally growing daily even though we can't "see" it. If it is dying, then we know it must need something like food or water. God uses this same illustration to teach us His **TRUTHS** about our Spiritual growth. It takes our **FAITH** for us to grow in our lives - to know it is taking place even though we may not "see" or "feel" it. God has given us this insight and encouragement along our way as He guides and directs us with His Word and with the aid of His Holy Spirit. We also need His "food" and "water" to keep us healthy, Spiritually. As our **FAITH** grows we can know about God's love and grace for us, and "see" a difference in our lives.

Hebrews 11:1
Now faith is the substance of things hoped for, the evidence of things not seen.

Hebrews 12:2
Looking unto Jesus the author and finisher of our faith;

Matthew 8:26
And He (Jesus) saith unto them, Why are ye fearful, O ye of little faith?

Luke 17:5
And the apostles said unto the Lord, Increase our faith.

John 15:5
I am the Vine, ye are the branches: He that abideth in Me, and I in him, the same bringeth forth much fruit: for without Me ye can do nothing.

Romans 10:17
So then faith cometh by hearing, and hearing by the Word of God.

JANUARY 6

ABIDE IN ME

"**Abiding**" is a matter of our choice - giving up our will to what God wants for us. Mentally, we know this is where we desire to be and it would be so grand to constantly abide with Him, but often we lose sight and concentration on Him through our own human efforts and the events that surround us. So today, be aware and alert when you leave or are not thinking about His presence.

<u>Psalms 91:1, 2</u>
He that dwelleth in the secret place of the Most High shall abide under the shadow of the Almighty. I will say of the Lord, He is my refuge and my fortress: my God; in Him will I trust.

<u>John 15:4</u>
Abide in Me, and I in you. As the branch cannot bear fruit of itself, except it abide in the Vine;

<u>I John 2:24, 25</u>
Let that therefore abide in you, which ye have heard from the beginning. If that which ye have heard from the beginning shall remain in you, ye also shall continue in the Son, and in the Father. And this is the promise that He hath promised us, even eternal life.

<u>I John 2:28</u>
And now, little children, abide in Him; that, when He shall appear, we may have confidence, and not be ashamed before Him at His coming.

<u>II Timothy 2:13</u>
If we believe not, <u>yet He abideth faithful</u>: He cannot deny Himself. Being born again, not of corruptible seed, but of incorruptible, by the Word of God, which liveth and abideth forever.

JANUARY 7

I AM THE VINE

Have you ever observed a Vine over time? This is another example of how God illustrates Himself and His people as such; Vine and Branches (with leaves, fruit). My children have a "Wandering Jew" plant which is amazing. It grows so fast you can almost see it from day to day but the branches need pruning often to keep it under control and from growing wild. In this observation, we are observing how **JESUS** is the **VINE**. We know in our hearts here is where we should abide and be pruned; but have you ever wondered why **JESUS** is called the Vine (out of the root of Jesse – a Jew: born of a virgin)? Take a look below and see how beautiful this picture is and where we stand.

Isaiah 11:1, 2, 4, 5 *(Prophetic picture of Christ)*
And there shall come forth a rod (JESUS) out of the stem of Jesse, and a Branch shall grow out of His roots:
And the spirit of the Lord shall rest upon Him, the spirit of wisdom and understanding, the spirit of counsel and might, the spirit of knowledge and of the fear of the Lord;
But with righteousness shall He judge the poor, and reprove with equity for the meek of the earth: and He shall smite the earth with the rod of His mouth, and with the breath of His lips shall He slay the wicked. And righteousness shall be the girdle of His loins, and faithfulness the girdle of His reins.

Romans 15:12
And again, Esaias saith, There shall be a Root of Jesse, and He (JESUS) that shall rise to reign over the Gentiles; in Him shall the Gentiles trust.

John 15:1, 4
I (JESUS) am the true Vine, and My Father (GOD) is the Husbandman. Abide in Me, and I in you. As the branch cannot bear fruit of itself . . .

JANUARY 8

PUT ON

Often, when I think of "Putting On," I immediately think of clothing. You have probably heard that when a mother is cold, she tells her children to put on a sweater or coat as they leave the house? Well, garments are so important to our society today – the right style or uniform. We are told our dress, style and accessories are so important to make a good first impression so that we can get ahead in this world. Clothing over the centuries has drastically changed for the masses and the powerful; and clothes then and now tell us at a glance - Who is who; or who we are pretending to be. God's Word teaches us a different view! The many other things to "Put On" while walking this earth with Him – The King of kings and Lord of lords!

<u>I Samuel 16:7</u>
. . . for the Lord seeth not as man seeth; for man looketh on the outward appearance, but the Lord looketh on the heart.

<u>Romans 13:12, 14</u>
. . . and let us put on the armor of light. Put ye on the Lord Jesus Christ, and make not provision for the flesh, to fulfil the lusts thereof.

<u>Galatians 3:26, 27</u>
For ye are all the children of God by faith in Christ Jesus. For as many of you as have been baptized into Christ have <u>put on Christ</u>.

<u>Ephesians 4:24</u>
And that ye put on the new man, which after God is created in righteousness and true holiness.

<u>Ephesians 6:11</u>
Put on the whole armor of God, that ye may be able to stand against the wiles of the devil.

JANUARY 9

OMNIPOTENT, OMNIPRESENT, OMNISCIENT

The **Attributes** of God are important to knowing Him. Teach them to your children early so they too know these awesome words even though they will understand them better later on. Let's begin with:

OMNIPOTENT – All Powerful is our God!
Revelation 19:6
For the Lord God Omnipotent reigneth. **Hallelujah.**

First, know and believe in you heart that this is true

Mark 22:24
Let us not err by not knowing the Scriptures, nor the power of God.

I Chronicles 29:11
Thine, O Lord, is the greatness, and the power, and the glory, and the victory, and the majesty: for all that is in the heaven and in the earth is Thine; Thine is the kingdom, O Lord, and Thou art exalted as Head above all.

Job 37:23
Touching the Almighty, we cannot find Him out: He is excellent in power, and in judgment, and in plenty of justice: He will not afflict.

Isaiah 40:26
Lift up your eyes on high, and behold who hath created these things, that bringeth out their host by number: he calleth them all by names by the greatness of his might, for that he is strong in power; not one faileth.

Matthew 9:6
But that ye may know that the Son of man hath power on earth to forgive sins,

JANUARY 10

OMNIPOTENT, **OMNIPRESENT**, OMNISCIENT

Continuing . . . to know how important it is to know the **Attributes** of God! **Secondly:**

OMNIPRESENT – Everywhere Present

Hebrews 13:5, 6
I will never leave thee, nor forsake thee. So that we may boldly say, The Lord is my helper, and I will not fear what man shall do unto me.

Matthew 26:64
Hereafter shall ye see the Son of man <u>sitting on the right hand</u> of power, and coming in the clouds of heaven.

John 10:18
No man taketh it (My life) from Me, but I lay it down of Myself. I have power to lay it down, and I have power to take it again.

Romans 1:20
For the <u>invisible things of Him from the creation</u> of the world are clearly seen, being understood by the things that are made, even His eternal power and Godhead;

Romans 9:17
. . . and that My Name might be declared <u>throughout all the earth</u>.

Romans 15:13
Now the God of hope <u>fill you</u> with all joy and peace in believing, that ye may abound in hope, through the power of the Holy Ghost.

I Peter 1:5
Who are kept by the power of God through faith unto salvation ready <u>to be revealed in the last time</u>.

JANUARY 11

OMNIPOTENT, OMNIPRESENT, **OMNISCIENT**

Continuing . . . to know how important it is to know the **Attributes** of God! **Thirdly:**

OMNISCIENT – All knowing

Genesis 2:9
And out of the ground the Lord God made to spring up every tree that is pleasant to the sight and good for food. The tree of life was in the midst of the garden, and the tree of the knowledge of good and evil.

Numbers 35:31
. . . and He has filled him with the Spirit of God, with skill, with intelligence, with knowledge, and with all craftsmanship,

I Samuel 2:3
Talk no more so very proudly, let not arrogance come from your mouth; for the Lord is a God of knowledge, and by Him actions are weighed.

Proverbs 2:4 - 6
. . . if you seek it like silver and search for it as for hidden treasures, then you will understand the fear of the Lord and find the knowledge of God. For the Lord gives wisdom; from His mouth come knowledge and understanding.

Ephesians 3:19
. . . to know the love of Christ that surpasses knowledge, that you may be filled with all the fullness of God.

Revelation 11:17
Saying, We give thee thanks, O Lord God Almighty, which art, and wast, and art to come; because Thou hast taken to Thee Thy great power, and hast reigned.

JANUARY 12

ON A HIGH

We have all heard, "don't be so Heavenly minded so that you are no earthly good!"

I'd like to say, if you really want a "**High,**" ask God to help you to be more Heavenly minded! Why? When you think of Heaven, you can't help but think of our God! Then you will be ready to be earthly good, while He still allows you to be here on His earth. Think on our Creator and who He really is. He created the whole world, universe and all that is therein. And God has thoughts of peace towards us and not of evil, so you can go around doing good just as Jesus did. What a God – our Creator!

Genesis 1:14, 15
And God said, Let there be lights in the firmament of the heaven to divide the day from the night; and let them be for signs, and for seasons, and for days, and years: . . . And God made two great lights; the greater light to rule the day, and the lesser light to rule the night: He made the stars also.

Job 22:12
Is not God in the height of heaven? and behold the height of the stars, how high they are!

Psalms 8:1, 3, 4
O Lord our Lord, how excellent is Thy Name in all the earth! Who hast set Thy glory above the heavens. When I consider Thy heavens, the work of Thy fingers, the moon and the stars, which Thou hast ordained; What is man, that Thou art mindful of him?

Isaiah 40:12
Who hath measured the waters in the hollow of His hand, and meted out heaven with the span, and comprehended the dust of the earth in a measure, and weighed the mountains in scales, and the hills in a balance?

JANUARY 13

TREASURES

God in His mercy and loving-kindness has given us many treasures here on earth. Look around and see what He has done for you. He also in His wisdom has given us the opportunity for us, to build up **Treasure** in His Heaven. Look ahead - to Heaven. Are we so earth bound and planning our own treasures here on earth that we overlook storing up **Treasures** in Heaven? This is very short-sighted and Jesus had something to say about this.

Matthew 6:21
For where your treasure is, there will your heart be also.

Matthew 12:35, 36
. . . for out of the abundance of the heart the mouth speaketh. A good man out of the good treasure of the heart bringeth forth good things:

Matthew 19:21
Jesus said unto him, If thou wilt be perfect, go and sell that thou hast, and give to the poor, and thou shalt have treasure in heaven: and come and follow Me.

Luke 12:20, 21
But God said unto him, Thou fool, this night thy soul shall be required of thee: then whose shall those things be, which thou hast provided? So is he that layeth up treasure for himself, and is not rich toward God.

I Timothy 6:19
Laying up in store for themselves a good foundation against the time to come, that they may lay hold on eternal life.

Isaiah 33:6
And wisdom and knowledge shall be the stability of thy times, and strength of salvation: the fear of the Lord is his treasure.

JANUARY 14

STUDY
To KNOW God's Word – HIS TRUTH

No matter how old we are we need to keep studying and learning. Especially, **Study** the Word of God. It is He that sustains us each day. Ask anyone over 80. It takes courage and strength to face each day; health wise, etc. Some can no longer read or hear, but depend on what they learned in the past from His Word, more than ever before. So now is the time to study, study, study and learn. Know that there is a difference between **Study** and just reading. Ask for wisdom as you read God's Word.

II Timothy 2:15
Study to shew thyself approved unto God, a workman that needeth not to be ashamed, rightly dividing the word of truth.

John 17:17
Sanctify them through Thy TRUTH: Thy Word is TRUTH.

Hebrews 11:6
. . . He is a rewarder of them that diligently seek Him.

John 7:16
My (Jesus) doctrine is not Mine, but His that sent Me.

I John 3:2
Beloved, now are we the sons of God, and it doth not yet appear what we shall be: but we KNOW that, when He shall appear, we shall be like Him; for we shall see Him as He is. And every man that hath this hope in him purifieth himself, even as He is pure.

I John 5:20
And we know that the Son of God is come, and hath given us an understanding, that we may KNOW Him that is true, and we are in Him that is true, even in His Son Jesus Christ. This is the true God, and eternal life.

JANUARY 15

BIRTHDAYS

Most of us like celebrating Birthdays. Some of us even go on trips with family or friends to make it even greater. However, we had no choice by whom, where or when we would be born. But God knew all about you! Being born is a gift. Without our being born we could not anticipate being with our Creator for all eternity. Thus, the most important **Birth** on earth was **the Birth of Jesus Christ**.

His Birth changed the whole world from death to life eternal. He brought with Him the plan of redemption that paid our sin debt through His death on the cross, and His resurrection to give us eternal life. Because He loved us so, He showed to us His marvelous mercy, grace, and forgiveness for our sins. **Now** we have been given the choice to receive this New Birth! We all have a free will to choose – Life in Christ, or death in our sin. Choose **LIFE**. – **Born Again to a New Life in Christ!**

Isaiah 9:6
For unto us a child is born, unto us a Son is given: and the government shall be upon His shoulder: and His name shall be called Wonderful, Counsellor, The mighty God, The everlasting Father, The Prince of Peace.

Psalms 127:3-5
Lo, children are an heritage of the Lord: and the fruit of the womb is his reward. As arrows are in the hand of a mighty man; so are children of the youth. Happy is the man that hath his quiver full of them:

Ecclesiastes 11:5
As thou knowest not what is the way of the spirit, nor how the bones do grow in the womb of her that is with child: even so thou knowest not the works of God who maketh all.

JANUARY 16

ETERNITY – FOR EVER

Have you <u>ever</u> used the word "<u>ever</u>" in a sentence? I'm sure you have, we all have. Were you just thinking of your lifetime or exaggerating? I recall saying to my children, "Don't you ever do that again," and probably with anger. How can we even imagine or comprehend "For Ever" (eternity)? We cannot see it! It is a God thing. Only God could create eternity and know everything about it! It takes faith on our part to believe Him. God tells us, His Word will stand "For Ever" (eternity)! Believe it or not – Our choice! We can count on all that we find and read in Scripture to be true. God does not lie. Believe His blessings and goodness, and His warnings - the good and the bad; His forgiveness, and His judgments; His love and mercy, and His wrath.

<u>Psalms 119:89, 90</u>
Forever, O Lord, Thy word is settled in heaven. Thy faithfulness is unto all generations: Thou hast established the earth, and it abideth.

<u>Jeremiah 31:3</u>
The Lord hath appeared of old unto me, saying, Yea, I have loved thee with an everlasting love: therefore with loving kindness have I drawn thee.

<u>Exodus 15:18</u>
The Lord shall reign for ever and ever.

<u>John 10:28</u>
And I give unto them eternal life; and they shall never perish, neither shall any man pluck them out of My hand.

<u>Romans 5:21</u>
So that, as sin reigned in death, grace also might reign through righteousness leading to eternal life through Jesus Christ our Lord.

JANUARY 17

LEARN OF ME

Jesus attached a promise to this command.

<u>Matthew 11:29</u>.
Learn of Me. Ye shall find rest unto your souls.

How can we help but not want to know the One who gave up His life for us? Even **while we were yet sinners!** (Romans 5:8). We need to come to Him before we can learn and know Him. Just as it was told of Timothy in Paul's book in the Bible, I can also testify and be so thankful that from a child I was taught God's Word.

<u>II Timothy 3:15</u>
And that from a child thou hast known the Holy Scriptures, which are able to make thee wise unto salvation <u>through faith which is in Christ Jesus</u>.

I look back and remember that my parents, as new Christians, were very diligent to teach me about Jesus and His Word. The world will certainly not tell us about Him, sometimes even churches fail, but my parents embraced their responsibly. So, this **Devotional** wants to pass it on.

<u>Deuteronomy 4:10</u>
. . . and I will make them hear My words, that they may learn to fear Me all the days that they shall live upon the earth, and that they may <u>teach their children</u>.

<u>John 6:45</u>
. . . Every man therefore that hath heard, and hath learned of the Father, cometh unto Me (Jesus).

<u>Romans 15:4</u>
For whatsoever things were written aforetime were written for our learning, that we through patience and comfort of the scriptures might have hope.

JANUARY 18

AWESOME GOD

Do you know anyone you would call "**awesome**"? Hopefully, your spouse, children, or a special friend comes to mind, but compared with God, we all fall short. The world throws this word around very casually; usually about sport heroes, actors, actresses, performers of all kinds, etc., reflecting their temporary fame. These passing tributes are just that – passing. But attributed to God, <u>He is truly</u> **awesome** – in the past, the present, and for all eternity!

<u>Deuteronomy 10:21</u>
He is thy praise, and He is thy God,
that hath done for thee these great and awesome things,
which thine eyes have seen.

<u>Job 37:22 - 24</u>
Fair weather cometh out of the north:
with God is terrible (awesome) majesty.
Touching the Almighty, we cannot find Him out: He is excellent in power, and in judgment, and in plenty of justice: He will not afflict. Men do therefore fear him: He respecteth <u>not</u> any that are wise of heart.

<u>Psalms 65:5</u>
By terrible (awesome) things in righteousness wilt Thou answer us, O God of our salvation; Who art the confidence of all the ends of the earth, and of them that are afar off.

<u>Psalms 99:3</u>
Let them praise Thy great and terrible (awesome) Name; for it is holy.

<u>Psalms 145:6</u>
And men shall speak of the might of Thy terrible (awesome) acts: and I will declare Thy greatness.

JANUARY 19

"PECULIAR *(chosen)* PEOPLE"

The words "**Peculiar People**" are not my words but they are used in both the Old and New Testaments, to describe the followers of God and Jesus Christ respectively. "Peculiar" is a word in our language that has a negative connotation. No one likes to be called peculiar but in God's language it is a wonderful and a great privilege to be called (chosen to be set apart) by Him. Look below and find out why.

Deuteronomy 14:2
For thou art an holy people unto the Lord thy God, and the Lord hath chosen thee to be a <u>Peculiar</u> people unto Himself, above all the nations that are upon the earth.

Psalms 135:4, 5
For the Lord hath chosen Jacob unto Himself, and Israel for His <u>Peculiar</u> treasure. For I know that the Lord is great, and that our Lord is above all gods.

Matthew 22:14
For many are called, but few are chosen.

John 15:16 - 20
Ye have not chosen Me, but I have chosen you, and ordained you, that ye should go and bring forth fruit, and that your fruit should remain: that whatsoever ye shall ask of the Father in My name, He may give it you. These things I command you, that ye love one another. If the world hate you, ye know that it hated Me before it hated you. If ye were of the world, the world would love his own: but because ye are not of the world, but I have chosen you out of the world, therefore the world hateth you. <u>Remember</u> the word that I said unto you, The servant is not greater than his lord. If they have persecuted Me, they will also persecute you; if they have kept My saying, they will keep yours also.

JANUARY 20

MEDITATION

Often, when I see or hear this word "meditation," I just can't help but think of those sitting on the ground, cross-legged with hands together pointed up to heaven. I don't believe this is what God had in mind when He told us to meditate, day and night. However, **"meditate"** is a Biblical term, so let us examine God's desire for us, through King David in the Book of Psalms. David shares his "inner" thoughts and prayers which illustrate his love, devotion, and dependency on God.

Psalms 1:8
*But his delight is in the law of the Lord; and in His law
doth he meditate day and night.*

Psalms 19:14
*Let the words of my mouth, and the meditation of my heart, be acceptable in
Thy sight,
O Lord, my strength, and my Redeemer.*

Psalms 63:6, 7
*When I remember Thee upon my bed, and meditate on Thee in the night
watches. Because
Thou hast been my help, therefore in the shadow of Thy wings will I rejoice.*

Psalms 104:34
My meditation of Him shall be sweet: I will be glad in the Lord.

Psalms 107:43
*Whoso is wise, and will observe these things,
even they shall understand the loving kindness of the Lord.*

Psalms 143:5
*I remember the days of old; I meditate on all Thy works; I muse on the work of
Thy hands. I stretch forth my hands unto Thee: my soul thirsteth after Thee, as a
thirsty land. Selah.*

JANUARY 21

THINK HEAVEN

"Heaven is a wonderful place, full of glory and grace! I want to see my Savior's face, Heaven is a wonderful, Heaven is a glorious, Heaven is a wonderful place."

This is another chorus from my "teen years." It was almost true for me then, but truer for me today. **"I want to see my Savior's face!"** I was a little scared <u>then</u> because I was too young, and only thought about how much I would miss in this life: children and grandchildren, etc. But <u>now</u> I have learned so much more and know Him better! It <u>will be</u> "**Heaven**" to be in His presence!

<u>II Corinthians 5:1</u>
For we (I) know that if our earthly house of this tabernacle were dissolved, we (I) have a building of God, an house not made with hands, eternal in the heavens.

THINK HEAVEN, and you can't help but **THINK of GOD**.

<u>Daniel 12:3</u>
And they that be wise shall shine as the brightness of the firmament; and they that turn many to righteousness as the stars for ever and ever.

<u>Matthew 6:9, 10</u>
*Our Father which art in heaven, Hallowed be Thy name.
Thy kingdom come. Thy will be done in earth, as it is in heaven.*

<u>Philippians 3:20</u>
*For our conversation (life) is in heaven; from whence also
we look for the Saviour, the Lord Jesus Christ:*

<u>Hebrews 8:1</u>
Now of the things which we have spoken <u>this is the sum</u>: We have such an High Priest, Who is set on the right hand of the throne of the Majesty in the heavens;

JANUARY 22

THE HAND

Just looking at <u>our hands</u> you wouldn't think that there could be so much activity involved with them. If you really think about it, they demonstrate many acts of work and pleasure, and can even show our attitudes that give away our inner self; even our Faith. Our hands are tools that can be used for honor or dishonor - for good or evil as we choose. Some of us can't even talk without using our hands. Also, the expression "is at hand," is used as a "time line" indicating now or soon.

Genesis 9:2, 3
And God blessed Noah and his sons, and said unto them, Be fruitful, and multiply, and replenish the earth. And the fear of you and the dread of you shall be upon every beast of the earth, and upon every fowl of the air, upon all that moveth upon the earth, and upon all the fishes of the sea; <u>into your hand</u> are they delivered.

Ecclesiastes 9:10
Whatsoever thy hand findeth to do, <u>do</u> it with thy might

Proverbs 19:24
A slothful man hideth his hand in his bosom, and will not so much as bring it to his mouth again.

Ecclesiastes 5:15
As he came forth of his mother's womb, naked shall he return to go as he came, and shall take nothing of his labour, which he may carry away in his hand.

Matthew 4:17
From that time Jesus began to preach, and to say, Repent: for the kingdom of heaven <u>is at hand</u>.

Luke 9:62
And Jesus said unto him, No man, having put his hand to the plough, and looking back, is fit for the kingdom of God.

JANUARY 23

THE HAND OF GOD

The Hand of God can bring guidance, blessings, honor, help, etc.; but it can also bring correction, terror, and judgment. Who are we to decide what we should receive from the Hand of God? He knows us and what He desires for our lives. Our part is to be aware and have faith to follow wherever He leads. We are not to go our own way. Our thoughts are not His thoughts. We cannot even think of what He has prepared for us. O how wonderful - His right hand will guide us.

Psalms 144:7, 8
Send Thine hand from above; rid me, and deliver me out of great waters, from the hand of strange children; whose mouth speaketh vanity, and their right hand is a right hand of falsehood.

Psalms 31:14
But I trusted in Thee, O Lord: I said, Thou art my God. My times are in Thy hand:

Psalms 48:10
According to Thy name, O God, so is Thy praise unto the ends of the earth: Thy right hand is full of righteousness.

Isaiah 62:3
Thou shalt also be a crown of glory in the hand of the Lord, and a royal diadem in the hand of thy God.

John 3:35
The Father loveth the Son, and hath given all things into His hand.

Romans 8:34
. . . It is Christ that died, yea rather, that is risen again, Who is even at the right hand of God, Who also maketh intercession for us.

JANUARY 24

"IT IS WELL WITH MY SOUL"
by Horatio G. Spafford (1828-1888)

If you have the inclination and then the desire; find a hymn book that has this song in it (or find it on the Internet). It is worth your while to look it up and meditate on it. It is amazing to me some hymn books still have songs being sung today, that were written in the 700's (example: "Be Thou My Vision," an Irish hymn – eighth century). But back to this one, "**It is well with my Soul**." Look at what the "poet" (Horatio G. Spafford, 1828-1888) was so sure about – the security of his soul and in the promises of God – forever!

Isaiah 48:18 . . . "**Peace** like a river"
O that thou hadst hearkened to My commandments! then had Thy <u>peace been as a river</u>, and Thy righteousness as the waves of the sea:

II Corinthians 7:10 . . . "**Sorrow**"
For godly <u>sorrow</u> worketh repentance to salvation not to be repented of: but the <u>sorrow</u> of the world worketh death.

Psalms 46:1 . . . "**Whatever** my lot"
<u>God is our refuge and strength, a very present help in trouble.</u>

Isaiah 26:3, 4 . . . "**Taught** me"
Thou wilt keep him in perfect peace, whose <u>mind is stayed on Thee</u>: because he <u>trusteth in Thee</u>. Trust ye in the Lord for ever: for in the Lord Jehovah is everlasting strength:

Isaiah 32:17 . . . "**Assurance**"
And the work of righteousness shall be peace; and the effect of righteousness quietness and <u>assurance</u> forever.

Colossians 1:14 . . . "**Shed HIS own Blood**"
In Whom we have redemption through <u>His blood</u>, the forgiveness of sins, according to the riches of His grace;

JANUARY 25

RESURRECTION

Yes, Christ shed His own blood on a cruel cross in our place. He was buried, and on the third day – HE AROSE from the dead! Now that is our hope in Him – we too will be raised from death unto life eternal. If Jesus had not come back to life after His crucifixion, it would have been all for nothing. Nothing more than a lie and a great hokes. <u>But</u> He did! An historical fact! Jesus was resurrected and we too shall live with Him for all eternity.

<u>Job 19:26, 27</u>. . . **Resurrection** of the body **foretold**:
And though after my skin worms destroy this body, yet in my flesh shall I see God: Whom I shall see for myself, and mine eyes shall behold, and not another;

<u>Psalms 17:15</u>
As for me, I will behold Thy face in righteousness:
I shall be satisfied, when I awake, with Thy likeness.

<u>Matthew 22:31 – 33</u>
. . . **Resurrection** proclaimed by **Christ**:
But as touching the <u>resurrection</u> of the dead, have ye not read that which was spoken unto you by God, saying, I am the God of Abraham, and the God of Isaac, and the God of Jacob? <u>God is not the God of the dead, but of the living</u>. And when the multitude heard this, they were astonished at His doctrine.

<u>John 5:28</u>
Marvel not at this: for the hour is coming, in the which all that are in the graves shall hear His voice, And shall come forth; they that have done good, unto the <u>resurrection</u> of life; and they that have done evil, unto the <u>resurrection</u> of damnation.

<u>Acts 4:2</u>
. . . **Resurrection** preached by the **Apostles**:
. . . <u>preached through Jesus the resurrection from the dead</u>.

JANUARY 26

WISDOM – ASK OF GOD

Scripture uses the word Wisdom not only as instructions, but it includes skill and understandings; given to us by God, with Spiritual insights. For this reason alone, we should ask for it and search for these treasures. As in life, everything seems to have a beginning so we find the getting of Wisdom begins with our fear (and awe) of the Lord. As you look below, Proverbs is the place to start to search for Wisdom – God's Wisdom. It is also an attribute of God and refers to Him as Wisdom interchangeably. See this great mystery.

Proverbs 1:2-4, 6; gives us the synopsis of knowing and applying wisdom:
To know wisdom and instruction; to perceive the words of understanding; To receive the instruction of wisdom, To give subtilty to the simple, to the young man knowledge and discretion. To understand a proverb, and the interpretation; the words of the wise, and their dark sayings.

Proverbs 1:7
*The fear of the Lord is the beginning of knowledge:
but fools despise wisdom and instruction.*

Proverbs 2:4 – 6
If thou seekest her as silver, and searchest for her as for hid treasures; Then shalt thou understand the fear of the Lord, and find the knowledge of God. For the Lord giveth wisdom: out of His mouth cometh knowledge and understanding.

Proverbs 2:10 - 12, 14, 15
When wisdom entereth into thine heart, and knowledge is pleasant unto thy soul; Discretion shall preserve thee, understanding shall keep thee: To deliver thee from the way of the evil man, from the man that speaketh froward things; Who rejoice to do evil, and delight in the frowardness of the wicked Whose ways are crooked, and froward in their paths:

JANUARY 27

WAIT! BLESSINGS ARE ON THE WAY

It seems it all began in my generation, so to speak! We want instant gratification - and we want it now! Waiting is so hard! But waiting can teach us many lessons in the process, and rushing ahead without it can bring disappointments. We easily see it in others but we don't like to see it in ourselves. We try to ignore waiting and continue on the path of hurriedness, and miss out on God's blessings. Put God's timing into perspective God – and His reasons.

II Peter 3:8, 9
But, beloved, be not ignorant of this one thing, that one day is with the Lord as a thousand years, and a thousand years as one day. The Lord is not slack concerning His promise, as some men count slackness; but is longsuffering to us-ward, not willing that any should perish, but that all should come to repentance.

Psalms 62:5 - 7
My soul, wait thou only upon God; for my expectation is from Him. He only is my rock and my salvation: He is my defence; I shall not be moved. In God is my salvation and my glory: the Rock of my strength, and my Refuge, is in God.

Isaiah 40:31
But they that wait upon the Lord shall renew their strength; they shall mount up with wings as eagles; they shall run, and not be weary and they shall walk, and not faint.

Hosea 12:6
Therefore turn thou to thy God: keep mercy and judgment, and wait on thy God continually.

Romans 8:25
For we are saved by hope: but hope that is seen is not hope:

JANUARY 28

THINK!

Think what? We are bombarded with subjects all around us. How do we choose what to think about wisely? Often our thoughts drift away throughout the day. Memories may just pop up about things from the distant past, like music, or negative things that make us feel depressed. This should give us pause to evaluate what we deliberately see, hear, or read. The Bible gives us a true way to sift out our thoughts that our brain is contemplating and use the control we have, and <u>will</u> to change the subject that is harmful to us.

Philippians 4:8
*Finally, brethren, whatsoever things are true,
whatsoever things are honest, whatsoever things are just,
whatsoever things are pure, whatsoever things are lovely,
whatsoever things are of good report; if there be
any virtue, and if there be any praise, think on these things.*

Proverbs 23:7
For as he thinketh in his heart, so is he:

Matthew 9:4
And Jesus knowing their thoughts said, Wherefore think ye evil in your hearts?

Matthew 22:42
. . . Jesus asked them, Saying, What think ye of Christ? Whose Son is He?

Romans 12:3
For I say, through the grace given unto me, to every man that is among you, not to think of himself more highly than he ought to think; but to think soberly, according as God hath dealt to every man the measure of faith.

JANUARY 29

HARMLESS AS DOVES

Matthew 10:16
Behold, I (Jesus) send you forth as sheep in the midst of wolves: be ye therefore wise as serpents, and harmless as <u>doves</u>.

We have not been called to be Apostles of Jesus Christ, but if we are believers in Him we are called to be His Disciples. Therefore, the above admonition is written for us to apply to our lives. Sheep? We're like Sheep? Just read the 23rd Psalm again and we know we are like Sheep. But the promises of God can give us confidence because He is our Shepherd and equips us as needed. The above verse lists Sheep, Wolves, Serpents, and Doves. All were created very differently from each other, and the lowest of the low as far as defense goes are Sheep (us). This makes us very dependent on our Shepherd! But as Scripture tells us we want to go our own way and we are given the will to do so. This is where **we** make the choice. Are we willing to follow our Master or what? "**Harmless as Doves**"? No one is afraid of a Dove! In our day; we even use them as a peace symbol.

Genesis 3:1
Now the serpent was more <u>subtil</u> than any beast of the field which the Lord God had made.

Matthew 3:16, 17
And Jesus, when He was baptized, went up straightway out of the water: and, lo, the heavens were opened unto Him, and He saw the Spirit of God descending like a dove, and lighting upon Him: And lo a voice from heaven, saying, This is My beloved Son, in Whom I am well pleased.

Psalms 55:6
And I said, Oh that I had wings like a dove! for then would I fly away, and be at rest.

JANUARY 30

COUNT THE COST

Do we really know what the word cost means?
When you look it up in a dictionary, you see that cost requires a payment – a price. As we know, some things cost more than others and some pay a higher price than others; such, as the crude example of the price of airplane tickets on the same plane – same destination. This is also true Spiritually. Yes, Salvation is a free gift from God but Jesus paid the (specific) price of death for our sins on the cross

<u>Romans 6:23</u>
For the wages (payment) of sin is death; but the gift of God is eternal life through Jesus Christ our Lord.

Sin cost Christ His life for the payment of our sins. We cannot even compare our cost of being one of His disciples with the price He paid. But there is a cost for us to pay (not from Him, but from the world), to be His disciple and we need to Count the Cost that Jesus illustrated in three Parables:

<u>Luke 14:28 - 33</u>
*A builder – to build a tower
A king – contemplating war
A disciple – following His Master, JESUS*

Jesus also said in <u>verses 25 - 27</u>
And there went great multitudes with Him: and He turned, and said unto them, If any man come to Me, and hate not his father, and mother, and wife, and children, and brethren, and sisters, yea, <u>and his own life also</u>, he cannot be My disciple. And whosoever doth not bear his cross, and come after Me, cannot be My disciple.

From Jesus' very words we must hear Him, and count the Cost of discipleship.

JANUARY 31

BENEATH THE CROSS OF JESUS

Let us end this month with a hymn of <u>DEDICATION</u>. This is a word not used very often these days but that is what it takes to be a disciple of Jesus Christ. I can still recall the time I went forward in church to "consecrate" my life. God has been so good to me even though I have failed often.

"BENEATH THE CROSS OF JESUS"
by Elizabeth C. Clephane (180-1869)

Beneath the Cross of Jesus, <u>I fain would take my stand</u>
The shadow of a mighty Rock within a weary land;
A home within the wilderness,
a rest upon the way –
From the burning of the noon-day heat
And the burden of the day.

Upon that cross of Jesus Mine eye at times can see
The very dying form of One Who suffered there for me;
And from my smitten heart with tears
** <u>Two</u> wonders I confess –
* The wonders of His glorious love
* And my own worthlessness.

<u>I take, O cross</u>, thy shadow <u>for my abiding place</u>-
I ask no other sunshine than The sunshine of His face;
Content to let the world go by,
To know no gain nor loss,
My sinful self my only shame,
<u>My glory all the cross</u>. Amen!

FEBRUARY

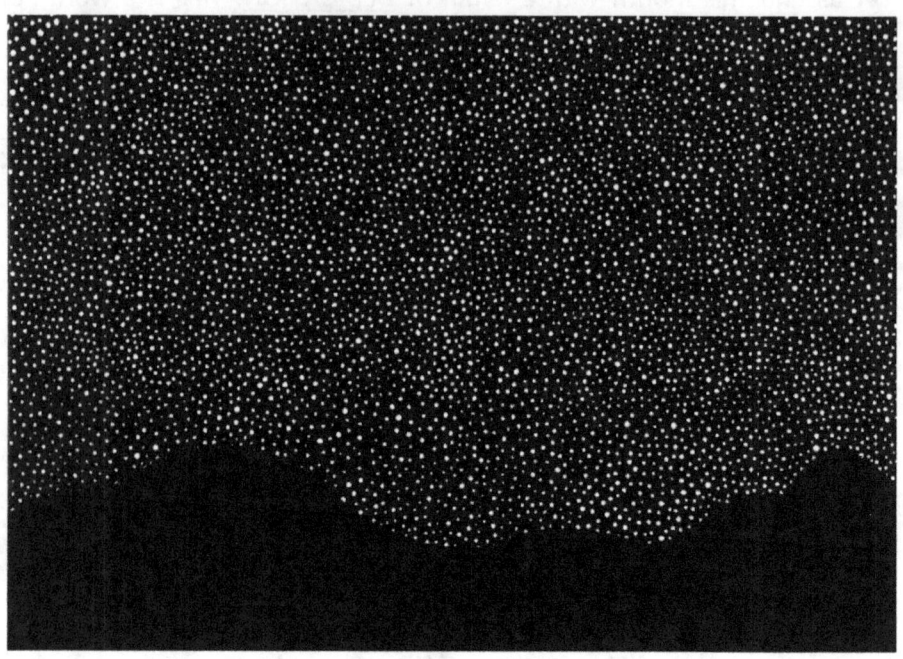

THY HEAVENS

Psalms 8:3 - 6

When I consider Thy heavens, the work of Thy fingers, the moon and the stars, which Thou hast ordained; What is man, that Thou art mindful of him? and the Son of man, that Thou visitest Him? For Thou hast made Him a little lower than the angels, and hast crowned Him with glory and honour. Thou madest Him to have dominion over the works of Thy hands; Thou hast put all things under His feet

FEBRUARY 1

ROOTS

Again, we want to look at Scriptures using nature to illustrate TURTHS; particularly, Roots! With my limited knowledge, I cannot recall a plant without roots, but if God created even one, then it is so. See how Roots relate to the great lessons about our relationship to God. Psalm 1 tells us in simple terms the whole story about being "planted," a word that implies Roots.

Psalm 1
Blessed is the man that walketh not in the counsel of the ungodly, nor standeth in the way of sinners, nor sitteth in the seat of the scornful. But his delight is in the law of the Lord; and in His law doth he meditate day and night. And he shall be like a tree planted by the rivers of water, that bringeth forth his fruit in his season; his leaf also shall not wither; and whatsoever he doeth shall prosper. The ungodly are not so: but are like the chaff whch the wind driveth away. Therefore the ungodly shall not stand in the judgment, nor sinners in the congregation of the righteous. For the Lord knoweth the way of the righteous: but the way of the ungodly shall perish.

Matthew 15:13
But He answered and said, Every plant, which My heavenly Father hath not planted, shall be rooted up.

Colossians 2:6, 7
As ye have therefore received Christ Jesus the Lord, so walk ye in Him: Rooted and built up in Him, and stablished in the faith, as ye have been taught, abounding therein with thanksgiving.

Ephesians 3:16 - 19
That Christ may dwell in your hearts by faith; that ye, being rooted and grounded in love . . .

FEBRUARY 2

CHEER UP

Sometimes, to "Cheer Up" is easier said than done. There is much to be said about why we need to cheer up. I don't even have to make a list because you know them for yourself. It is not that we should ignore hard times but we are to know that God's Spirit dwells within us and there is much to "cheer up" about. He helps us to get through tough times when we dwell on Him. Even King David experienced difficulties and asked himself a very important question that we need to ask ourselves too.

Psalms 43:5
Why art thou cast down, O my soul? and why art thou disquieted within me? - He even gives us the cure . . . hope in God: *for I shall yet* praise Him, *Who is the health of my countenance, and my God.*

Psalms 27:1
The Lord is my light and my salvation; whom shall I fear? the Lord is the strength of my life; of whom shall I be afraid?

Psalms 126:5,6
They that sow in tears shall reap in joy. He that goeth forth and weepeth, bearing precious seed, shall doubtless come again with rejoicing, bringing his sheaves with him.

Matthew 9:2
And, behold, they brought to Him a man sick of the palsy, lying on a bed: and Jesus seeing their faith said unto the sick of the palsy; Son, be of good cheer; *thy sins be forgiven thee.*

Matthew 14:27
But straightway Jesus spake unto them, saying, Be of good cheer; *it is I; be not afraid.*

John 16:33
. . . In the world ye shall have tribulation: but be of good cheer; *I have overcome the world.*

FEBRUARY 3

Let's Go – Go On

Get busy and keep on going, going on! Do not give up in doing good or slacking by just sitting around waiting for something to do. Look around! There are opportunities everywhere if we just open our eyes and see, then do.

Matthew 25:35 - 39
For I was an hungred, and ye gave Me meat: I was thirsty, and ye gave Me drink: I was a stranger, and ye took Me in: Naked, and ye clothed me: I was sick, and ye visited Me: I was in prison, and ye came unto Me. Then shall the righteous answer Him, saying, Lord, when saw we Thee an hungred, and fed Thee? or thirsty, and gave Thee drink? When saw we Thee a stranger, and took Thee in? or naked, and clothed Thee? Or when saw we thee sick, or in prison, and came unto Thee? And the King shall answer and say unto them, Verily I say unto you, Inasmuch <u>as ye have done it unto one of the least of these My brethren, ye have done it unto Me.</u>

Philippians 3:13, 14
. . . this one thing I do, forgetting those things which are behind, and reaching forth unto those things which are before, I press toward the mark for the prize of the high calling of God in Christ Jesus.

Hebrews 6:10, 12
For God is not unrighteous to forget your work and labour of love, which ye have shewed toward His name, in that ye have ministered to the saints, and do minister. That ye be not slothful, but followers of them who through faith and patience inherit the promises.

Psalms 71:16
I will go in the strength of the Lord God:

Isaiah 6:8
Also I heard the voice of the Lord, saying, Whom shall I send, and who will go for us? Then said I, Here am I; send me.

FEBRUARY 4

LIVE OUT LOUD

Psalms 107:2; *Let the Redeemed of the Lord say so . . .* and,
Galatians 3:13; *Christ hath redeemed us from the curse of the law, being made a curse for us: for it is written, Cursed is every one that hangeth on a tree*:

It is the fear of man and what he might think of us if we share what we believe. This is our pride and Satan's ploy to make us of no effect. But Jesus said in Matthew 10:28:

Fear not them which kill the body, but are not able to kill the soul: but rather fear Him which is able to destroy both soul and body in hell.

If we only could go back and tell those we knew before what God has done in our lives. This we cannot do but we can move forward in all honesty and in confidence that God's Spirit will give us words to speak and actions to do, just as He gives to us the opportunity to witness. We can depend on Him. Often, fear makes me hesitate to speak up. Don't let that happen to you.

Ephesians 6:19
And for me (Paul), that utterance may be given unto me, that I may open my mouth boldly, to make known the mystery of the gospel . . .

Matthew 10: 27
What I (Jesus) tell you in darkness, that speak ye in light: and what ye hear in the ear, that preach ye upon the housetops.

Luke 12:4, 5
And I say unto you My friends, Be not afraid of them that kill the body, and after that have no more that they can do. But I will forewarn you whom ye shall fear: Fear Him, which after He hath killed hath power to cast into hell; yea, I say unto you, Fear Him.

FEBRUARY 5

SUNRISE

"Early to bed, early to rise makes a man healthy, wealthy, and wise."

This could be true but it also may be just an old <u>wives</u>' tale. Believe it or not! Because of man-made Daylight Savings time laws, it is easier to see the sun come up in March. It can happen on our way to school or work; or may even really wake us up if going east to get there. In Bible times, I believe they used daylight more efficiently. It ruled the day and when it was dark it was time to go to bed. It still was a temptation to be slothful and ignore nature's calling of the Sunrise, but Scriptures give us examples of this beautiful time of the day.

<u>Mark 1:35</u>
And in the morning, rising up a great while before day,
He (Jesus) went out, and departed into a solitary place, and there prayed.

<u>Genesis 19:27</u>
And Abraham gat up early in the morning to the place where he stood before the Lord:

<u>Exodus 34:4</u>
And he hewed two tables of stone like unto the first; and Moses rose up early in the morning, and went up unto mount Sinai, as the Lord had commanded him, and took in his hand the two tables of stone.

<u>Psalms 5:3</u>
My voice shalt thou hear in the morning, O Lord; in the morning will I direct my prayer unto Thee, and will look up.

<u>Mark 16:2</u>
And very early in the morning the first day of the week,
they came unto the sepulchre at the rising of the sun.

FEBRUARY 6

HOSEA 7:8

There is a particular phrase and lesson in Hosea 7 to be aware of today and apply to our lives. **Ephraim hath mixed himself among the people; <u>Ephraim is a cake unturned</u>.**

The word-picture brought to my mind a pancake, because it was cooked only on one side and not turned over. Not a pancake I would like to eat. So, what does this passage imply? A pancake not turned over is soon burnt on the side closest to the flame while the upside is not cooked properly. As one famous preacher* explained this, "the Lord needs to turn us over from getting burnt black with bigoted zeal or charred to a cinder with conceit." For instance: "a saint in public and a devil in private - in flour by day and in soot by night." The conclusion to be learned is to ask the Lord, so to speak, in repentance, "turn us over." Turn our unsanctified (old) nature in the fire of His love. If we are left like a "pancake unturned" and do not receive God's grace, we will be consumed in the burning.

Hosea 7:2 – 10
And they consider not in their hearts that I remember all their wickedness: now their own doings have beset them about; they are before My face. They make the king glad with their wickedness, and the princes with their lies. They are all adulterers . . . , <u>as an oven</u> heated by the baker, In the day of our king the princes have made him sick with bottles of wine; he stretched out his hand with scorners. For they have made <u>ready their heart like an oven</u>, whiles they lie in wait: their baker sleepeth all the night; in the morning it burneth as a flaming fire. They are all hot as an oven, and have devoured their judges; all their kings are fallen: there is none among them that calleth unto Me. <u>Ephraim, he hath mixed himself among the people; Ephraim is a cake not turned.</u> Strangers have devoured his strength, and he knoweth it not: yea, gray hairs are here and there upon him, yet he knoweth not. And the pride of Israel testifieth to his face: and they do not return to the Lord their God, nor seek Him for all this.

* Spurgeon, Charles H., *Morning and Evening: Daily Readings*. Hendrickson Publishers, Inc., 1995, page 350.

FEBRUARY 7

ALIENS, PILGRIMS and STRANGERS

Sometimes, don't we feel like a stranger? Like a "fish out of water," particularly when we get out of our comfort zone. Other times include being where someone else thinks we should be, or doing something we know goes against what we believe. We are all individuals in the sight of God and we need to remember all He has taught and given us, and what He asked us to do. We are not of this world. We are looking forward to our new home – Heaven, and seeing Christ face-to-face.

Acts 13:17
The God of this people of Israel chose our fathers, and exalted the people when they dwelt as <u>strangers</u> in the land of Egypt, and with an high arm brought He them out of it.

Ephesians 2:12, 13, 18, 19
That at that time ye were without Christ, being <u>aliens</u> from the commonwealth of Israel, and <u>strangers</u> from the covenants of promise, having no hope, and <u>without God</u> in the world: <u>But now in Christ Jesus ye who sometimes were far off are made nigh by the blood of Christ</u>. For through Him we both have access by one Spirit unto the Father. Now therefore ye are no more <u>strangers</u> and <u>foreigners</u>, but <u>fellow-citizens</u> with the saints, and <u>of the household of God</u>

Hebrews 11:13, 14, 16
. . . confessed that they were <u>strangers</u> and <u>pilgrims</u> on the earth. For they that say such things declare plainly that they seek a country . . . a better country, that is, an heavenly: wherefore God is not ashamed to be called their God: for He hath prepared for them a city.

I Peter 2:11
Dearly beloved, I beseech you as <u>strangers</u> and <u>pilgrims</u>, abstain from fleshly lusts, which war against the soul;

FEBRUARY 8

LOOK FORWARD

We are all interested in what the future holds for us. That's one reason why fortune-tellers have become so popular here in the past few years. As believers in Christ, we can know much about what He has planned for us and the future. It behooves us to know what He has to say and not consult those who would lead us astray. Just reading the verses below gives us a lot to look at and think about for <u>our</u> future. Some would say, what will happen tomorrow is not mentioned, but do they really believe anyone but God really knows? It is alright to plan ahead and to be responsible for our schedule, but be flexible for any change to the will and knowledge of God. Only He knows.

<u>Deuteronomy 18:14</u>
For these nations, which thou shalt possess, hearkened unto observers of times, and unto diviners: but as for thee, the Lord thy God hath not suffered thee so to do.

<u>Jeremiah 27:9</u>
Therefore hearken not ye to your prophets, nor to your diviners, nor to your dreamers, nor to your enchanters, nor to your sorcerers, which speak unto you

<u>Psalms 4:5 - 6</u>
Stand in awe, and sin not: <u>commune</u> with your own heart upon your bed, and <u>be still</u>. Selah. Offer the sacrifices of righteousness, and <u>put your trust in the Lord</u>. There be many that say, Who will shew us any good? Lord, lift Thou up the light of Thy countenance upon us.

<u>Proverbs 4:25 - 27</u>
Let thine eyes look right on, and let thine eyelids look straight before thee. Ponder the path of thy feet, and let all thy ways be established. Turn not to the right hand nor to the left: remove thy foot from evil.

FEBRUARY 9

FOLLOW WHERE HE LEADS

I remember very vividly hymns of commitment and consecration. The congregation was encouraged to follow God wherever God would lead us. The chorus of the hymn, "Where He Leads Me," stands out strongly in my mind reminding me of baptism services at church. It would remind us of our promise to follow Him. Jesus has called us to follow Him, many times. Read the words of the hymn, and see that it will touch your heart too.

"WHERE HE LEADS ME"
By William A. Ogden (1841- 1897)

*I can hear my Savior calling, I can hear my Savior calling,
I can hear my Savior calling, "Take thy cross and follow, follow Me."*

*I'll go with Him thru the garden, I'll go with Him thru the garden,
I'll go with Him thru the garden, I'll go with Him, with Him all the way.*

*He will give me grace and glory, He will give me grace and glory,
He will give me grace and glory, And go with me, with me all the way.*

Chorus
Where He leads me I will follow. Where He leads me I will follow. Where He leads me I will follow. I'll go with Him, with Him all the way.

Hosea 6:3
Then shall we know, if we follow on to know the Lord: His going forth is prepared as the morning; and He shall come unto us as the rain,

Luke 9:23
And he said to them all, If any man will come after me, let him deny himself, and take up his cross daily, and follow me.

GIVE UP YOUR RIGHTS, GLADLY

"I want to do it myself."

This often comes from the mouth of many a five-year-old! This is the childlike trait we must put aside when it comes to giving up our rights to God and let His way be done in our lives. We slip and slide about this every day even when we don't mean to; happening without our realization. We like to plan ahead and then resist when plans are changed for us by the will of God. See if this happens to you today. Remember you are God's dear "little child" and He knows which way you should go – go with His choice. In the Book of Job, we have evidence of a complete turn-about face of Job's will and accepting what God wills, with repentance.

Job 7:11
Therefore I will not refrain my mouth; I will speak in the anguish of my spirit; I will complain in the bitterness of my soul.

Job 10:15
If I be wicked, woe unto me; and if I be righteous, yet will I not lift up my head. I am full of confusion; therefore see thou mine affliction;

Job 9:20
*If I justify myself, mine own mouth shall condemn me:
if I say, I am perfect, it shall also prove me perverse.*

Job 27:6
*My righteousness I hold fast, and will not let it go:
my heart shall not reproach me so long as I live.*

Job 42:5, 6
*I have heard of Thee by the hearing of the ear: but now mine eye seeth Thee.
Wherefore I abhor myself, and repent in dust and ashes.*

FEBRUARY 11

SECURITY

Do you have a security system in your home? We don't, but maybe we should. I don't have the statistics on how many do, but I can imagine it is a lot. Even a large number of houses are arming themselves because of the fear of harm, or a sense of living responsibly to protect the family in case of danger. Many bad things do happen to take away Security in our time. However, God does not want us to fear and be afraid to the point it stops us in our tracks. Precautions are fine unless that is what we totally depend on and not the Lord's care and protection. There will be a time when those that trust in the Lord, will be safe forever.

Psalms 91:2
I will say of the Lord, He is my refuge and my fortress:
my God; in Him will I trust.

Psalms 119:115 - 117
Depart from me, ye evildoers: for I will keep the commandments of my God. Uphold me according unto Thy Word, that I may live: and let me not be ashamed of my hope. Hold Thou me up, and I shall be safe:

Proverbs 18:10
The name of the Lord is a strong tower: the righteous runneth into it, and is safe.

Proverbs 29:25
The fear of man bringeth a snare: but whoso putteth his trust in the Lord shall be safe.

Ezekiel 23:28
And they shall no more be a prey to the heathen, neither shall the beast of the land devour them; but they shall dwell safely, and none shall make them afraid.

FEBRUARY 12

FOCUS

All our daily lives there are things we must Focus on to see and understand, and do. Can you name a few in your schedule today? Even just driving a car takes our and full concentration and Focus! But there is a special Focus we need to compensate when we get busy and occupied with daily living. Of course, you can guess – it is the person of Christ Jesus. Besides being our Savior and Friend, He is always there to help and guide us throughout our day. I know I need that.

Psalms 27:13,14
I had fainted, unless I had believed to see the goodness of the Lord in the land of the living. Wait on the Lord: be of good courage, and He shall strengthen thine heart:
wait, I say, on the Lord.

Psalms 34:9
O fear the Lord, ye His saints: for there is no want to them that fear Him.

Psalms 36:9, 10
For with Thee is the fountain of life: in Thy light shall we see light. O continue Thy lovingkindness unto them that know Thee; and Thy righteousness to the upright in heart.

Psalms 40:3, 4
And He hath put a new song in my mouth, even praise unto our God: many shall see it, and fear, and shall trust in the Lord. Blessed is that man that maketh the Lord his trust, and respecteth not the proud, nor such as turn aside to lies.

Psalms 63:2 - 4
To see Thy power and Thy glory, so as I have seen Thee in the sanctuary. Because Thy lovingkindness is better than life, my lips shall praise Thee. Thus will I bless Thee while I live: I will lift up my hands in Thy name.

FEBRUARY 13

LIGHT OF THE WORLD

Darkness needs the LIGHT!

The whole world lives in a darkness even when there is bright sunshine. You read and hear the evidence every day from newspapers, the television, and radio. Then came Jesus! He is the LIGHT of the World, so that we don't have to live in darkness any longer.

John 8:12
Then spake Jesus again unto them, saying, <u>I am the light of the world</u>: he that followeth Me shall not walk in darkness, but shall have the light of life.

Psalms 119:105
Thy word is a lamp unto my feet, and a light unto my path.

Matthew 5:14 - 16
Ye are the light of the world. A city that is set on an hill cannot be hid. Neither do men light a candle, and put it under a bushel, but on a candlestick; and it giveth light unto all that are in the house. <u>Let your light so shine before men</u>, that they may see your good works, and <u>glorify your Father which is in heaven</u>.

John 9:5
As long as I am in the world, I am the light of the world.

II Corinthians 4:4
In whom the god of this world hath blinded the minds of them which believe not, lest the Light of the glorious gospel of Christ, Who is the image of God, should shine unto them.

I John 1:7
But if we walk in the light, as He is in the light, we have fellowship one with another, and the blood of Jesus Christ His Son cleanseth us from all sin.

FEBRUARY 14

"IT" NEVER JUST ARRIVES

No matter what we think "IT" is; "IT" never just happens! For good or bad, "IT" takes an action of something or on somebody's part to make "IT" happen. I thought and thought about happenings in my experiences and can't think of anything that happened without a person, the order of nature, or without God being involved. Can you? The question about God is, does He <u>cause</u> "IT" - or <u>permit</u> "IT" to happen? Many of our negative "ITS" happen because of the <u>consequences of sin</u>. Think about it.

<u>Psalms 42:8</u>
Yet the Lord will command His lovingkindness *in the daytime, and in the night His song shall be with me, and my prayer unto the God of my life.*

<u>Psalms 102:1, 2</u>
Hear my prayer, O Lord, and let my cry come unto Thee. Hide not Thy face from me in the day when I am in trouble; incline Thine ear unto me: in the day when I call answer me speedily.

<u>Psalms 143:1, 2</u>
Hear my prayer, O Lord, . . .
Enter not into judgment with thy servant; for no man living is righteous before Thee;

<u>Jeremiah 17:9.</u>
The heart is deceitful above all things and desperately corrupt; who can understand it?

<u>Romans 12:12</u>
Rejoicing in hope; patient in tribulation; continuing instant in prayer;

<u>I Peter 4:7</u>
But the end of all things is at hand: be ye therefore sober, and watch unto prayer.

FEBRUARY 15

GRACE, GRACE, and MORE GRACE

We here on earth are privileged to receive Grace, Grace, and more Grace. This free gift from God is sometimes used flippantly and taken for granted because we haven't thought through what it really means, or what it really cost God. God is the only one who can bestow it on us. It is a God thing that so often is refused, to our own peril. Be sure this day you know the GRACE of God in Truth!

Acts 20:32
And now, brethren, I commend you to God, and to the word of His grace, which is able to build you up, and to give you an inheritance among all them which are sanctified.

Romans 5:2
By Whom also we have access by faith into this grace wherein we stand, and rejoice in hope of the glory of God.

Ephesians 2:8, 9
For by grace are ye saved through faith; and that not of yourselves: it is the gift of God: Not of works, lest any man should boast.

Colossians 1:5, 6
For the hope which is laid up for you in heaven, whereof ye heard before in the Word of the truth of the Gospel; Which is come unto you, as it is in all the world; and bringeth forth fruit, as it doth also in you, since the day ye heard of it, and knew the grace of God in truth:

II Peter 1:2, 3
Grace and peace be multiplied unto you through the knowledge of God, and of Jesus our Lord, According as His divine power hath given unto us all things that pertain unto life and godliness . . .

FEBRUARY 16

SHARED "MYSTERIES" FROM GOD

We have learned the Book of Job, in the **Old Testament**, is probably the first book written in the Bible - even before the books Abraham wrote. Job listed so many facts of God's creation that it would have taken us much more time to learn them from experience than just by reading **JOB**. It is very fascinating and is a must reading for all to learn how wonderful our Creator is. I want to list <u>some of these creation facts</u> below before I go to some of the <u>mysteries</u> in the **New Testament** that Jesus revealed - His <u>mysteries</u> from God. Jesus' actions consistently fulfilled Old Testament <u>mysteries</u> and promises regarding the Kingdom and the Messiah, **Jesus Christ**.

<u>Job 26:7 - 9</u>
He stretcheth out the north over the empty place, and hangeth the earth upon nothing. He bindeth up the waters in His thick clouds; and the cloud is not rent under them. He holdeth back the face of His throne, and spreadeth His cloud upon it.

<u>Job 28:5, 6; 10, 11</u>
As for the earth, out of it cometh bread: and under it is turned up as it were fire. The stones of it are the place of sapphires: and it hath dust of gold. He cutteth out rivers among the rocks; and His eye seeth every precious thing. He bindeth the floods from overflowing; and the thing that is hid bringeth He forth to light.
(search for more in the Book of **JOB**)

<u>Isaiah 61:1, 2)</u>
The Spirit of the Lord God is upon me; because the Lord hath anointed me to preach good tidings unto the meek; He hath sent Me to bind up the brokenhearted, to proclaim liberty to the captives, and the opening of the prison to them that are bound; To proclaim the acceptable year of the Lord, and the day of vengeance of our God; to comfort all that mourn;

Now for the **New Testament - <u>SHARED "MYSTERIES"</u>**

Matthew 13:10, 11
Who hath ears to hear, let him hear. And the disciples came, and said unto Him, Why speakest Thou unto them in parables? He answered and said unto them, Because <u>it is given unto you to know the mysteries</u> of the kingdom of heaven, but to them it is not given.

Luke 4:20 - 22
And He closed the book, and He gave it again to the minister, and sat down. And the eyes of all them that were in the synagogue were fastened on Him. And He began to say unto them, <u>This day is this scripture fulfilled</u> in your ears. And all bare Him witness, and wondered at the gracious words which proceeded out of His mouth.
<u>And they said, Is not this Joseph's son?</u>

Matthew 13:17
For verily I say unto you, That many prophets and righteous men have desired to see those things which ye see, and have not seen them; and to hear those things which ye hear, and have not heard them.

Mark 14:22 - 24
. . . Jesus took bread, and blessed, and brake it, and gave to them, and said, Take, eat: <u>this is My body</u>. And He took the cup, and when He had given thanks, He gave it to them: and they all drank of it. And He said unto them, This is <u>My blood of the New Testament</u>, which is shed for many.

John 1:10 - 12
He was in the world, and the world was made by Him, and the world knew Him not. He came unto His own (Jews), and His own received Him not. But as many as received Him, to them gave he power to become the sons of God, even to them that believe on His name:

FEBRUARY 17

HOLY IS THE LORD

"Because it is written, Be ye holy; for I am holy" (I Peter 1:16).

What does this mean? Is this possible? Take a look below and understand whatever God will teach you personally on this matter. His Word and the Holy Spirit always gives us insight when we ask and seek it. Don't be afraid of the word and actions of being "holy" because you as a child of God will be led into all holiness in Christ Jesus. It is not what you do but what He does through your willingness. Thank God that He is Holy, because we would not want to worship any other god to reign supreme in our lives.

<u>Leviticus 11:44</u>
I am the Lord your God. Consecrate yourselves therefore, and be holy, for I am holy.

<u>Leviticus 19:2</u>
Speak to all the congregation of the people of Israel and say to them, You shall be holy, for I the Lord your God am Holy.

<u>Leviticus 20:26</u>
You shall be holy to me, for I the Lord am holy and have separated you from the peoples, that you should be mine.

<u>I Peter 1:15</u>
But as He which hath called you is Holy, so be ye holy <u>in all manner of conversation</u> (life);

<u>II Peter 3:9, 11 - 14</u>
The Lord is not slack concerning His promise, . . . but is longsuffering to us-ward, not willing that any should perish, but that all should come to repentance. . . . what manner of persons ought ye to be <u>in all holy conversation and godliness</u>, Looking for and hasting unto the coming of the day of God, . . . look for new heavens and a new earth, wherein dwelleth righteousness. Wherefore, . . .be diligent - found of Him in peace, without spot, and blameless.

FEBRUARY 18

THIS HOPE IN YOU

Life without hope is "hopeless," of course! Before we go on, let's review the meaning of **hopeless**: bleak, no possibility of a solution, impossible. Hope can be used as a noun or a verb but both refer to action! Our action is either, to believe in, and/or to apply to your life. We don't even have to imagine a world without hope because we can see it vividly in these times, on television every day all over the world and that is tragic.

Many of us have felt this way at one time or another, but that doesn't have to be. Let's study where real HOPE comes from.

The HOPE of the world is JESUS!

John 10:10
The thief cometh not, but for to steal, and to kill, and to destroy: I (Jesus) am come that they might have life, and that they might have it more abundantly.

Psalms 146:5, 6
Happy is he that hath the God of Jacob for his help, whose hope is in the Lord his God: Which made heaven, and earth, the sea, and all that therein is: which keepeth truth for ever:

Jeremiah 17:7
Blessed is the man that trusteth in the Lord, and whose hope the Lord is.

Romans 5:1, 2
Therefore, since we have been justified by faith, we have peace with God through our Lord Jesus Christ. Through him we have also obtained access by faith into this grace in which we stand, and we rejoice in hope of the glory of God.

Romans 8:24
Now hope that is seen is not hope. For who hopes for what he sees?

FEBRUARY 19

LIVE INTENTIONALLY

How then shall we live? Do we make a plan of action? Do we have purpose?

To live INTENTIONALLY is a life lived willingly, on purpose (a choice) with an aim that guides our actions! This implies that we must be firmly fixed on an intention; having a mind fastened upon a goal. Hopefully, that aim is to praise and honor God and to do His will in whatever we do. God's Word gives instructions and teaches us how we can focus on this goal and give our love to Him.

Psalms 27:11
Teach me Thy way, O Lord, and lead me in a plain path . . .

Philippians 2:13, 14
For it is God which worketh in you both to will and to do of His good pleasure. Do all things without murmurings and disputings:

Hebrews 13:21
Make you <u>perfect</u> in every good work <u>to do His will</u>, working in you that which is well-pleasing in His sight, <u>through Jesus Christ</u>; to Whom be glory for ever and ever. Amen.

Romans 12:2
And be not conformed to this world: but <u>be ye transformed</u> by the renewing of your mind, that ye may prove what is that good, and acceptable, and <u>perfect, will of God</u>.

Ephesians 6:6
Not with eye-service, as men-pleasers; but as the servants of Christ, <u>doing the will of God</u> from the heart;

I Peter 4:2
That he no longer should <u>live</u> the rest of his time in the flesh to the lusts of men, but <u>to the will of God</u>.

FEBRUARY 20

CHRIST'S SECOND COMING
HE IS COMING SOON

Most of the world knows of Christ's first coming: His birth, born of a virgin. The Son of God, the "Son of the Highest" and His Name shall be called JESUS. This account of His first coming is so beautiful as told to us in Luke 1:27 - 35. Keep on reading through Luke, Chapter 2, and be blessed again by the whole event.

As wonderful and exciting as this was, JESUS' second coming will be magnificent. He will claim His Kingdom with power and judgment. Both the Old and New Testaments prophesied Christ's return but fewer people know of this or have never heard. Those who have heard either do not believe it or do not care to think about it. They rationalize that it has been so long now since it has been written, that it won't be in their lifetime. This is very short-sighted for we are told it may be today.

<u>Jude 14, 15</u>
And Enoch also, the seventh from Adam, prophesied of these, saying, Behold, the Lord cometh with ten thousands of His saints, to execute judgment upon all, and to convince all that are ungodly among them of all their ungodly deeds which they have ungodly committed, and of all their hard speeches which ungodly sinners have spoken against Him.

<u>Mark 14:61, 62</u>
. . . Art thou the Christ, the Son of the Blessed? And Jesus said, I am: and ye shall see the Son of man sitting on the right hand of power, and coming in the clouds of heaven.

<u>Acts 1:11</u>
Ye men of Galilee, why stand ye gazing up into heaven? This same Jesus, which is taken up from you into heaven, shall so come in like manner as ye have seen Him go into heaven.

<u>II Peter 3:3-5, 8</u>
Knowing this first, that there shall come <u>in the last days scoffers</u>, walking after their own lusts, and saying, <u>Where is the promise of His coming</u>? for since the fathers fell asleep, all things continue as they were from the beginning of the creation. For this they <u>willingly are ignorant</u> . . .But, <u>beloved, be not ignorant of this one thing</u>, that one day is with the Lord as a thousand years, and a thousand years as one day.

II Peter 3:10 - 14

But the day of <u>the Lord will come</u> as a thief in the night; in the which the heavens shall pass away with a great noise, and the elements shall melt with fervent heat, the earth also and the works that are therein shall be burned up. Seeing then that all these things shall be dissolved, <u>what manner of persons ought ye to be</u> in all holy conversation and godliness, <u>Looking</u> for and hasting unto the coming of the day of God, wherein the heavens being on fire shall be dissolved, and the elements shall melt with fervent heat? Nevertheless we, according to His promise, <u>look for</u> new heavens and a new earth, wherein dwelleth righteousness. Wherefore, beloved, seeing that ye look for such things, <u>be diligent</u> that ye may be found of Him in peace, without spot, and blameless.

Revelation 1:7, 8

Behold, He cometh with clouds; and every eye shall see Him, and they also which pierced Him: and all kindreds of the earth shall wail because of Him. Even so, Amen. I am Alpha and Omega, the beginning and the ending, saith <u>the Lord, Which is, and Which was, and Which is to come, the Almighty</u>.

Revelation 22:7

Behold, I come quickly: blessed is he that keepeth the sayings of the prophecy of this book.

FEBRUARY 21

WAIT and ENDURE
(to the end joyfully)

It is possible to meet all our difficulties with love and laughter since we can know God is with us to the end. Trials are God's way of training us on to maturity and righteousness in Him. With His help, endure and rest your soul in His power, joy, and peace. And be aware and conscious of His presence with thanksgiving. As He said, "**I will never leave you nor forsake you.**"

WAIT

Hebrews 13:5, 6
Let your conversation (life) be without covetousness; and be content with such things as ye have: for He hath said, I will never leave thee, nor forsake thee. So that we may boldly say, The Lord is my helper, and I will not fear what man shall do unto me.

Psalms 25:5, 21
Lead me in Thy truth, and teach me: for Thou art the God of my salvation; on Thee do I wait all the day. Let integrity and uprightness preserve me for I wait on Thee.

Psalms 27:14
Wait on the Lord: be of good courage, and He shall strengthen thine heart: wait, I say, on the Lord.

Psalms 62:5, 7, 8
My soul, wait thou only upon God; for my expectation is from Him. In God is my salvation and my glory: the rock of my strength, and my refuge, is in God. Trust in Him at all times; ye people, pour out your heart before Him: God is a refuge for us. Selah.

Psalms 130:5
I wait for the Lord, my soul doth wait, and in His Word do I hope.

Lamentations 3:26
It is good that a man should both hope and quietly wait for the salvation of the Lord.

ENDURE

Matthew 24:13, 14
But he that shall endure unto the end, the same shall be saved. And this gospel of the kingdom shall be preached in all the world for a witness unto all nations; and then shall the end come.

II Timothy 2:3, 4
Thou therefore endure hardness, as a good soldier of Jesus Christ. No man that warreth, entangleth himself with the affairs of this life; that he may please him who hath chosen him to be a soldier.

Hebrews 12:7
If ye endure chastening, God dealeth with you as with sons; for what son is he whom the father chasteneth not?

James 5:11
Behold, we count them happy which endure. Ye have heard of the patience of Job, and have seen the end of the Lord; that the Lord is very pitiful, and of tender mercy.

Peter 2:19, 20, 21
For this is thankworthy, if a man for conscience toward God endure grief, suffering wrongfully. For what glory is it, if, when ye be buffeted for your faults, ye shall take it patiently? but if, when ye do well, and suffer for it, ye take it patiently, this is acceptable with God. For even hereunto were ye called: because Christ also suffered for us, leaving us an example, that ye should follow His steps:

FEBRUARY 22

YOUR WAGE
If you don't have it – don't spend it!

All that we have comes from the hand of God – not from our employers, our businesses or the government. Be a good steward of all that we have been given. If you are in debt stop spending and especially stop using credit cards unless it is an absolute emergency. Sad to say at least one credit card seems to be a must in our present society, but we all too often use them frivolously. Get out of debt so you can GIVE first (back to God and anyone in need), SAVE secondly, and LIVE on the rest. Our first reaction to this is "I just can't do that!" Ask God to help you find a way – His way. As we have learned during the "war on drugs," "just say NO" to spending more than you have. This takes planning and discipline and turning back over to God what He so generously provided. Get free of the trap of debt and released from the hook of spending what you cannot pay!

Job 13:23
How many are mine iniquities and sins? make me to know my transgression and my sin.

Proverbs 3:9
Honour the Lord with thy substance, and with the first-fruits of all thine increase:

Proverbs 15:16
Better is little with the fear of the Lord than great treasure and trouble therewith.

Proverbs 21:20
There is treasure to be desired and oil in the dwelling of the wise; but a foolish man spendeth it up.

Proverbs 22:7
The rich ruleth over the poor, and the borrower is servant to the lender.

FEBRUARY 23

TRUTH WILL SET YOU FREE

We can be completely confident that God's Word is **TRUTH!** God tells us so and He cannot lie! "**God be true, but every man a liar**" **TRUTH** is in Jesus – "**I am the way, the TRUTH and the life.**" Seek to KNOW more and more of Christ's risen life in us. Rise above all fears and go out and meet the Lord Jesus Who waits for you with open arms. How can we ignore or neglect such a great invitation? God will even give us the gift of His Holy Spirit to guide us to **TRUTH** and understanding if we will only ask Him. God's **TRUTH** is joined together with mercy and kindness so study God's Word and examine what He wants you to KNOW!

Hebrews 6:17 - 19
Wherein God, willing . . . to shew . . . by an oath: That by two immutable things, in which it was impossible for God to lie . . . for refuge . . . lay hold upon the hope set before us: Which hope we have as an anchor of the soul, both sure and stedfast.

John 2:22
When therefore He was risen from the dead, His disciples remembered that He had said this unto them; and they believed the scripture, and the word which Jesus had said.

Psalms 25:5
Lead me in Thy truth, and teach me: for Thou art the God of my salvation; on Thee do I wait all the day.

I John 5:20
And we know that the Son of God is come, and hath given us an understanding, that we may know Him that is true, and we are in Him that is true, even in His Son Jesus Christ. This is the true God, and eternal life.

FEBRUARY 24

YOUR BOOKS – BE CHOOSY

Add "Astronomy" to your Library!

Looking up into the sky has always given me great joy – the forming of the clouds by day and the stars by night. That was the extent of my knowledge – what I could see. Then I remembered that one of our groomsmen at our wedding had taught high school Astronomy in Minnesota, for years and I thought what a fantastic career. One can't help but believe there is a God when seeing how vast the heavens are, with greater wonders beyond – the **"heaven of heavens."**

Deuteronomy 10:14
Behold, the heaven and the heaven of heavens is the Lord's thy God, the earth also, with all that therein is.

Get a book on Astronomy (**not astrology**) and be overwhelmed by the magnitude of our God and the love He has for us. Become a **"stargazer."**

Genesis 1:16
And God made two great lights; the greater light to rule the day, and the lesser light to rule the night: he made the stars also.

II Chronicles 2:6
But who is able to build Him an house, seeing the heaven and heaven of heavens cannot contain Him? who am I then, that I should build Him an house, save only to burn sacrifice before Him?

Psalms 8:3,4
When I consider thy heavens, the work of thy fingers, the moon and the stars, which thou hast ordained; What is man, that thou art mindful of him? and the son of man, that thou visitest him?

FEBRUARY 25

THE LIGHT FOR MY PATH

Once, my Dad and I were out on an errand after dark, and the car ran out of gas. We had to walk down a dark street to get some. A man approached and asked my Dad what was going on. It must have looked like he shouldn't have had a small young girl out at that time of night. In my mind, I was afraid until I saw he was a policeman trying to help us. Then I wasn't afraid anymore since I was with my Dad. This is a small illustration of how the truth of knowing who you are with, and their love, can chase away the fear of darkness and circumstances. Almost everything you read in the Bible is a lesson for us and *"a light to your path."* I can hardly imagine a life without it.

Luke 1:79
To give light to them that sit in darkness and in the shadow of death, to guide our feet into the way of peace.

Another illustration of darkness is the complete darkness when you go deep into a cave. We only want to see what it is like for just a moment before we want a light to be turned on. God has provided Spiritual Light for us to bring us out of the darkness of wandering around in sin and on our own.

Genesis 1:3, 4
And God said, Let there be light: and there was light. And God saw the light, that it was good: and God divided the light from the darkness.

Isaiah 5:20
Woe unto them that call evil good, and good evil; that put darkness for light, and light for darkness; that put bitter for sweet, and sweet for bitter!

Ephesians 5:8
For ye were sometimes darkness, but now are ye light in the Lord: walk as children of light:

FEBRUARY 26

A PRAYER FOR OLD AGE

You may not be ready for old age yet, but you must know someone who is. Getting through even the better days takes a lot of courage and faith. Many new lessons must be learned. Read Psalms 71:1 – 24, for yourself for now, or your future then share it with someone who needs encouragement today.

I remember reading the autobiography of the inspiring singer, Ethel Waters, many years ago. She claimed that Psalms 71 was a great comfort to her in her old age.

Psalms 71:1 - 24
1. In Thee, O Lord, do I put my trust: let me never be put to confusion.
2. Deliver me in Thy righteousness, and cause me to escape: incline Thine ear unto me, and save me.
3. Be Thou my strong habitation, whereunto I may continually resort: Thou hast given commandment to save me; for Thou art my rock and my fortress.
4. Deliver me, O my God, out of the hand of the wicked, out of the hand of the unrighteous and cruel man.
5. For Thou art my hope, O Lord God: Thou art my trust from my youth.
6. By Thee have I been holden up from the womb: Thou art He that took me out of my mother's bowels: my praise shall be continually of Thee.
7. I am as a wonder unto many; but Thou art my strong refuge.
8. Let my mouth be filled with Thy praise and with Thy honour all the day.
9. Cast me not off in the time of old age; forsake me not when my strength faileth.
10. For mine enemies speak against me; and they that lay wait for my soul take counsel together,
11. Saying, God hath forsaken him: persecute and take him; for there is none to deliver him. O God, be not far from me:
12. O my God, make haste for my help.
13. Let them be confounded and consumed that are adversaries to my soul; let them be covered with reproach and dishonour that seek my hurt.
14. But I will hope continually, and will yet praise Thee more and more.
15. My mouth shall shew forth Thy righteousness and Thy salvation all the day; for I know not the numbers thereof.
16. I will go in the strength of the Lord God: I will make mention of Thy righteousness, even of Thine only.
17. O God, Thou hast taught me from my youth: and hitherto have I declared Thy wondrous works.
18. Now also when I am old and gray-headed, O God, forsake me not; until I have shewed thy strength unto this generation, and Thy power to everyone that is to come.
19. Thy righteousness also, O God, is very high, Who hast done great things: O God, who is like unto thee!
20. Thou, which hast shewed me great and sore troubles, shalt quicken me again, and shalt bring me up again from the depths of the earth.
21. Thou shalt increase my greatness, and comfort me on every side.
22. I will also praise Thee with the psaltery, even Thy truth, O my God: <u>unto Thee will I sing</u> with the harp, O thou Holy One of Israel.
23. My lips shall greatly rejoice when I sing unto Thee; and my soul, which thou hast redeemed.
24. My tongue also shall talk of Thy righteousness all the day long: for they are confounded, for they are brought unto shame, that seek my hurt.

FEBRUARY 27

THE LOVE OF GOD

God's love is eternal and forever. This is His promise.

Jeremiah 31:3
The Lord hath appeared of old unto me, saying, Yea, I have loved thee with an everlasting love: therefore with lovingkindness have I drawn thee.

You can see God's love all around us starting each day with the sunrise. All throughout your day, if you look for it, you will see how He cares for you moment by moment. Then as the sun goes down we can see the beautiful moon He has given us for our light by night and enjoyment. Watch today for the many signs of God's love toward you personally. If you are so inclined, make a list.

Psalms 89:1
I will sing of the steadfast love of the LORD, forever; with my mouth I will make known Your faithfulness to all generations.

Psalms 136:2, 3
Give thanks to the God of gods, for His steadfast love endures <u>forever</u>. Give thanks to the Lord of lords, for His steadfast love endures <u>forever</u>.

Jeremiah 33:11
Give thanks to the Lord of hosts, for the Lord is good, <u>for His steadfast love endures forever</u>!

Romans 8:38, 39
For I am sure that neither death nor life, nor angels nor rulers, nor things present nor things to come, nor powers, nor height nor depth, nor anything else in all creation, will be able to separate us from the love of God in Christ Jesus our Lord.

FEBRUARY 28

MY REFLECTIONS

Look up the word "reflections" for yourself and you will find at least two meanings to think about today: like looking in a mirror and seeing oneself, and to think and consider what you saw or heard. After serious considerations, you might be called upon to react – either with a yes or no, or simply ignore. WOW! There are so many choices to make as we go along, even moment by moment, thought by thought. Today, be especially aware of your reflections and your responses.

James 1:22
But be ye doers of the word, and not hearers only, deceiving your own selves.

Ephesians 4:32
And be ye kind one to another, tenderhearted, forgiving one another, even as God for Christ's sake hath forgiven you.

Psalms 37:1, 3, 4, 5, 7, 8
Fret not thyself because of evildoers, neither be thou envious against the workers of iniquity. Trust in the Lord, and do good; . . . Delight thyself also in the Lord. . . . Commit thy way unto the Lord; . . . Rest in the Lord, and wait patiently for Him: . . . Cease from anger, and forsake wrath: fret not thyself in any wise to do evil.

John 6:61
When Jesus knew in Himself that His disciples murmured at it, He said unto them, Doth this offend you?

II Corinthians 3, 4
But if our gospel be hid, it is hid to them that are lost: In whom the god of this world hath blinded the minds of them which believe not, lest the light of the glorious gospel of Christ, Who is the image of God, should shine unto them.

FEBRUARY 29

LEAP YEAR

MARCH

JOSEPH'S COAT

<u>Genesis 37:3</u>
Now Israel (Jacob) loved Joseph more than all his children, because he was the son of his old age: and he made him a coat of many colours.

MARCH 1

A "TO DO" EXERCISE

If we all spend more time reading the Bible we will have an increased desire to know God and His Word. I have learned a way to be consistent and blessed daily; I was taught this **"to do"** exercise: read Proverbs and Psalms together in the months that have 30 days. Why only the 30–day months? Because Proverbs has 30 Chapters (1 each day) and Psalms has 150 (5 each day). Therefore, it is easy to keep track of where you left off.

This commitment of time and effort will result in getting to know God! Desire to know and hear from Him as you read. Don't just read to read; but listen as your priority. If it takes you longer than a month, just continue on into the next month. You will be blessed.

Psalms 119:11
Thy Word have I hid in mine heart, that I might not sin against Thee.

Psalms 119:15, 16
I will meditate in Thy precepts, and have respect unto Thy ways. I will delight myself in Thy statutes: I will not forget Thy Word.

Psalms 119:105, 133
Thy Word is a lamp unto my feet, and a light unto my path.
Order my steps in Thy Word: and let not any iniquity have dominion over me.

Psalms 119:160, 162
Thy Word is true from the beginning:
and every one of Thy righteous judgments endureth forever.
I rejoice at Thy Word, as one that findeth great spoil.

MARCH 2

REMEMBERANCE

Most of what we have learned we either may forget or we don't use or think about. Other times we may even have to be reminded of or re-study information we used to know. I believe this is why the Bible uses the word "remembrance" to refer to specific times, events, places, or actions. We do the same thing. Besides birthdays and anniversaries, think of other important items you bring to your "remembrance." See how Scriptures use the word:

Luke 22:18 - 20
For I (Jesus) say unto you, I will not drink of the fruit of the vine, until the kingdom of God shall come. And He took bread, and gave thanks, and brake it, and gave unto them, saying, This is My body which is given for you: this do in remembrance of Me. Likewise, also the cup after supper, saying, This cup is the New Testament in My blood, which is shed for you.

John 14:26
But the Comforter, which is the Holy Ghost, Whom the Father will send in My name, He shall teach you all things, and bring all things to your remembrance, whatsoever I have said unto you.

II Peter 1:3, 4, 12
According as his divine power hath given unto us all things that pertain unto life and godliness, through the knowledge of him that hath called us to glory and virtue: Whereby are given unto us exceeding great and precious promises: that by these ye might be partakers of the divine nature, having escaped the corruption that is in the world through lust.
Wherefore I will not be negligent to put you always in remembrance of these things, though ye know them, and be established in the present truth.

MARCH 3

"TRUST and OBEY"
A chorus from a hymn from my childhood:
By J. H. Sammis (1846-1919)

<u>Trust</u> and <u>Obey</u>
For there's no other way
To be happy in Jesus
But to <u>Trust</u> and Obey

Where we put our trust and who we trust is an important matter. I ask myself, do I obey God or man? We must answer this question honestly. Do I really trust God in all things, through every changing phase of life? We cannot obey God if this choice is not settled in our hearts and minds. Jesus is our perfect example as He lived in a time of a very cruel society and government. We need His wisdom to know how we should live.

TRUST

<u>Psalms 40:4</u>
Blessed is that man that maketh the Lord his trust, and respecteth not the proud, nor such as turn aside to lies.

<u>Psalms 71:5</u>
For Thou art my hope, O Lord God: Thou art my trust from my youth.

<u>Proverbs 29:25</u>
The fear of man bringeth a snare: but whoso putteth his trust in the Lord shall be safe.

<u>II Samuel 22:3</u>
The God of my rock; in Him will I trust: He is my shield, and the horn of my salvation, my high tower, and my refuge, my saviour; Thou savest me from violence.

MARCH 4

"TRUST and OBEY," By J. H. Sammis (1846-1919)

**Trust and Obey
For there's no other way
To be happy in Jesus
But to Trust and Obey**

Continue today with this train of thought of obedience in this chorus above from yesterday. Like our children find it hard to obey us or authorities over them, we find it just as hard to be obedient to our Heavenly Father. We may also often find ourselves not wanting to obey those over us in government or work.

OBEY

I Peter 2:18, 19
Servants, be subject to your masters (employers) with all fear (respect); not only to the good and gentle, but also to the forward (harsh).

I Timothy 2:1 - 3
I exhort therefore, that, first of all, supplications, prayers, intercessions, and giving of thanks, be made for all men; For kings, and for all that are in authority; that we may lead a quiet and peaceable life in all godliness and honesty. For this is good and acceptable in the sight of God our Saviour;

Acts 5:29
Then Peter and the other apostles answered and said, We ought to obey God rather than men.

Romans 2:8 - 11
But unto them that are contentious, and do not obey the truth, but obey unrighteousness, indignation and wrath, Tribulation and anguish, upon every soul of man that doeth evil, of the Jew first, and also of the Gentile; But glory, honour, and peace, to every man that worketh good . . .For there is no respect of persons with God.

MARCH 5

WHATSOEVER YE DO

I like the old English word "whatsoever" as used in the Bible. What other word could replace it? It implies: whatever you please to do. Mostly used in commands, whatsoever is as an all-inclusive word giving both positive and negative actions. So, let us "do" the positives to honor God in all that we "do."

Let us also look at a few negatives of what "not to do" which would bring dishonor to God. King Solomon wrote in Ecclesiastes, his conclusion of all wisdom (given to him by God).

Ecclesiastes 12:13, 14
Let us hear the conclusion of the whole matter: Fear God, and keep His commandments: for this is the whole duty of man. For God shall bring every work into judgment, with every secret thing, whether it be good, or whether it be evil.

Ecclesiastes 9:10
<u>Whatsoever</u> thy hand findeth to do, do it with thy might; for there is no work, nor device, nor knowledge, nor wisdom, in the grave, whither thou goest.

Matthew 7:12
Therefore all things <u>whatsoever</u> ye would that men should do to you, do ye even so to them: for this is the law and the prophets.

Matthew 28:20
Teaching them to observe all things <u>whatsoever</u> I have commanded you: and, lo, I am with you alway, even unto the end of the world. Amen.

John 15:14, 16a
Ye are My friends, if ye do <u>whatsoever</u> I command you.
Ye have not chosen Me, but I have chosen you and ordained you, that ye should go and bring forth fruit.

MARCH 6

BITTERNESS and MALICE

We hear: Bitterness only hurts you! Not true! Bitterness is the twin of malice and is contagious, meaning it can spread from one person to another if we are not careful. If you have bitterness and/or malice, how's it working for you? I'm sure not so good. It can harm your attitude, health, personality and especially your relationships. Most of all, it affects your relationship with God. Call it what it is – bitterness is sin against God. Ask God to heal you before it eats you up.

Job 21:25
And another dieth in the bitterness of his soul, and never eateth with pleasure.

Isaiah 38:17
Behold, for peace I had great bitterness: but Thou hast in love to my soul delivered it from the pit of corruption: for Thou hast cast all my sins behind Thy back.

Acts 8:23
For I perceive that thou art in the gall of bitterness, and in the bond of iniquity.

Romans 3:14 - 18
Whose mouth is full of cursing and bitterness: Their feet are swift to shed blood: Destruction and misery are in their ways: And the way of peace have they not known: There is no fear of God before their eyes.

Ephesians 4:31, 32
Let all bitterness, and wrath, and anger, and clamour, and evil speaking, be put away from you, with all malice: And be ye kind one to another, tenderhearted, forgiving one another, even as God for Christ's sake hath forgiven you.

MARCH 7

CHOOSING WISELY

We have so many choices to make in our lifetime. Each decision has good or bad consequences. Sometimes these results don't show up immediately and too often we have to learn the hard way. Our God-given free will, that He created in us, has everything to do with our decisions. If we choose, we can become one of His children. At times, God will let us have our own way while other times He will intervene. Who can know the mind of God? But we do know He deals with us as individuals – on a very personal level. Only God knows our future and what is best for us. Believing in Him takes our faith and ability to trust His Word.

Deuteronomy 30:19, 20a
I call heaven and earth to record this day against you, that I have set before you, life and death, blessing and cursing: therefore, <u>choose life</u>, that both thou and thy seed may live: That thou mayest love the Lord thy God, and that thou mayest obey His voice, and that thou mayest cleave unto Him: for <u>He is thy life</u>, and the length of thy days:

Joshua 24:15a, c
And if it seem evil unto you to serve the Lord, <u>choose</u> you this day whom ye will serve . . . <u>as for me and my house, we will serve the Lord</u>.

Psalms 25:12
What man is he that feareth the Lord? him shall He teach in the way that he shall choose.

Proverbs 1:28, 29
Then shall they call upon Me, but I will not answer; they shall seek Me early, but they shall not find Me: For that they hated knowledge, and <u>did not choose the fear of the Lord</u>:

MARCH 8

WORKS OF THE FLESH

We refer to deeds of human nature and frailty as "works of the flesh." We often make excuses for such wrongdoings and weaknesses. In our hearts, we know these selfish acts are sin but we do them anyway. They become evidence of straying away from our walk with God. As we rationalize our behavior, we claim some of our actions were meant for good. But when our eyes are opened to the hurting of ourselves and others, we know better, and need God to forgive us. Paul, in Romans, explains this dilemma we are in, here in our earthly bodies. Take the time and pray to comprehend the full understanding and meaning of our works of the flesh.

Romans 7:14 - 25

For we know that the law is <u>spiritual</u>: but I am <u>carnal</u>, sold under sin. For that which I do I allow not: for what I would, that do I not; but what I hate, that do I. If then I do that which I would not, I consent unto the law that it is good. Now then it is no more I that do it, but sin that dwelleth in me. For I know that in me (that is, <u>in my flesh</u>,) dwelleth no good thing: <u>for to will is present with me; but how to perform that which is good I find not. For the good that I would I do not</u>: but the evil which I would not, that I do. Now if I do that I would not, it is no more I that do it, but sin that dwelleth in me. <u>I find then a law, that, when I would do good, evil is present with me</u>. For I delight in the law of God after the inward man: But I see another law in my members, warring against the law of <u>my mind</u>, and bringing me into captivity to the law of sin which is in <u>my members</u>. O wretched man that I am! <u>who shall deliver me from the body of this death? I thank God through Jesus Christ our Lord</u>. So then with <u>the mind</u> I myself serve the law of God; but with <u>the flesh</u> the law of sin.

MARCH 9

FEAR NOT

Fear is a big and reoccurring problem in each of our lives. So big is it, the Bible tells us over and over to "**fear not,**" giving us ways not to give into fear – believe God, His power, give reverence to Him and foremost, His love to man. His only command <u>to fear</u> is to fear (respect) Him (with awe).

Matthew 10:28
And fear not them which kill the body, but are not able to kill the soul: but rather <u>fear Him</u> which is able to destroy both soul and body in hell.

Deuteronomy 31:8
And the Lord, He it is that doth go before thee; He will be with thee, He will not fail thee, neither forsake thee: fear not, neither be dismayed.

Exodus 20:20
And Moses said unto the people, Fear not: for God is come to prove you, and that His fear may be before your faces, that ye sin not.

I Chronicles 28:20a, b
And David said to Solomon his son, Be strong and of good courage, and do it: fear not, nor be dismayed: for the Lord God, even my God, will be with thee; He will not fail thee . .

Isaiah 41:10, 13
Fear thou not; for I am with thee: be not dismayed; for I am thy God: I will strengthen thee; yea, I will help thee; yea, I will uphold thee with the right hand of my righteousness. For I the Lord thy God will hold thy right hand, saying unto thee, Fear not; I will help thee.

Isaiah 44:8
Thus saith the Lord the King of Israel, and his Redeemer the Lord of hosts; I am the first, and I am the last; and beside me there is no God. Fear ye not, neither be afraid: have not I told thee . . . Is there a God beside Me? yea, there is no God; I know not any.

MARCH 10

JOY UNSPEAKABLE

What does Joy Unspeakable mean?
"Happiness" is an empty pursuit, and is different from real Joy. Joy rises above <u>feelings</u> and circumstances - knowing our true standing with God – He loves me! I am His child! He bore my sins with His own body on the cross! I shall see Him face-to-face for all eternity, when He shall appear. This is our JOY UNSPEAKABLE! Recognize it and recall it whenever you need to "feel" it. What a wonderful God and Savior we have in Christ Jesus! **JOY UNSPEAKABLE!**

I Peter 1:8
Whom having not seen, ye love; in Whom, though now ye see Him not, yet believing, ye rejoice with joy unspeakable and full of glory:

I John 1:4
And these things write we unto you, that your joy may be full.

Psalms 32:11
Be glad in the Lord, and rejoice, ye righteous: and shout for joy, all ye that are upright in heart.

Psalms 51:12
Restore unto me the joy of Thy salvation; and uphold me with Thy free spirit.

Ecclesiastes 2:26 a
For God giveth to a man that is good in His sight wisdom, and knowledge, and joy: . . .

MARCH 11

"GREAT IS THY FAITHFULNESS"
by Thomas O. Chrisolm (1866-1960)

Great is Thy faithfulness, O God my Father!
There is no shadow of turning with Thee;
Thou changest not, Thy compassions, they fail not:
As Thou hast been Thou forever wilt be.

This hymn comes to my mind and encourages me whenever I think of God and His faithfulness. Being full of truth, we are reminded, God is our Father, and has pardoned our sin and gives us enduring peace. He gives us strength for today and a hope for tomorrow. He gives each of us blessings. He provides all we need by His mighty hand. He is forever Faithful!

Psalms 36:5
Thy mercy, O Lord, is in the heavens; and Thy faithfulness
reacheth unto the clouds.

Psalms 40:10
I have not hid Thy righteousness within my heart; I have declared Thy
faithfulness and Thy salvation:
I have not concealed Thy lovingkindness
and Thy truth from the great congregation.

Psalms 89:5
And the heavens shall praise Thy wonders, O Lord:
Thy faithfulness also in the congregation of the saints.

Psalms 119:90
Thy faithfulness is unto all generations:
Thou hast established the earth, and it abideth.

Lamentations 3:22, 23
It is of the Lord's mercies that we are not consumed, because His compassions
fail not.
They are new every morning: great is thy faithfulness.

MARCH 12

SECOND (Chance) BIRTH

Some are given the blessings of a <u>Second (Chance) Birth</u> - <u>physically</u>, when they come so close to death that they remember if not for the grace of God they would have died. Possibly through an accident, health issue, or other causes, both these individuals, and loved ones are so grateful for this "<u>second chance birth</u>" here on earth. However, there is a Spiritual new birth which is the most important birth. Jesus told us about – an <u>Eternal New birth;</u> He said, "Ye must be born again." This Second Chance Birth gives us an opportunity to examine ourselves for the assurance we have <u>received the New Birth</u> offered by Christ through His death on the cross, in our place for our sins. This is the <u>Eternal New Birth</u>. We will live forever with Him.

<u>Jeremiah 21:8b</u>
Thus saith the Lord; Behold, I set before you the way of <u>life</u>, and the way of death.

<u>John 3:5 – 7</u>
Jesus answered, Verily, verily, I say unto thee, Except a man be born of water and of the Spirit, he cannot enter into the kingdom of God. That which is born of the flesh is flesh; and that which is born of the Spirit is spirit. Marvel not that I said unto thee, <u>Ye must be born again</u>.

<u>I John 5:1, 4, 5, 19</u>
Whosoever believeth that Jesus is the Christ is born of God: For whatsoever is born of God overcometh the world: and this is the victory that overcometh the world, even our faith. Who is he that overcometh the world, but he that believeth that Jesus is the Son of God? And we know that we are of God, and the whole world lieth in wickedness.

MARCH 13

PLEASURES FOREVER

Feeling good in various ways is a pleasure unto itself. This verse comes to mind when I think of beautiful godly pleasures:

Psalms 16:11
Thou wilt shew me the path of life: in Thy presence is fullness of joy; at Thy right hand there are <u>pleasures</u> for evermore.

So different from the "happiness" we seek here on earth, be it sports, movies, entertainment, or anything else you can think of. Happiness occurs when our lives are comfortable and secure in a momentary space of time. But the pleasures from God are not subject to change like "happiness," at a moment's notice. <u>Real pleasures</u> are lasting in the Person of Jesus Christ and the promise of all eternity.

Psalms 36:8 - 10
They shall be abundantly satisfied with the fatness of Thy house; and Thou shalt make them drink of the river of <u>Thy pleasures</u>. For with Thee is <u>the fountain of life</u>: in Thy light shall we see light. O continue Thy lovingkindness unto them that know Thee; and Thy righteousness to the upright in heart.

Titus 3:3
For we ourselves also were sometimes foolish, disobedient, deceived, serving divers lusts and pleasures, living in malice and envy, hateful, and hating one another.

Isaiah 47:8a, 10
Therefore hear now this, thou that art given to pleasures, that dwellest carelessly, that sayest in thine heart, I am, and none else beside me; . . . For thou hast trusted in thy wickedness: thou hast said, None seeth me. Thy wisdom and thy knowledge, it hath perverted thee; and thou hast said in thine heart, I am, and none else beside me.

MARCH 14

ONE DAY AT A TIME

One day at a time! Sometimes we borrow troubles from tomorrows that may not even happen. We can name this as worry. Possibly the most common trait among mankind. We should pay attention to what the Bible says about worry. An old song has used this title and even an old television program borrowed this phrase as its own title. So, we apparently need this prompting.

<u>Matthew 6:31-- 34</u>
Therefore take no thought, saying, What shall we eat? or, What shall we drink? or, Wherewithal shall we be clothed? (For after all these things do the Gentiles seek:) for your heavenly Father knoweth that ye have need of all these things. But seek ye first the kingdom of God, and His righteousness; and all these things shall be added unto you. Take therefore no thought for the morrow: for the morrow shall take thought for the things of itself. Sufficient unto the day is the evil thereof.

<u>Romans 8:32</u>
He that spared not His Own Son, but delivered Him up for us all, how shall He not with Him also freely give us all things?

<u>Philippians 3:13, 14</u>
Brethren, I count not myself to have apprehended: but this one thing I do, forgetting those things which are behind, and reaching forth unto those things which are before I press toward the mark for the prize of the high calling of God in Christ Jesus.

<u>Hebrews 12:1, 2a</u>
Therefore, since we are surrounded by so great a cloud of witnesses, let us also lay aside every weight, and sin which clings so closely, and let us run with endurance the race that is set before us, looking to Jesus . . .

MARCH 15

FROWARD

Scripture uses "froward" (obstinate, stubborn) mostly in the Old Testament, but it also pertains to us in our relationship to God.

I Corinthians 10:11
Now all these things happened unto them for ensamples: and they are written for our admonition, upon whom the ends of the world are come.

This interesting study has a very negative meaning; provides an eye opener of our behavior. Man"s wisdom tells us to always try to think positive, but sometimes this is bad advice since we learn (the hard way) great lessons from our negative choices. In more recent translations, "froward" has been replaced by the word perverse which thankfully, I have never heard in a casual conversation. I can see my own behavior (stubbornness) at times in a different light – not a pretty sight! I found this so important I want to continue on to the next page!

Deuteronomy 32:20
And He said, I will hide My face from them, I will see what their end shall be: for they are a very froward generation, children in whom is no faith.

Psalms 101:4, 5
A froward heart shall depart from Me: I will not know a wicked person. Whoso privily slandereth his neighbour, him will I cut off: him that hath an high look and a proud heart will not I suffer.

Proverbs 2:12 - 15
To deliver thee from the way of the evil man, from the man that speaketh froward things; Who leave the paths of uprightness, to walk in the ways of darkness; Who rejoice to do evil, and delight in the frowardness of the wicked; Whose ways are crooked, and they froward in their paths:

Proverbs 6:12 - 15
A naughty person, a wicked man, walketh with a froward mouth. He winketh with his eyes, he speaketh with his feet, he teacheth with his fingers; Frowardness is in his heart, he deviseth mischief continually; he soweth discord. Therefore shall his calamity come suddenly; suddenly shall he be broken without remedy.

Proverbs 8:13
The fear of the Lord is to hate evil: pride, and arrogancy, and the evil way, and the froward mouth, do I hate.

Proverbs 11:20
They that are of a froward heart are abomination to the Lord: but such as are upright in their way are His delight.

Proverbs 16:28 - 30
A froward man soweth strife: and a whisperer separateth chief friends. A violent man enticeth his neighbour, and leadeth him into the way that is not good. He shutteth his eyes to devise froward things: moving his lips he bringeth evil to pass.

Proverbs 17:20
*He that hath a froward heart findeth no good:
and he that hath a perverse tongue falleth into mischief.*

MARCH 16

NEED WISDOM?

We all need the wisdom of God. Man's wisdom is a trap and snare for us even if it seems right or aligns with the Scriptures we know. We must have sure knowledge where wisdom is coming from, and reject all of man's ways and motives, even our own. Know it for yourself from God, and do not take man's word for it. As we go along moment by moment in this life, examine if what we are doing or thinking is pleasing and honoring God.

Ask for His wisdom in every situation and in every thought. He is right there in your heart and will instruct you in His ways and wisdom. Read and re-read the Book of Proverbs. We can know and understand how God wants us to live. Just ask Him.

James 1:5, 6
If any of you lack wisdom, let him ask of God, that giveth to all men liberally, and upbraideth (rebuketh) not; and it shall be given him. But let him ask in faith, nothing wavering. For he that wavereth is like a wave of the sea driven with the wind and tossed.

Psalms 19:7
The law of the Lord is perfect, converting the soul: the testimony of the Lord is sure, making wise the simple.

Proverbs 4:7
Wisdom is the principal thing; therefore get wisdom: and with all thy getting get understanding.

Matthew 10:16
Behold, I send you forth as sheep in the midst of wolves: be ye therefore wise as serpents, and harmless as doves.

Romans 1:16
. . . Be not wise in your own conceits.

MARCH 17

HEAR and HEARKEN

What good is it if you "hear and not hearken"? These two words are partners, as though you "can't have one without the other" when you listen with a firm purpose. For our study here, let's deliberately apply our hearing and hearkening to the Word of God and concentrate on what we hear, discerning what God is saying to us, then apply or hearken it to our lives. I believe hearkening is the application of whatever we truly hear. We either accept or deny it. Don't let what you hear from Him "go in one ear and out the other," but honestly fix it to your life. When you seriously read and study His Word, "hear and hearken."

Deuteronomy 12:28
Observe and hear all these words which I command thee, that it may go well with thee, and with thy children after thee forever, when thou doest that which is good and right in the sight of the Lord thy God.

Jeremiah 6:10
To whom shall I (Jeremiah) speak, and give warning, that they may hear? behold, their ear is uncircumcised, and they cannot hearken: behold, the Word of the Lord is unto them a reproach; they have no delight in it.

II Chronicles 9:23
And all the kings of the earth sought the presence of Solomon, to hear his wisdom, that God had put in his heart.

Proverbs 8:33, 34
Hear instruction, and be wise, and refuse it not. Blessed is the man that heareth Me (God's wisdom), watching daily at My gates, waiting at the posts of My doors. For whoso findeth me findeth life, and shall obtain favour of the Lord.

MARCH 18

SIN

Sin? "Don't even go there," some people say. "You might offend someone." Guilt and punishment turn people off. However, we must face the true facts and the warning about sin recorded in God's Word; not my words or thoughts, but the very Word of God.

First of all, it is important to know Romans 3:23, 24.
For all have sinned, and come short of the glory of God (the Fact!); Being justified freely by His grace through the redemption that is in Christ Jesus (our hope):

Second, we say, what debt do I owe? See Romans 6:23
For the wages of sin is death (the Fact); but the gift of God is eternal life through Jesus Christ our Lord (Jesus paid the debt for our sin).

Third, our *"propitiation"* II Corinthians 5:21 *For He hath made Him to be sin for us (Fact, on the cross), who knew no sin; that we might be made the righteousness of God in Him.*

I Peter 2:24, 25
Who His own self bare our sins in His own body on the tree, that we, being dead to sins, should live unto righteousness: by Whose stripes ye were healed. For ye were as sheep going astray; but are now returned unto the Shepherd and Bishop of your souls.

Wait, there's more . . .

John 8:34
Jesus answered them, Verily, verily, I say unto you, Whosoever committeth sin is the servant of sin.

Wait. Wait. James 4:17
Therefore to him that knoweth to do good, and doeth it not, to Him it is sin.

MARCH 19

FORGIVENESS

We are so blessed! God Himself promises us His forgiveness, even when we are in our deep, deep sin. He first loved us and gave Himself for us. With our limited understanding, we can only believe in His forgiveness by faith. Only His words and the His Holy Spirit's words through the authors in the Bible, can give us this hope through faith, believing. Be blessed by the Scriptures below. Believe, believe, believe.

Acts 3:18, 19
But those things, which God before had shewed by the mouth of all His prophets, that Christ should suffer, He hath so fulfilled. Repent ye therefore, and be converted, that your sins may be blotted out, when the times of refreshing shall come from the presence of the Lord;

Colossians 1:13 - 15
Who hath delivered us from the power of darkness, and hath translated us into the kingdom of His Dear Son: In Whom we have redemption through His blood, even the forgiveness of sins: Who is the image of the invisible God, the firstborn of every creature:

Hebrews 10:17
And their sins and iniquities will I remember no more.

I John 1:9
If we confess our sins, He is faithful and just to forgive us our sins and to cleanse us from all unrighteousness.

Psalms 103:12
As far as the east is from the west, so far hath He removed our transgressions from us.

Isaiah 43:25
I, even I, am He that blotteth out thy transgressions for Mine own sake, and will not remember thy sins.

MARCH 20

STAR SPANGLED BANNER

Because of the current national events, I must reconfirm my love for this country, the belief that God knows what is happening and will take care of the problems we see <u>according to His will</u>. We are admonished in the Bible to pray for our country and leaders because they are put in office by the will of God.

<u>Romans 13:1, 2</u>
Let every soul be subject unto the higher powers. For there is no power but of God: the powers that be are ordained of God. Whosoever therefore resisteth the power, resisteth the ordinance of God: and they that resist shall receive to themselves damnation.

So, here is the song of our loyalty and faith we sing about our dear country:

"THE STAR - SPANGLED BANNER"
by Francis Scott Key

OUR NATIONAL ANTHEM

O say can you see, by the dawn's early light,
What so proudly we hail'd at the twilight's last gleaming,
Whose broad stripes and bright stars through the perilous fight
O'er the ramparts we watch'd were so gallantly streaming?
And the rocket's red glare, the bombs bursting in air,
Gave proof through the night that Our flag was still there,
O say does that star – spangled banner yet wave
O'er the land of the free and the home of the brave?

MARCH 21

CARRYING A GRUDGE?

Are **you** carrying a grudge? If so, you are carrying a load of sin around night and day! What a heavy burden, but there is a remedy for this before it affects your life, health, and eternity. Forgiveness! Think how Christ forgives us over and over again, and since we are His followers, we can forgive as we have been forgiven. We likewise should not only forgive but also forget. God puts our sins in the **depths of the sea**, and remembers them no more.

Micah 7:19c
. . . Thou wilt cast all their sins into the depths of the sea.

Isaiah 43:25
I, even I, am he that blotteth out thy transgressions for mine own sake, and will not remember thy sins.

Forgiveness starts by asking God to first to forgive us for holding a grudge against another. Then He may also require us, if at all possible, to go to the specific person and ask their forgiveness. Now is the time to examine and rid ourselves of every grudge, giving life and health to our souls.

Matthew 6:14, 15
For if ye forgive men their trespasses, your heavenly Father will also forgive you: But if ye forgive not men their trespasses, neither will your Father forgive your trespasses.

Matthew 18:21, 22
. . . Lord, how oft shall my brother sin against me, and I forgive him? till seven times? Jesus saith unto him, I say not unto thee, Until seven times: but, until seventy times seven.

Luke 6:37
Judge not, and ye shall not be judged: condemn not, and ye shall not be condemned: forgive, and ye shall be forgiven:

MARCH 22

TEACHABLE MOMENTS

Many times, we can recognize teachable moments for our own good. A chance for us to learn or re-learn an important lesson for our lives and our Spiritual growth. To see these opportunities, we must be diligent and aware to spot them. These moments may be an answer to a puzzling question, or may appear as we go about our day. Either way, these lessons are important influences in our lives.

Exodus 4:12
Now therefore go, and I will be with thy mouth, and teach thee what thou shalt say.

Deuteronomy 4:9
Only take heed to thyself, and keep thy soul diligently, lest thou forget the things which thine eyes have seen, and lest they depart from thy heart all the days of thy life: but teach them thy sons, and thy sons' sons;

Psalms 25:4, 5, 9, 11, 12
Shew me Thy ways, O Lord; teach me Thy paths. Lead me in Thy truth, and teach me: for Thou art the God of my salvation; on Thee do I wait all the day.

Psalms 90:12
So teach us to number our days, that we may apply our hearts unto wisdom.

Psalms 143:10, 11
Teach me to do Thy will; for Thou art my God: Thy spirit is good; lead me into the land of uprightness. Quicken me, O Lord, for Thy name's sake: for Thy righteousness' sake bring my soul out of trouble.

Luke 11:1
And it came to pass, that, as He was praying in a certain place, when He ceased, one of His disciples said unto Him, Lord, teach us to pray, as John also taught his disciples.

MARCH 23

CHOOSE RELATIONSHIPS WISELY

Ask God how to discern and choose good relationships. Sometimes we don't have a choice, be it at work, or schools, or even neighbors, but we are to give honor unto all men because we are all created by God. We do have a choice how deeply involved we become with those who are not good for our well-being. In fact, Scripture warns us of unhealthy relationships:

I Corinthians 6:9 - 12, particularly in verses 11 and 12.
Know ye not that the unrighteous shall not inherit the kingdom of God? Be not deceived: neither fornicators, nor idolaters, nor adulterers, nor effeminate, nor abusers of themselves with mankind, Nor thieves, nor covetous, nor drunkards, nor revilers, nor extortioners, shall inherit the kingdom of God.
And such were some of you: but ye are washed, but ye are sanctified, but ye are justified in the Name of the Lord Jesus, and by the Spirit of our God. All things are lawful unto me, but all things are not expedient: all things are lawful for me, but I will not be brought under the power of any.

Proverbs 18:24
A man that hath friends must shew himself friendly: and there is a Friend that sticketh closer than a brother.

Proverbs 27:6
Faithful are the wounds of a friend; but the kisses of an enemy are deceitful.

Proverbs 22:24, 25
Make no friendship with an angry man; and with a furious man thou shalt not go: Lest thou learn his ways, and get a snare to thy soul.

MARCH 24

PRIORITIES

Here is a quote from Dwight Eisenhower, one of our beloved presidents.
"Taking first things first often reduces the most complex human problem to a manageable proportion."

Then, our true source about time and priorities, scripture; gives us another viewpoint.

<u>Ecclesiastes 3:1-9</u>
To everything there is a season, and a time to every purpose under the heaven: A time to be born, and a time to die; time to plant, and a time to pluck up that which is planted; A time to kill, and a time to heal; a time to break down, and a time to build up; A time to weep, and a time to laugh; a time to mourn, and a time to dance; A time to cast away stones, and a time to gather stones together; a time to embrace, and a time to refrain from embracing; A time to get, and a time to lose; a time to keep, and a time to cast away; A time to rend, and a time to sew; a time to keep silence, and a time to speak; A time to love, and a time to hate; a time of war, and a time of peace. What profit hath he that worketh in that wherein he laboureth?

All of us have the same allotted time each day. Wisdom helps us to spend it wisely. Some of us can do more in an hour than others do in a week. We choose how to navigate our accomplishments. We are all different and we work at different paces - some go very slow and others go frantically. Our skills, needs, duties, and unexpected circumstances determine much. Even our physical stamina can influence the outcome. However, we must put our priorities in order to make the most of our day. Do the most pressing or demanding things first; but keep the other priorities foremost in your mind, and do them too.

MARCH 25

"TIME IS MONEY"

"_They_" say, "Time is money!"

Sometimes, but time and money are connected to our priorities. What do we do with our time and money? Do we squander them or spend wisely? There are many activities that don't include making or using money. Most important is what we do for others: family, friends and neighbors; everything from a kind smile, to housework, reading to our children, etc. Of course, the most valuable time spent is with God and His Word learning how to live for His glory.

Ephesians 5:15 – 17
See then that ye walk circumspectly, not as fools, but as wise, Redeeming the time, because the days are evil. Wherefore be ye not unwise, but understanding what the will of the Lord is.

Colossians 3:23a
And whatsoever ye do, do it heartily, as to the Lord . . .

Colossians 4: 6
Let your speech be alway with grace, seasoned with salt, that ye may know how ye ought to answer every man.

I Timothy 4:7, 8
But refuse profane and old wives' fables, and exercise thyself rather unto godliness. For bodily exercise profiteth little: but godliness is profitable unto all things, having promise of the life that now is, and of that which is to come.

James 4:13, 14
Go to now, ye that say, To day or to morrow we will go into such a city, and continue there a year, and buy and sell, and get gain: Whereas ye know not what shall be on the morrow. For what is your life? It is even a vapour, that appeareth for a little time, and then vanisheth away.

MARCH 26

CHOOSE A QUIET TIME

What are you thinking of? A nap?
A good place to look for an answer is to look at the life of King David.

Acts 13:22b
. . . I (the Lord) have found David the son of Jesse, a man after Mine own heart, which shall fulfil all My will.

Even though David had many enemies and dangerous times, he always knew to trust and turn to God in quietness for His comfort, help, and guidance. So it is for us to include this same quiet time and confidence into our own lives. When consistent, we are eager to seek God in prayer whether in need or in happiness. As new questions and emotions sneak up on us, we know to go to Him in love with all our hearts; in prayer, reading His Word, or singing praise - in our own quiet time.

Psalms 3:3
But Thou, O Lord, art a shield for me; my glory, and the lifter up of mine head.

Psalms 4:3, 4
But know that the Lord hath set apart him that is godly for Himself: the Lord will hear when I call unto Him. Stand in awe, and sin not: commune with your own heart upon your bed, and be still. Selah.

Psalms 14:2
The Lord looked down from heaven upon the children of men, to see if there were any that did understand, and seek God.

Psalms 50:15
And call upon Me in the day of trouble: I will deliver thee, and thou shalt glorify Me.

MARCH 27

MAKE HASTE or PROCRASTINATE?

Be committed to action!

Make haste or procrastinate? This is today's question. As you read the verses below, you will find one of my favorite stories about Jesus and **Zacchaeus**. Would you have made haste like **Zacchaeus**? or would you procrastinate? Procrastinate - the "putting off until tomorrow," the decision about God, which can have many consequences. Concerning our relationship to God Himself, if we delay, He cannot be a friend, comforter, helper, or guide. **Zacchaeus** saw this in Jesus immediately and "made haste." What would we do if God had the attitude of procrastination toward us? God forbid! God is not bound by time! Thank Him!

<u>Luke 19:3 - 6</u>
And he sought to see Jesus who He was; and could not for the press, because he was little of stature. And he ran before, and climbed up into a sycamore tree to see Him: for He was to pass that way. And when Jesus came to the place, He looked up, and saw him, and said unto him, <u>Zacchaeus,</u> <u>make haste</u>, and come down; for today I must abide at thy house. And he <u>made haste</u>, and came down, and received Him joyfully.

<u>Ephesians 4:22 - 24</u>
That ye <u>put off</u> concerning the former conversation the old man, which is corrupt according to the deceitful lusts; And be renewed in the spirit of your mind; And that ye <u>put on</u> the new man, which after God is created in righteousness and true holiness.

<u>Psalms 119:59, 60</u>
I <u>thought</u> on my ways, and turned my feet unto Thy testimonies. I <u>made haste</u>, and <u>delayed not</u> to keep Thy commandments.

MARCH 28

"SHOULD – HAVES"

Looking back with I "should-have" done this or that is futile! This is one of Satan's ploys that puts the emphasis on the past instead of looking forward to the "high calling" of the Lord. **Paul**, in his letter to the Philippians (Chapter 3), gives us such a picture of not looking back. If anyone had the right to look back with either pride or regret, he did. He was the Hebrew of all Hebrews and then rounded up the Christians at that time, for jail or punishment. But instead he said, *"I press toward the mark for the prize of <u>the high calling of God in Christ Jesus</u>"*

<u>Philippians 3:3b – 14</u>

. . . and (we) rejoice in Christ Jesus, and have no confidence in the flesh. Though I might also have confidence in the flesh. If any other man thinketh that he hath whereof he might trust in the flesh, I more: <u>Circumcised</u> the eighth day, of the stock of Israel, of the tribe of Benjamin, an Hebrew of the Hebrews; as touching the law, a <u>Pharisee</u>; Concerning <u>zeal, persecuting the church</u>; touching the righteousness which is in the law, blameless. But what things were gain to me, <u>those I counted loss for Christ</u>. Yea doubtless, and I count all things but loss for the excellency of the knowledge of Christ Jesus my Lord: for Whom I have suffered the loss of all things, and do count them but dung, <u>that I may win Christ, And be found in Him</u>, not having mine own righteousness, which is of the law, but that which is through the faith of Christ, the righteousness which is of God by faith: <u>That I may know Him</u>, and the power of His resurrection, and the fellowship of His sufferings, being made conformable unto His death; If by any means I might attain unto the resurrection of the dead. Not as though I had already attained, either were already perfect: but I follow after, if that I may apprehend that for which also I am apprehended of Christ Jesus . . . but <u>this one thing I do</u>, forgetting those things which are behind, and <u>reaching</u> forth unto <u>those things which are before</u>, I press toward the mark for the prize of <u>the high calling of God in Christ Jesus.</u>

MARCH 29

CONSIDER THIS . . .

Deuteronomy 4:39
Know therefore this day, and <u>Consider</u> it in thine heart, that the Lord He is God in heaven above, and upon the earth beneath: <u>there is none else</u>.

This is where it all begins!

Until we have settled this "consideration" in our hearts and minds, we have not begun to live. Life on our own is truly a struggle and often unbearable. Some people think they have it all together, but if truth be known, they are insecure, fearful, and frustrated when dealing with unwanted circumstances. If you ask them, "what are you going to do now," they really don't know even if they tell you some wild scheme. Even believers may say the same thing, but when they are settled and confidently trust that God knows all about the circumstance (and what will be done) according to His will, His wisdom, and plans He has for them, they can have a confidence and peace, knowing God is in charge.

Deuteronomy 32:29
O that they were wise, that they understood this, that they would <u>consider</u> their latter end!

I Samuel 12:24
Only fear the Lord, and serve Him in truth with all your heart: for <u>consider</u> how great things He hath done for you.

Job 37:14
Hearken unto this, O Job: stand still, and <u>consider</u> the wondrous works of God.

Psalms 8:3, 4
When I <u>consider</u> Thy heavens, the work of Thy fingers, the moon and the stars, which Thou hast ordained; What is man, that Thou art mindful of him?

MARCH 30

GOD'S WAYS ARE ETERNAL

What if God changed His mind anytime He wanted to? That's what we do all the time, making life unstable for our family, friends, and society. We see it all around us. Good intentions go astray. Bad judgments are based on lies. But God in His wisdom has told us He is the same, yesterday, and forever! You can count on it, He will not change His mind – HIS WAYS and promises ARE ETERNAL. By faith, we stake our life and all of eternity on Him.

II Corinthians 5:1
For we know that if our earthly house of this tabernacle were dissolved, we have a building of God, an house not made with hands, eternal in the heavens.

I Timothy 1:17
Now unto the King eternal, immortal, invisible, the only wise God, be honour and glory for ever and ever. **Amen.**

Hebrews 5:8, 9
Though He were a Son, yet learned He obedience by the things which He suffered; And being made perfect, He became the author of eternal salvation unto all them that obey Him;

Titus 1:2
In hope of eternal life, which God, that cannot lie, promised before the world began;

Titus 3:5 - 7
Not by works of righteousness which we have done, but according to His mercy He saved us by the washing of regeneration, and renewing of the Holy Ghost; Which He shed on us abundantly through Jesus Christ our Saviour; That being justified by His grace, we should be made heirs according to the hope of eternal life.

MARCH 31

SALT

There is a whole history of salt: how it was found, used, bought and sold, etc. To flavor something is good and this is how salt is commonly used. But more importantly, salt is used for <u>preservation</u> – to keep various things from spoiling. We can see these illustrations in Scripture as Jesus taught us. Lowly salt is so important. Even way back in Genesis we find that a Sea was known as the Salt Sea. Take a look.

<u>Genesis 14:3</u>
All these were joined together in the vale of Siddim, which is the salt sea.

<u>Leviticus 2:13</u>
And every oblation of thy meat offering shalt thou season with salt; neither shalt thou suffer the salt of the covenant of thy God to be lacking from thy meat offering: with all thine offerings thou shalt offer salt.

<u>Job 6:6</u>
Can that which is unsavoury be eaten without salt? or is there any taste in the white of an egg?

<u>Matthew 5:13</u>
Ye are the salt of the earth: but if the salt have lost his savour, wherewith shall it be salted?

<u>Mark 9:50</u>
Salt is good: but if the salt have lost his saltness, wherewith will ye season it? Have salt in yourselves, and have peace one with another.

<u>Colossians 4:6</u>
Let your speech be alway with grace, seasoned with salt, that ye may know how ye ought to answer every man.

APRIL

BLOOM WHERE PLANTED

Psalms 1:3
And he shall be like a tree planted by the rivers of water, that bringeth forth his fruit in his season; his leaf also shall not wither; and whatsoever he doeth shall prosper.

APRIL 1

ABILITY vs. AVAILABILITY

Ability and availability are gifts from God. He gives us the desire and love for Him and the AVAILABILITY to use these talents for Him, whether at "work" or "play." God is able to do what He wills - what He wants us to do through Him. For His glory and praise we are privileged to serve Him with our gifts and talents. The willingness is our decision to be available. We don't need to depend on our own abilities to be successful because we have the help of the Holy Spirit within us to will and to do whatever God is asking us to do. All gifts are not given at one time because whenever our willingness is our decision to be available so we are able to do what He asks us to do. He provides what we need, but we are to be willingly available to act accordingly. Be thankful with joy as you serve.

II Corinthians 9:8
And God is able to make all grace abound toward you; that ye, always having all sufficiency in all things, may abound to every good work:

Titus 1:9
. . . holding fast the faithful word as he hath been taught, that he may be able by sound doctrine both to exhort and to convince the gainsayers.

Romans 15:14
And I myself also am persuaded of you, my brethren, that ye also are full of goodness, filled with all knowledge, able also to admonish one another.

Ephesians 3:20
Now unto Him that is able to do exceeding abundantly above all that we ask or think, according to the power that worketh in us,

APRIL 2

WHEN THEY HAD SUNG AN HYMN . . .

<u>Matthew 26:30</u>
And when they had sung an hymn, they went out into the mount of Olives.

Easter celebrations for this year may be over but I can't get the above phrase out of my thoughts. Christ knew what was about to happen; His darkest hour, yet He sang. I never thought much about Him singing before, but He was going to the cross and He could sing with His disciples. Doesn't this tell us something about how we should face our testings and trials? When we compare ours to His, ours are very minor. In our darkest times, we can sing and trust the Lord to bring us through it - as He wills. We do not know what is ahead for us, but He does and He is in control. Be joyful and sing His praises.

<u>Mark 14:27, 28</u>
All ye shall be offended because of Me this night: for it is written, I will smite the shepherd, and the sheep shall be scattered. But after that I am risen, I will go before you into Galilee.

<u>Ephesians 5:19, 20</u>
Speaking to yourselves in psalms and hymns and spiritual songs, singing and making melody in your heart to the Lord; <u>Giving thanks always for all things</u> unto God and the Father in the Name of our Lord Jesus Christ;

<u>Acts 16:25, 26</u>
And at midnight Paul and Silas prayed, and sang praises unto God: and the prisoners heard them. And suddenly there was a great earthquake, so that the foundations of the prison were shaken: and immediately all the doors were opened, and every one's bands were loosed.

<u>II Chronicles 29:30</u>
. . . bowed themselves, and worshipped.

The hymn for me to sing today:

"I WILL SING THE WONDROUS STORY"
by Francis H. Rowley (1854-1952)

I Will Sing the Wondrous Story
Of the Christ Who died for me -
How He left His home in glory
For the cross of Calvary

<u>Chorus</u>
Yes, I'll sing the wondrous story
Of the Christ Who died for me,
Sing it with the saints in glory,
Gathered by the crystal sea.

I was lost but Jesus found me –
Found the sheep that went astray,
Threw His loving arms around me,
Drew me back into His way.

Days of darkness still come o'er me,
Sorrow's paths I often tread,
But the Savior still is with me –
By His hand I'm safely led.

He will keep me till the river
Rolls its waters at my feet;
Then He'll bear me safely over,
Where the loved ones I shall meet.

APRIL 3

EDIFICATION

Edification (instruction, enlightenment) may need to return into our spiritual vocabulary. Maybe not used in everyday conversation, but to know it and be aware of this important word that describes a powerful virtue in the Bible. There are many ways to build up one another and especially the Church of Christ as a whole. Below are verses to open our eyes on how we view and apply edification to our lives.

Ephesians 4:12, 13, 29
For the perfecting of the saints, for the work of the ministry, for the edifying of the body of Christ: Till we all come in the unity of the faith, and of the knowledge of the Son of God, unto a perfect man, unto the measure of the stature of the fulness of Christ: Let no corrupt communication proceed out of your mouth, but that which is good to the use of edifying, that it may minister grace unto the hearers.

I Corinthians 14: 12
Even so ye, forasmuch as ye are zealous of spiritual gifts, seek that ye may excel to the edifying of the church.

Acts 9 :31
Then had the churches rest throughout all Judaea and Galilee and Samaria, and were edified; and walking in the fear of the Lord, and in the comfort of the Holy Ghost, were multiplied.

Romans 14:19
Let us therefore follow after the things which make for peace, and things wherewith one may edify another.

I Corinthians 8:1b
Knowledge puffeth up, but charity (love) edifieth.

APRIL 4

PROVIDENCE

Although found in the dictionary, providence seems to be a "Christianese" word - only found in the Bible as a clarification in the margin replacing the word for "provision" in Acts 24:2. People may want to have this power over us to guide our futures. Think about it. Who has such power? Who do you want to be in charge of your future? We can choose to rest in our God, because: <u>He is the One</u> in control – no matter what! <u>He is the One</u> who sees and cares for us, and completely knows our future with His foresight! <u>He is the One</u> who gives us His Divine Guidance! So, study on – find everything God gives us in Psalms 23 . . . His care, His provision, His foresight, His divine direction, and even His house - forever.

<u>Psalms 23</u>
The Lord is my shepherd; I shall not want.
He maketh me to lie down in green pastures:
He leadeth me beside the still waters.
He restoreth my soul: He leadeth me in the paths of righteousness
for His name's sake.
Yea, though I walk through the valley of the shadow of death, I will fear no evil:
for Thou art with me; Thy rod and Thy staff they comfort me.
Thou preparest a table before me in the presence of mine enemies:
Thou anointest my head with oil; my cup runneth over.
Surely goodness and mercy shall follow me all the days of my life:
and I will dwell in the house of the Lord for ever.

APRIL 5

HALLELUJAH

With Easter fresh on my mind, I recall Handel's *Messiah* – "The Hallelujah Chorus." What a glorious word; a joyful, wonderful tribute to our Lord Jesus Christ and our God! Wondering how many times Hallelujah is used in scripture - I thought I would find too many to list. In a couple Bible Concordances, I found only **four** listed as *Alleluia*; all in Revelation 19. This surprised me so I continued my search. I thought surely the angels used Hallelujah at Jesus' birth. But No! The multitude of the heavenly host praised God **saying**, "**Glory to God in the highest, and on earth peace, good will toward men."** – Not Hallelujah! (Luke 2:13, 14). Heard and used so casually, I didn't realize that Hallelujah is such a hallowed and special word as what **the redeemed** in haven will say. However, it is the "voice of many people" rejoicing **GOD'S VICTORY** over the harlot after the great tribulation; giving God praise for His salvation (redemption), glory, honor, and power.

Revelation 19:6b
Alleluia (Hallelujah)**! For the Lord God Omnipotent reigneth**

Revelation 19:1 - 7
And after these things I heard a great voice of much people in heaven, saying, *Alleluia*; Salvation, and glory, and honor, and power, unto the Lord our God:

For true and righteous are His judgments: for He hath judged the great whore, which did corrupt the earth with her fornication, and hath avenged the blood of His servants at her hand.

And again they said, *Alleluia*. And her smoke rose up for ever and ever.

And the four and twenty elders and the four beasts fell down and worshipped God that sat on the throne, saying, Amen; *Alleluia*.

And a voice came out of the throne, saying, Praise our God, all ye His servants, and ye that fear Him, both small and great.

And I heard as it were the voice of a great multitude, and as the voice of many waters, and as the voice of mighty thunderings, saying, *Alleluia*: for the Lord God omnipotent reigneth.

Let us be glad and rejoice, and give honor to Him: for the marriage of the Lamb is come, and his wife hath made herself ready.

Editor's note: Although Hallelujah and Alleluia share a common root - Hallelujah has come to be used as a shout to God, like Praise the Lord! Alleluia still refers to a praising chant or chorus.

APRIL 6

CALLED TO NEW LIFE

Who is calling to us?
There are many voices we hear trying to get our attention, but there is One Voice we should hear. Are we listening to the right voice? Let's hear the message from God's Word.

Luke 5:31, 32
And Jesus answering said unto them, They that are whole need not a physician; but they that are sick.
I came not to call the righteous, but sinners to repentance.

I Peter 5:10
But the God of all grace, Who hath called us unto His eternal glory by Christ Jesus, after that ye have suffered a while, make you perfect, stablish, strengthen, settle you.

Hebrews 10:31
It is a fearful thing to fall into the hands of the living God.

I Corinthians 1:9
God is faithful, by Whom ye were called unto the fellowship of His Son Jesus Christ our Lord.

I Corinthians 7:24
Brethren, let every man, wherein he is called, therein abide with God.

Ephesians 4:1 - 3
I (Paul) therefore, the prisoner of the Lord, beseech you that ye walk worthy of the vocation wherewith ye are called, With all lowliness and meekness, with longsuffering, forbearing one another in love; endeavouring to keep the unity of the Spirit in the bond of peace.

Colossians 3:15
And let the peace of God rule in your hearts, to the which also ye are called in one body; and be ye thankful.

APRIL 7

II PETER (3 Chapters)

While reading ***Real Stories for the Soul***, by Robert J. Morgan.* One story grabbed my attention, titled "Read It Some More," relating a conversation between the great preacher and Bible teacher, Dr. Torrey and Dr. Conglon. He complained to him (Dr. Torrey) he could get nothing out of his Bible reading – "it was dry as dust." Dr. Torrey suggested, "Read It Some More," To make the long story short, the instructions were to start with: read the book of II Peter, and read it **12 times a day for a month**. Dr. Conglon and his wife took his advice and committed to three or four times in the morning; two or three times; at noon; and two or three times at dinner for a month! What a commitment! After marking up passages with crayons and tears, humbly on their knees; they confessed the pages were smudged but their hearts were bright!

So, if Scripture is boring, dry, or simply not meeting your heart's need, try this approach and see what God will do in your life.

Part I. The Great Christian Virtues
II Peter 1:1 - 4
Simon Peter, a servant and an apostle of Jesus Christ, to them that have obtained like precious faith with us through the righteousness of God and our Saviour Jesus Christ: Grace and peace be multiplied unto you through the knowledge of God, and of Jesus our Lord, According as His divine power hath given unto us all things that pertain unto life and godliness, through the knowledge of Him that hath called us to glory and virtue: Whereby are given unto us exceeding great and precious promises: that by these ye might be partakers of the divine nature, having escaped the corruption that is in the world through lust.

II Peter 1:5 - 9
And beside this, giving all diligence, add to your faith virtue; and to virtue knowledge; and to knowledge temperance; and to temperance patience; and to patience godliness; and to godliness brotherly kindness; and to brotherly kindness charity. For if these things be in you, and abound, they make you that ye shall neither be barren nor unfruitful in the knowledge of our Lord Jesus Christ. But he that lacketh these things is blind, and cannot see afar off, and hath forgotten that he was purged from his old sins.

II Peter 1:10, 11
Wherefore the rather, brethren, give diligence to make your calling and election sure: for if ye do these things, ye shall never fall: For so an entrance shall be ministered unto you abundantly into the everlasting kingdom of our Lord and Saviour Jesus Christ.

Part II. The Scriptures Exalted
II Peter 1:16 - 19

For we (Apostles) have not followed cunningly devised fables, when we made known unto you the power and coming of our Lord Jesus Christ, but were eyewitnesses of His majesty.

For He received from God the Father honour and glory, when there came such a voice to Him from the excellent glory, <u>This is My beloved Son, in Whom I am well pleased</u>.

And this voice which came from heaven we heard, when we were with Him in the holy mount.

We have also a more sure word of prophecy; whereunto ye do well that ye take heed, as unto a light that shineth in a dark place, until the day dawn, and the day star arise in your hearts:

CONTINUE ON! II Peter - Chapters 2 and 3

* Morgan, Robert J. *Real Stories for the Soul*. Thomas Nelson Publishers. 1952

APRIL 8

CONVERSATION
(Manner of Life)

Our behavior tells a great deal about us. How we act and respond in any situation reveals what is coming out of our heart, be it good or bad. Our "conversation" (manner of life) requires a conversion before we can show love and honor. Power comes from God through the gift of His Holy Spirit. He is ever present! Be aware and trust in the Lord always throughout each day – one day at a time. Read Psalm 37, for a good understanding of trusting in the Lord and responding to life through our actions.

Psalms 37:1 - 6
Fret not thyself because of evildoers, neither be thou envious against the workers of iniquity. For they shall soon be cut down like the grass, and wither as the green herb. Trust in the Lord, and do good; so shalt thou dwell in the land, and verily thou shalt be fed. Delight thyself also in the Lord; and He shall give thee the desires of thine heart. Commit thy way unto the Lord; trust also in Him; and He shall bring it to pass. And He shall bring forth thy righteousness as the light, and thy judgment as the noonday.

Psalms 37:7 - 9
Rest in the Lord, and wait patiently for Him: fret not thyself because of him who prospereth in his way, because of the man who bringeth wicked devices to pass. Cease from anger, and forsake wrath: fret not thy self in any wise to do evil. For evildoers shall be cut off: but those that wait upon the Lord, they shall inherit the earth.

Psalms 37:10 - 13
For yet a little while, and the wicked shall not be: yea, thou shalt diligently consider his place, and it shall not be. But the meek shall inherit the earth; and shall delight themselves in the abundance of peace. The wicked plotteth against the just, and gnasheth upon him with his teeth. The Lord shall laugh at him: for He seeth that His day is coming.

Psalms 37:16 - 18
A little that a righteous man hath is better than the riches of many wicked. For the arms of the wicked shall be broken: but the Lord upholdeth the righteous. The Lord knoweth the days of the upright: and their inheritance shall be forever.

Psalms 37:23, 24
The steps of a good man are ordered by the Lord: and he delighteth in His way. Though he fall, he shall not be utterly cast down: for the Lord upholdeth him with His hand.

Psalms 37:25 - 33

I have been young, and now am old; yet have I not seen the righteous forsaken, nor his seed begging bread. He is ever merciful, and lendeth; and his seed is blessed. Depart from evil, and do good; and dwell for evermore. For the Lord loveth judgment, and forsaketh not His saints; they are preserved for ever: but the seed of the wicked shall be cut off. The righteous shall inherit the land, and dwell therein for ever. The mouth of the righteous speaketh wisdom, and his tongue talketh of judgment. The law of his God is in his heart; none of his steps shall slide. The wicked watcheth the righteous, and seeketh to slay him. The Lord will not leave him in his hand, nor condemn him when he is judged.

Psalms 37:34 - 40

Wait on the Lord, and keep His way, and He shall exalt thee to inherit the land: when the wicked are cut off, thou shalt see it. I have seen the wicked in great power, and spreading himself like a green bay tree. Yet he passed away, and, lo, he was not: yea, I sought him, but he could not be found. Mark the perfect man, and behold the upright: for the end of that man is peace. But the transgressors shall be destroyed together: the end of the wicked shall be cut off. But the salvation of the righteous is of the Lord: He is their strength in the time of trouble. And the Lord shall help them, and deliver them: He shall deliver them from the wicked, and save them, because they trust in Him.

Psalms 50:23

Whoso offereth praise glorifieth Me: and to him that ordereth his conversation aright will I shew the salvation of God.

APRIL 9

RIGHT is *WRONG*
WRONG is RIGHT

Today, while listening to the radio, there was discussion about right being wrong and wrong being right. It brought to mind what I read somewhere in the Bible. It took a little time but it is found in *Isaiah 5:20**. In fact, this chapter lists six **WOES** we should heed. This Prophet prophesied to Israel punishment was to come because of their behavior toward God and His commands. We are living through some of these same **WOES** of disobedience. Let us be vigilant!

Isaiah 5:8, 11, 18, 20 - 23
5. Woe unto them that join house to house, that lay field to field, till there be no place, that they may be placed alone in the midst of the earth!
11. Woe unto them that rise up early in the morning, that wine inflame them!
18. Woe unto them that draw iniquity with cords of vanity, and sin as it were with a cart rope:
20. *Woe unto them that call evil good, and good evil; that put darkness for light, and light for darkness; that put bitter for sweet, and sweet for bitter!
21. Woe unto them that are wise in their own eyes, and prudent in their own sight!
22. Woe unto them that are mighty to drink wine, and men of strength to mingle strong drink:
23. Which justify the wicked for reward, and take away the righteousness of the righteous from him!

APRIL 10

A NEW DAY

This is a new day!
This is the day which the Lord hath made; we will rejoice and be glad in it
(Psalms 118:24).

*. . . **joy** cometh in the morning!* (Psalms 30:5b)

In contrast to all the trouble King David had around him, he still praised the Lord. Let us do the same. In David's 100th Psalm, he gives us much to learn, think about, and do:

Make a joyful noise unto the Lord, all ye lands. Serve the Lord with gladness: come before His presence with singing. Know ye that the Lord He is God: it is He that hath made us, and not we ourselves; we are His people, and the sheep of His pasture. Enter into His gates with thanksgiving, and into His courts with praise: be thankful unto Him, and bless His name. For the Lord is good; His mercy is everlasting; and His truth endureth to all generations.

Psalms 5:3
My voice shalt Thou hear in the morning, O Lord; in the morning will I direct my prayer unto Thee, and will look up.

Psalms 59:16
But I will sing of Thy power; yea, I will sing aloud of Thy mercy in the morning: for Thou hast been my defence and refuge in the day of my trouble.

Psalms 64:10
The righteous shall be glad in the Lord, and shall trust in Him; and all the upright in heart shall glory.

Psalms 143:8
Cause me to hear Thy lovingkindness in the morning; for in Thee do I trust: cause me to know the way wherein I should walk; for I lift up my soul unto Thee.

APRIL 11

WALKING

A warm spring day is a good time to resume daily physical walks after a long, cold winter! The beauty of nature reminds us of the love and mercy God has for us. For this reason, we want to review and know how to <u>walk with Him</u> by our side. He is ever present! God is a friend! Be aware and acknowledge how He longs to be close to you. No matter what happens, we shall not fear – God Himself is with us in Christ Jesus.

Genesis 17:1b
<u>I am the Almighty God</u>; walk before Me, and be thou perfect.

Joshua 22:5b
. . . to love the Lord your God, and to walk in all His ways, and to keep His commandments, and to <u>cleave unto Him</u>, and to serve Him with all your heart and with all your soul.

Psalms 86:11
Teach me Thy way, O Lord; I will <u>walk in Thy truth</u>: unite my heart to fear Thy name

Isaiah 40:31a
. . . but they that <u>wait upon the Lord</u> shall renew their strength; they shall mount up with wings as eagles; they shall run, and not be weary, . . .

Romans 6:6b
. . . so we also should <u>walk in newness of life</u>.

Romans 8:1b
. . . <u>walk not after the flesh</u>, but after the Spirit.

Colossians 1:10
That ye might walk worthy of the Lord unto all pleasing, being fruitful in every good work, and <u>increasing in the knowledge of God</u>;

APRIL 12

LIVING IN THE WORLD
(conversation-behavior)

Another hymn comes to my mind when I think about "living in the world"; "*I Need Thee Every Hour*" - written in the 1800's, by Thomas O. Chrisolm (1866-1960). Although in this "modern-age", old hymns have been set aside but they do remind us of our need and dependence on God and all that He gives us hour by hour. Also, the chorus of "**Moment by Moment**" written by Daniel W. Whittle (1840-1901). What a heritage we have been given; a love for God's Word and the singing of hymns written in the forgotten past. Besides the scriptures below, find a hymn book and sing these songs and be blessed today.

"I NEED THEE EVERY HOUR"
"I need Thee, O I Need Thee, Ev'ry hour I need Thee!
O bless me now, my Savior – I come to Thee"

"MOMENT BY MOMENT"
Moment by Moment I'm kept in His love,
Moment by moment I've life from above;
Looking to Jesus till glory doth shine
Moment by Moment, O Lord, I am Thine."

II Corinthians 1:12
For our rejoicing is this, the testimony of our conscience, that in simplicity and godly sincerity, not with fleshly wisdom, but by the grace of God, we have had our conversation (manner of life) in the world, and more abundantly to you-ward.

Philippians 1:27a
Only let your conversation be as it becometh the gospel of Christ:

I Peter 1:15, 16
. . . but as He which hath called you is holy, so be ye holy in all manner of conversation; Because it is written, Be ye holy; for I am holy.

APRIL 13

EVERLASTING

In our finite minds, everlasting is a long, long, time: forever! We know these words but cannot fully understand them. Everlasting is a God concept! It is the TRUTH of God's own making! – No beginning – No end. How can it be? – our own mortal minds ask!

God is good. If we ask Him, He will give us faith to believe! His Word tells us so!

Isaiah 54:8
In a little wrath I hid My face from thee for a moment; but with everlasting kindness will I have mercy on thee, saith the Lord thy Redeemer.

Matthew 25:41, 46
Then shall He say also unto them on the left hand, Depart from Me, ye cursed, into <u>everlasting fire</u>,
prepared for the devil and his angels:
And these shall go away into everlasting punishment: <u>but the righteous into life eternal</u>.

John 3:36
He that believeth on the Son hath everlasting life: And he that believeth not the Son shall not see life; but the wrath of God abideth on him.

John 5:24
Verily, verily, I say unto you, He that heareth My word, and believeth on Him that sent Me, hath everlasting life, and shall not come into condemnation; but is passed from death unto life.

Romans 6:22
But now being made free from sin, and become servants to God, ye have your fruit unto holiness, and the end everlasting life.

APRIL 14

WORDS DO MATTER

"Words Do Matter" is a fact!

The consequences of our words have a lasting effect on those who hear, so we try to teach our children at home and school to think before we speak. The status of our hearts is clearly heard in our words to one another. In some schools, teachers say they see bullying (including what they say to each other) as such a great problem they have had to make rules to protect their students.

If we search the scriptures, we will watch and control what we say to each other. All our words are **one** to **one** even if we are in a group or giving a speech to thousands. Each individual's ears hear us through their personal perspective. Make our goal to speak for good and encourage or edify each other. Take a look below, as we start with the Word of God. Both negative and positive examples are given to us.

Psalms 139:4
For there is not a word in my tongue, but, lo, O Lord, Thou knowest it altogether.

Proverbs 12:25
Heaviness in the heart of man maketh it stoop: but a good word maketh it glad.

Proverbs 13:2
A man shall eat good by the fruit of his mouth: but the soul of the transgressors shall eat violence.

Matthew 12:37
For by thy words thou shalt be justified, and by thy words thou shalt be condemned.

Proverbs 15:23
A man hath joy by the answer of his mouth: and a word spoken in due season, how good is it!

APRIL 15

RECONCILIATION

In our own way, we try to resolve disputes between ourselves and others. If our efforts are to be successful, a restored relationship takes the desire of both parties. Even if we do want to solve our conflict with someone, we may think all will be worked out by itself and refuse to take the first step.

There is a more important reconciliation we need to recognize: our sin separating us from God. Thanks be to God, He took the first step to reconcile with us.

He has reconciled us to Himself through Jesus Christ Who paid the debt for our sin at a great cost. He gave His life on a cruel cross to reconcile us to God. Christ is our example and <u>we are now given the ministry of reconciliation</u> also to bring others to God.

With God's direction, we can resolve any disputes in our lives, within our power to face, to not hinder anyone to receive God's reconciliation. Let us look at how Christ reconciled us to God.

II Corinthians 5:18, 19 - 21
And all things are of God, Who hath reconciled us to Himself <u>by Jesus Christ</u>, and hath given to us the ministry of reconciliation; To wit, that God was in Christ, reconciling the world unto Himself, not imputing their trespasses unto them; and hath <u>committed unto us the word of reconciliation</u>.

Matthew 5:23, 24
Therefore if thou bring thy gift to the altar, and there rememberest that thy brother hath ought against thee; Leave there thy gift before the altar, and go thy way; first be reconciled to thy brother, and then come and offer thy gift.

APRIL 16

WHAT LOVE IS THIS?

We see and flippantly use the word love everywhere – on television, in movies, in books, etc. Some stories are beautiful and encouraging, but most are troubling, deceitful and harmful. But stop and think, where does real love come from? There are all kinds of ways to look at love, but today, look at the Love of God. The Bible is God's "Love Letter" to us, and He desires we read it, learn, believe, and accept His eternal love toward us. See where we as humans fall so short. His love never changes and is kind, merciful, just, and forgiving. <u>His kind of love is true love that only He can create in us</u>, because:

GOD IS LOVE! There is no greater love! (I John 4:8b)

Jeremiah 31:3
The Lord hath appeared of old unto me, saying, Yea, I have loved thee with an everlasting love: therefore with loving kindness have I drawn thee.

Romans 8:35
Who shall separate us from the love of Christ? shall tribulation, or distress, or persecution, or famine, or nakedness, or peril, or sword?

Ephesians 3:17 - 19
That Christ may dwell in your hearts by faith; that ye, being rooted and grounded in love, may be able to comprehend with all saints what is the breadth, and length, and depth, and height; And to know the love of Christ, which passeth knowledge, that ye might be filled with all the fulness of God.

I John 4:7, 8
Beloved, let us love one another: for love is of God; and every one that loveth is born of God, and knoweth God. He that loveth not knoweth not God; for God is love.

APRIL 17

THE LOST SHEEP

THE NINETY AND NINE
Matthew 18:12 - 14
How think ye? if a man have an hundred sheep, and one of them be gone astray, doth he not leave the ninety and nine, and goeth into the mountains, and <u>seeketh that which is gone astray</u>? And if so be that he find it, verily I say unto you, he rejoiceth more of that sheep, than of the ninety and nine which went not astray. Even so it is not the will of your Father which is in heaven, that one of these little ones should perish.

THE LOST SHEEP

Scattered around our house are a few reminders of sheep either in pictures on the wall, or figurines, etc. This is a way I can keep my mind on Whose I am, a sheep of His pasture. I can also teach and remind my young grandchildren whenever they visit, that Jesus is the Lamb of God and how He looks for His lost sheep. He cares for us, is always present, and wants to be our guide. He is our Shepherd!

John 1:29
John (the Baptist) seeth Jesus coming unto him, and saith, Behold the Lamb of God, which taketh away the sin of the world.

References to sheep and shepherds are many in the Bible and are great pictures of the love God has for us. He offered His Son Jesus as a sheep before the slaughter - to take our place for the payment of our sin. There is no greater love!

Psalms 119:176a
I have gone astray like a lost sheep; . . .

All we like sheep have gone astray; we have turned everyone to his own way; and the Lord hath laid on Him the iniquity of us all.

John 10:14 - 18
I am the good shepherd, and know My sheep, and am known of Mine. As the Father knoweth Me, even so know I the Father: and I lay down My life for the sheep. And other sheep I have, which are not of this fold: <u>them also I must bring</u>, and they shall hear My voice; and there shall be One Fold, and One Shepherd. Therefore doth My Father love Me, because I lay down My life, that I might take it again. No man taketh it from Me, but I lay it down of Myself. I have power to lay it down, and I have power to take it again. This commandment have I received of My Father.

I Peter 2:24, 25
Who His own self bare our sins in His own body on the tree, that we, being dead to sins, should live unto righteousness: by Whose stripes ye were healed. For ye were as sheep going astray; but are now returned unto the Shepherd and Bishop of your souls.

APRIL 18

DISCIPLINE or LAZINESS

(slothfulness)

The difference between these two actions or inactions is attitude. One is much harder than the other, we often choose wrong, as we see from our past experiences. We have learned life is full of choices – one after another. Just think: God has given us this gift of "free will", which sets us apart from the animal world. We are not robots but are made in the image of God! Our choices make the difference of our accomplishments. The critical decision to become a Disciple of Christ - a true "Christian," seals our commitment and relationship with God. Discipline (1) is a derivative of the noun Disciple (2), and a good description of a follower of Christ. We especially need to choose Discipline (1) over laziness, the other (2) if being like God is our passion.

Genesis 1:27
So God created man in His own image, in the image of God created He him; male and female created He them.

Acts 11:26b
. . . And the disciples were called Christians first in Antioch.

Proverbs 24:30 - 34
I went by the field of the slothful, and by the vineyard of the man void of understanding; And, lo, it was all grown over with thorns, and nettles had covered the face thereof, and the stone wall thereof was broken down. Then I saw, and considered it well: I looked upon it, and received instruction. Yet a little sleep, a little slumber, a little folding of the hands to sleep: So shall thy poverty come as one that travelleth; and thy want as an armed man.

Theodore Roosevelt said, "If we seek merely swollen, slothful ease . . . then bolder and stronger peoples will pass us by."

APRIL 19

GOD HATES SIN

God is Love, God is Love, God is Love!

Did you know God also hates? Hate is a very strong word, but is used in His Word to describe His feelings in Proverbs 16: God hates sin! And by using another strong word – abominations – this should give us a new determination on how important it is for us to abstain from sin in our lives.

Proverbs 6:16-19 (look up, and read more)
These six things doth the Lord hate: yea, seven are an abomination unto Him: A proud look, a lying tongue, and hands that shed innocent blood, An heart that deviseth wicked imaginations, feet that be swift in running to mischief, A false witness that speaketh lies, and he that soweth discord among brethren.

Zechariah 8:17
And let none of you imagine evil in your hearts against his neighbour; and love no false oath: for all these are things that I hate, saith the Lord.

Matthew 6:24
No man can serve two masters: for either he will hate the one, and love the other; or else he will hold to the one, and despise the other. Ye cannot serve God and mammon.

Galatians 5:19-21
19. Now the works of the flesh are manifest, which are these; Adultery, fornication, uncleanness, lasciviousness,

20. Idolatry, witchcraft, hatred, variance, emulations, wrath, strife, seditions, heresies,

21. Envyings, murders, drunkenness, revellings, and such like: of the which I tell you before, as I have also told you in time past, that they which do such things shall not inherit the kingdom of God.

APRIL 20

NOURISHMENT

Physically, we must <u>eat to live</u>! God made us this way and provides food for our good. But if we <u>live to eat</u>, we have turned God's great gift of food upside down, into a curse. We know how to satisfy our physical hunger and thirst but we may not recognize our Spiritual hunger. We may be starving our souls without knowing it. God will never force us to feed our souls but tells us to desire Him. I know what physical foods I desire – but I must be disciplined with love for God, to desire to feed my soul through His Word, spiritually.

<u>Matthew 5:6</u>:
Hunger and thirst after Righteousness!

When we are physically hungry and cannot be satisfied, and want more food than we need, transfer this desire for physical food to a desire for "<u>Soul Food.</u>"

<u>Deuteronomy 8:3</u>
And He humbled thee, and suffered thee to hunger, and fed thee with manna, which thou knewest not, neither did thy fathers know; that He might make thee <u>know that man doth not live by bread only</u>, but by every Word that proceedeth out of the mouth of the Lord doth man live.

<u>Psalms 34:8</u>
O taste and see that the Lord is good: blessed is the man that trusteth in Him.

<u>Psalms 107:5, 9</u>
Hungry and thirsty, their soul fainted in them. For He satisfieth the longing soul, and filleth the hungry soul with goodness.

<u>Amos 8:11</u>
Behold, the days come, saith the Lord God, that I will send a famine in the land, not a famine of bread, nor a thirst for water, but of hearing the Words of the Lord:

April 21

THINK ON THESE THINGS

When we read this passage of God's Word, do we skim quickly, or take it seriously? "Positive thinking" is good and healthy reading from the Apostle Paul! More than that, it has been called the briefest biography of Christ Himself – our sanctuary!

Ponder the verses below and see each one as a virtue. <u>Virtues attributed to Christ</u> as He walked this earth – our example.

Philippians 4:8, 9
Finally, brethren,
whatsoever things are true,
whatsoever things are honest,
whatsoever things are just,
whatsoever things are pure,
whatsoever things are lovely,
whatsoever things are of good report;
if there be any virtue,
and if there be any praise,
<u>think on these things.</u>

(THINK on) Those things, which ye have both learned,
and received, and heard,
and seen in me (Paul), do:
and the God of peace shall be with you.

APRIL 22

SUDDENLY

Very few good things happen to us "suddenly." Most of what we do suddenly happens on an impulse and often does not turn out well. As we get older, it seems that for positive things to happen we must work for positive outcomes or at least wait for our hopes to be done - but not for God. There are some amazing examples of "suddenly" in scripture showing His power. His "suddenly" is according to His perfect will and purpose, and is always right in each incident. Some things in life take the course of time, unless God intervenes.

Proverbs 6:14, 15
Frowardness is in his heart, he deviseth mischief continually; he soweth discord. Therefore shall his calamity come suddenly; suddenly shall he be broken without remedy.

Luke 2:13, 14
And suddenly there was with the angel a multitude of the heavenly host praising God, and saying, Glory to God in the highest, and on earth peace, good will toward men.

Acts 2:1, 2
And when the day of Pentecost was fully come, they were all with one accord in one place. And suddenly there came a sound from heaven as of a rushing mighty wind, and it filled all the house where they were sitting.

Acts 16:25, 26
And at midnight Paul and Silas prayed, and sang praises unto God: and the prisoners heard them. And suddenly there was a great earthquake, so that the foundations of the prison were shaken: and immediately all the doors were opened, and every one's bands were loosed.

APRIL 23

YOUR CHOICE
Anger or Patience

So many choices – moment by moment of every waking hour. Practically every thought requires a decision to keep and use it or decide to discard and change our actions. Today we will delve into the choices between anger and patience – usually made in seconds with appropriate consequences!

Today, **Anger**

Remember: Proverbs 15:18 - *A wrathful man stirreth up strife: but he that is slow to anger appeaseth strife.*

Proverbs 19:11
The discretion of a man deferreth his anger; and it is his glory to pass over a transgression.

Ecclesiastes 7:9
Be not hasty in thy spirit to be angry: for anger resteth in the bosom of fools.

Psalms 37:8, 9
Cease from anger, and forsake wrath: fret not thyself in any wise to do evil. For evildoers shall be cut off: but those that wait upon the Lord, they shall inherit the earth.

Psalms 74:38, 39
But He, being full of compassion, forgave their iniquity, and destroyed them not: yea, many a time turned He His anger away, and did not stir up all His wrath. For He remembered that they were but flesh; a wind that passeth away, and cometh not again.

Proverbs 15:1 - 3
A soft answer turneth away wrath: but grievous words stir up anger. The tongue of the wise useth knowledge aright: but the mouth of fools poureth out foolishness. The eyes of the Lord are in every place, beholding the evil and the good.

APRIL 24

YOUR CHOICE (continued)
Anger or <u>Patience</u>

Now Today, **Patience**

Luke 8:15
But that on the good ground are they, which in an honest and good heart, having heard the Word, keep it, and bring forth fruit with patience.

Romans 5:3 - 5
And not only so, but we glory in tribulations also: knowing that tribulation worketh patience; And patience, experience; and experience, hope: And hope maketh not ashamed; because the love of God is shed abroad in our hearts by the Holy Ghost which is given unto us.

II Corinthians 6:4
But in all things approving ourselves as the ministers of God, in much patience, in afflictions, in necessities, in distresses,

Colossians 1:11
Strengthened with all might, according to His glorious power, unto all patience and longsuffering with joyfulness;

I Thessalonians 1:3
Remembering without ceasing your work of faith, and labour of love, and patience of hope in our Lord Jesus Christ, in the sight of God and our Father;

I Timothy 6:11, 12
But thou, O man of God, flee these things; and follow after righteousness, godliness, faith, love, patience, meekness. Fight the good fight of faith, lay hold on eternal life, whereunto thou art also called, and hast professed a good profession before many witnesses.

James 1:4
But let patience have her perfect work, that ye may be perfect and entire, wanting nothing.

APRIL 25

IN HIS PRESENCE

I pray today, O Lord, help me to remember: You are with me and in me, that I am in Your presence at all times, everywhere I go!

My desire is to be alive to Christ and dead to self, but I fail to remember these truths many times during the day. I go about doing my own thing, my own way. Help me O Lord, at all times, to be aware of Your ever presence and guide me to go Your way; do Your will, and obey Your new commandments. There is joy for evermore.

Psalms 139:7
Whither shall I go from Thy spirit?
or whither shall I flee from Thy presence?

Psalms 16:11
Thou wilt shew me the path of life: in Thy presence is fulness of joy; at Thy right hand there are pleasures for evermore.

Psalms 31:20
Thou shalt hide them in the secret of Thy presence from the pride of man: Thou shalt keep them secretly in a pavilion from the strife of tongues.

Psalms 51:11
Cast me not away from Thy presence; and take not Thy holy spirit from me. Restore unto me the joy of Thy salvation; and uphold me with Thy free spirit.

Psalms 100:2, 3
Serve the Lord with gladness: come before His presence with singing. Know ye that the Lord He is God: it is He that hath made us, and not we ourselves; we are His people, and the sheep of His pasture.

Psalms 140:13
Surely the righteous shall give thanks unto Thy name: the upright shall dwell in Thy presence.

APRIL 26

"godliness"
(to be like Jesus)

Before I knew better – I thought "godliness" was <u>just trying</u> to live right to please God. That's what I wanted to do – please God! But I did it my way according to my knowledge. Now I know better, through learning and experience, that "godliness" can <u>only</u> be done <u>through His Holy Spirit</u>, not my way. Christ is my example within my heart, and the God-sent Holy Spirit is the guide and power for me to do His will. I would be like Jesus!

<u>Acts 10:38</u>
God anointed Jesus of Nazareth with the Holy Ghost and with power: <u>Who went about doing good,</u> and healing all that were oppressed of the devil; for God was with Him.

<u>II Peter 1:3, 4</u>
According as His divine power hath given unto us all things that pertain unto life and godliness, through the knowledge of Him that hath called us to glory and virtue: Whereby are given unto us exceeding great and precious promises: that by these ye might be partakers of the divine nature, having escaped the corruption that is in the world through lust.

<u>II Peter 1:5-8</u>
And beside this, giving all diligence, add to your faith virtue; and to virtue knowledge; And to knowledge temperance; and to temperance patience; and to patience godliness; And to godliness brotherly kindness; and to brotherly kindness charity. For if these things be in you, and abound, they make you that ye shall neither be barren nor unfruitful in the knowledge of our Lord Jesus Christ.

<u>I Timothy 6:6, 11</u>
But godliness with contentment is great gain.
. . . follow after righteousness, godliness, faith, love, patience, meekness.

APRIL 27

DEATH UNTO NEW LIFE

From birth, we all start out on the path leading to death. When we accept God's gift to us, we have eternal LIFE. Show us the path to LIFE, O God. We have the desire to know. We come to You for we know the fountain of LIFE comes from You. Make us wise to salvation. Because of God's mercy, we can find our righteousness and **NEW LIFE** through His dear Son, Jesus Christ.

Romans 6:23
For the <u>wages</u> of sin is death; but the gift of God is eternal life through Jesus Christ our Lord.

But <u>continue on</u> to the New Life

Romans 3:23, 24, 25; - **our hope!**
For all have sinned, and come short of the glory of God; Being justified freely by His grace through the redemption that is in Christ Jesus: Whom God hath set forth to be a propitiation (the <u>payment</u> for our sin to God in our place) through faith in His blood, to declare His righteousness for the remission of sins that are past, through the forbearance of God;

Hebrews 2:9, 15
But we see Jesus, who was made a little lower than the angels for the suffering of death, crowned with glory and honour; that <u>He</u> by the grace of God <u>should taste death for every man</u>. And deliver them who through <u>fear of death were all their lifetime subject to bondage</u>.

Romans 7:24, 25a
O wretched man that I am! who shall deliver me from the body of this death? I thank God through Jesus Christ our Lord.

Proverbs 12:28
In the way of righteousness is life; and in the pathway thereof there is no death.

APRIL 28

SEIZE THE DAY

"Today is the first day of the rest of your life."
Forget the past, *"press toward the mark,"* (Philippians 3:14) and know He will work in your life as you have learned from experience. **Live in God's power today** The Holy Spirit is your guide and gives you power to do His will – to be like Jesus! Even a child can learn this lesson, from songs of my Sunday School days.

Challenge for today – **SEIZE THE DAY**

"JESUS BIDS US SHINE"
by S. Warner
JESUS bids us shine, *with a clear pure light,*
Like a little candle burning in the night;
In this world of darkness we must shine,
You in your small corner, and I in mine.

JESUS bids us shine, *first of all for Him;*
well He sees and knows it if our light is dim;
He looks down from heaven, sees us shine,
You in your small corner, and I in mine.

JESUS bids us shine, *then for all around.*
Many kinds of darkness in this world abound –
Sin, and want, and sorrow: we must shine,
You in your small corner, and I in mine.

JESUS bids us shine, *as we work for Him;*
Bringing those that wander in the paths of sin;
He will ever help us, if we shine,
You in your small corner, and I in mine.

Colossians 1:9, 10
. . . be filled with the knowledge of his will in all wisdom and spiritual understanding; That ye might walk worthy of the Lord unto all pleasing, being fruitful in every good work, and increasing in the knowledge of God;

APRIL 29

STRENGTH FOR TODAY

"Strength for today," is a phrase my father taught me long ago; it comes to my mind often, especially when I think of him. Strength from God; a hope for tomorrow. Renewed day by day but not stored up for the future needs we cannot fix. God wants us to be close to Him and see our need for Him and His supply. Ask Him for His strength throughout each day, whether bright or filled with trials.

Psalms 73:26, 28
My flesh and my heart faileth: but God is the strength of my heart, and my portion for ever. But it is good for me to draw near to God: I have put my trust in the Lord God, that I may declare all Thy works.

Job 12:13, 16a
With Him is wisdom and strength, He hath counsel and understanding. With Him is strength and wisdom:

Psalms 27:1
The Lord is my light and my salvation; whom shall I fear? The Lord is the strength of my life; of whom shall I be afraid?

Psalms 73:26
My flesh and my heart faileth: but God is the strength of my heart, and my portion for ever.

Psalms 84:5
Blessed is the man whose strength is in Thee; in whose heart are the ways of them.

Ephesians 6:10
Finally, my brethren, be strong in the Lord, and in the power of His might.

APRIL 30

DOOR

Besides the common definition of doors as a physical entry, a door also can be a metaphor for other entrances or opportunities, entry, a door, i.e. the "door to success." Deuteronomy 15:17 describes a dreadful use for a door: *"Then thou shalt take an aul, and thrust it through his ear unto the door, and he shall be thy servant for ever. And also unto thy maidservant thou shalt do likewise."*

So instead, read on for further uses for the word door in scripture. Here we will see <u>the all-sufficient door</u> as **Jesus** said in:

<u>John 10:7 - 11</u>
Then said Jesus unto them again, Verily, verily, I say unto you, <u>I am the door</u> of the sheep. All that ever came before Me are thieves and robbers: but the sheep did not hear them. <u>I am the door</u>: by Me if any man enter in, he shall be saved, and shall go in and out, and find pasture. The thief cometh not, but for to steal, and to kill, and to destroy:
I am come that they might have life, and that they might have it more abundantly. I am the good shepherd: <u>the good shepherd giveth His life for the sheep</u>.

<u>Psalms 141:3</u>
Set a watch, O Lord, before my mouth; keep the door of my lips.

<u>Proverbs 26:14</u>
As the door turneth upon his hinges, so doth the slothful upon his bed.

<u>Revelation 3:20</u>
Behold, I stand at the door, and knock:
if any man hear My voice, and open the door,
I will come in to him, and will sup with him, and he with Me.

MAY

LIFE'S PATHWAYS

Proverbs 3:5, 6
*Trust in the Lord with all thine heart;
and lean not unto thine own understanding.
In all thy ways acknowledge Him,
and He shall direct thy paths.*

MAY 1

IF you WILL, I WILL

God in His great power, wisdom, and mercy has created us with us a will and a soul, making us completely different from all the rest of His Creation. Above all else, we can read His Word and then can choose with our own free will to believe Him or not. God's desire is all people should believe and not perish. Every individual **must make this decision purposefully and knowingly.**

II Peter 3:9
The Lord is not slack concerning His promise, as some men count slackness; but is longsuffering to us-ward, not willing that any should perish, but that all should come to repentance.

Luke 8:21
(Jesus) answered and said unto them, My mother and My brethren are these which hear the word of God, and do it.

Philippians 2:13
For it is God which worketh in you both to will and to do of His good pleasure.

I Chronicles 28:9
. . . the Lord searcheth all hearts, and understandeth all the imaginations of the thoughts: if thou seek Him, He will be found of thee; but if thou forsake Him, He will cast thee off for ever.

John 15:14, 15
Ye are My friends, if ye do whatsoever I command you. Henceforth I call you not servants; for the servant knoweth not what his lord doeth: but I have called you friends; for all things that I have heard of My Father I have made known unto you.

MAY 2

TRY IT!

I chuckle as I search my memory and phrases pop up like: "Try it, you'll like it," "Let Mikey try it," or the spiritual one "<u>Try God</u>!" (even made into a lapel pin). So, staying on the "spiritual" plane, I transfer my thoughts to "trying in vain." Mankind has tried many things to fill up its empty, worthless feelings with everything else but God, and ends up worse than what it started. The Old and New Testaments give us positive and negative examples of their "trying." The last being, "Try God!"

<u>Psalms 2:1</u>
Why do the heathen rage, and the people imagine a vain thing?

<u>Isaiah 1:13, 14</u>
Bring no more vain oblations; incense is an abomination unto Me (God); the new moons and sabbaths, the calling of assemblies, I cannot away with; it is iniquity, even the solemn meeting. Your new moons and your appointed feasts My soul hateth: they are a trouble unto Me; I am weary to bear them.

<u>Romans 1:21 - 23</u>
Because that, when they knew God, they glorified Him not as God, neither were thankful; but became vain in their imaginations, and their foolish heart was darkened. Professing themselves to be wise, they became fools, and changed the glory of the incorruptible God into an image made like to corruptible man, and to birds, and four-footed beasts, and creeping things.

<u>Colossians 2:8 - 10</u>
Beware lest any man spoil you through philosophy and vain deceit, after the tradition of men, after the rudiments of the world, and not after Christ. For in Him dwelleth all the fulness of the Godhead bodily. And ye are complete in Him, which is the Head of all principality and power:

MAY 3

A PIG is a PIG

If you are familiar with any of Jesus' Parables, you probably know of the Prodigal Son, given to us in Luke 15:11 - 32. As I was reading "THRU THE BIBLE" with J. Vernon McGee * (Vol. V, pp. 742-744), I found where he used the illustration of a parable of the <u>Prodigal Pig</u>, a parallel to the son leaving his home. This pig did likewise and left his "pigsty." When the prodigal son came to his senses he returned to his father with the pig following behind. When his father saw him coming from afar, he welcomed him with open arms, because he was still his "son." As the illustration continues both the son and the pig were all cleaned and dressed up. The son was at home but the pig soon felt uneasy being squeaky clean and sleeping in a beautiful house. So, he returned to the pigpen where his father lived. He was also welcomed home – because he was still a "pig." A son is always a son. A pig is always a pig. Moral of the story: <u>Repent</u> and be a "child" of God, be a "son" of the King! Even if you stray away, He will always welcome and forgive you with open arms! **The Prodigal Son is not a story of how a son became a son (or how a pig became a pig), but how a son became a sinner – the telling of the results of repentance and forgiveness.**

J. Vernon McGee also shared this poem by Evelyn C. Sanders, which she gave to him, after she heard him use this illustration of the "prodigal pig."

<u>A PIG is a PIG</u>
Come home with me said the prodigal son.
We'll sing and dance and have lots of fun.
We'll wine and dine with women and song.
You'll forget you're a pig before very long.

So the pig slipped out while the momma was asleep,
Shook off the mud from mire so deep.
Around his neck was a bow so big,
He's gonna show the world, a pig's not a pig!

With his snout in the air he trotted along,
With the prodigal son who was singin' a song.
It must be great to be a rich man's son,
He would surely find out "for the day was done"!

It didn't take long to realize his mistake –
He'd been scrubbed and rubbed til his muscles ached!
He squealed when they put a gold ring in his nose

And winced with pain when the trimmed his toes.

He sat at the table on a stool so high,
A bib around his neck and a fork to try.
While the prodigal son, in his lovely robe,
Kept feeding his face, so glad to be home!

When the meat came around, the pig gave a moan –
It looked too much like a kind of his own.
He jumped from his chair with a grunt and a groan,
Darted through the door and headed for home.

His four little feet made the dust ride high
For he didn't stop till he reached that sty!
It's what's on the inside that counts, by friend,
For a pig is a pig to the very end!

* Mcgee, J. Vernon. *Thru the Bible*, Thomas Nelson Publishers, 1982, Vol. V, pp. 742-744

MAY 4

OTHERS
<u>Do</u> for Others

Repaying good for good and evil for evil is our natural instinct. But Christ gave us His new command to love our neighbors as ourselves, and not a respecter of persons. As He guides, we can follow His direction to do unto others as we would like to be treated; and help one another.

<u>Ephesians 4:32</u>:
Be ye kind one to another. Tenderhearted, forgiving one another. Even as God, for Christ's sake hath forgiven you

Kindness doesn't expect anything in return, but is our response and desire born out of our New Nature in Christ. "Love your neighbor as yourself." Whatever we do to others, we are doing to Christ Jesus. So, those brought across your path by God today, treat them as if they were Jesus Himself.

<u>Matthew 5:43-48</u>
Ye have heard that it hath been said, Thou shalt love thy neighbour, and hate thine enemy. But I (Jesus) say unto you, Love your enemies, bless them that curse you, do good to them that hate you, and pray for them which despitefully use you, and persecute you; That ye may be the children of your Father which is in heaven: for He maketh His sun to rise on the evil and on the good, and sendeth rain on the just and on the unjust. For if ye love them which love you, what reward have ye? do not even the publicans the same? And if ye salute your brethren only, what do ye more than others? do not even the publicans so? Be ye therefore perfect, even as your Father which is in heaven is perfect.

<u>Ephesians 5:1, 2</u>
Be ye therefore followers of God, as dear children; And walk in love, as Christ also hath loved us, and hath given himself for us an offering and a sacrifice to God for a sweetsmelling savour.

MAY 5

KNOW YOUR CREATOR BETTER

Don't you want to know Who created you better?

God knows how many hairs you have on your head: Matthew 10:30, **But the very hairs of your head are all numbered**. God, our Creator, is interested in every detail of our life. He wants to be our guide and help us make life's tough decisions. He is our Comforter when we are sad or distressed. He is ever-present. Our faith even comes from Him, so we don't have to worry. When we do worry, we are trying to "do life" by ourselves. King David's Psalms is a great place to start to know our God, as David did. Read all through the Psalms and underline all the "God is" phrases.

Isaiah 40:28a
Hast thou not known? hast thou not heard, that the everlasting God, the Lord, the Creator of the ends of the earth, fainteth not, neither is weary?

Psalms 10:4
The wicked, through the pride of his countenance, will not seek after God: God is not in all his thoughts.

Psalms 46:1 - 3
God is our refuge and strength, a very present Help in trouble. Therefore will not we fear, though the earth be removed, and though the mountains be carried into the midst of the sea; Though the waters thereof roar and be troubled, though the mountains shake with the swelling thereof. Selah.

Psalms 47:7a, 8b
For God is the King of all the earth: . . .God sitteth upon the throne of His holiness.

MAY 6

LOOKING FOR A KIND WORD

Many people today are looking for kind words, just like we are. Kind words are rare, but can mean so much. Instead of anger, rudeness, unkindness, etc., why don't we use kind words? We all desire to hear them. Let us be careful to think before we blurt out something "count to ten" to ensure our message is kind and thoughtful. Build up the person you are speaking to. We all need encouragement and kindness; demonstrating the love of God in us, as shown by kind words.

Mother Teresa saw everyone she met and cared for as if she were seeing Jesus Christ. Whatever she said and did, she was saying and doing <u>to</u> Him, not just <u>for</u> Him. This does not come automatically but must be a chosen thought as we go. We must ask the Holy Spirit in us for His help. We are God's instruments.

<u>Proverbs 12:25</u>
Heaviness in the heart of man maketh it stoop: but a good word maketh it glad.

<u>Matthew 25:35 - 46</u>
For I was an hungred, and ye gave Me meat: I was thirsty, and ye gave Me drink: I was a stranger, and ye took Me in: Naked, and ye clothed Me: I was sick, and ye visited Me: I was in prison, and ye came unto Me. Then shall the righteous answer Him, saying, Lord, when saw we Thee an hungred, and fed Thee? or thirsty, and gave Thee drink? When saw we Thee a stranger, and took Thee in? or naked, and clothed Thee? Or when saw we Thee sick, or in prison, and came unto Thee? And the King shall answer and say unto them, Verily I say unto you, Inasmuch as ye have done it unto one of the least of these My brethren,<u> ye have DONE it unto Me.</u>

MAY 7

START WALKING

Are you walking yet? I ask myself this question nearly every day. The leaves on the trees are so big we can now identify them. Don't let them grow any bigger before you start. They know to grow; we know to "wake up and smell the roses." The leaves of the trees are the announcements of spring, so let's leave the house and enjoy. With God's nature (not "mother" nature) we can have the faith to believe in Him and who He is.

Okay, I've convinced myself to start again after this long winter season. Please join me! Let's go!

Genesis 17:1b
I am the Almighty God; walk before Me, and be thou perfect

Galatians 5:16
This I say then, Walk in the Spirit, and ye shall not fulfil the lust of the flesh.

Ephesians 5:2, 8
And walk in love, as Christ also hath loved us, and hath given Himself for us an offering and a sacrifice to God for a sweet smelling savor. For ye were sometimes darkness, but now are ye light in the Lord: walk as children of light:

Colossians 1:10
That ye might walk worthy of the Lord unto all pleasing, being fruitful in every good work, and increasing in the knowledge of God;

I John 1:6, 7
If we say that we have fellowship with Him, and walk in darkness, we lie, and do not the truth: But if we walk in the light, as He is in the light, we have fellowship one with another, and the blood of Jesus Christ His Son cleanseth us from all sin.

MAY 8

GIVE CHEERFULLY

How we handle our finances matters and our priorities reflect our <u>giving</u>; how we give and to whom we give. Start by giving back to God and His work here on earth – blessing His storehouse.

<u>Proverbs 3:9a</u>
Honour the Lord with thy substance,

AND, <u>Malachi 3:8 – 10</u>: *Will a man rob God? Yet ye have robbed Me. But ye say, Wherein have we robbed Thee? In tithes and offerings. Ye are cursed with a curse: for ye have robbed Me, even this whole nation. Bring ye all the tithes into the storehouse, that there may be meat in Mine house, and prove Me now herewith, saith the Lord of hosts, if I will not open you the windows of heaven, and pour you out a blessing, that there shall not be room enough to receive it.*

AND, <u>Matthew 6:21</u> *For where your treasure is, there will your heart be also.*

God asks us to give back to Him because <u>He provides us with more than enough</u> so we can give to others in their need.

<u>Philippians 4:19</u>
But my God shall supply all your need according to his riches in glory by Christ Jesus.

As you give, **REMEMBER**: <u>II Corinthians 9:7</u> *Every man according as he purposeth in his heart, so let him give; not grudgingly, or of necessity: for <u>God loveth a cheerful giver.</u>*

<u>I Timothy 6:10</u>
For <u>the love of money</u> is the root of all evil: which while some coveted after, they have erred from the faith, and pierced themselves through with many sorrows.

<u>Matthew 10:8b</u>
. . . freely ye have received, freely give.

MAY 9

TOO WONDERFUL!

Who do we think we are? Our God is ridiculed, cursed and said to be "dead." To Job, God lists specifics about who He is in five chapters: Job, Chapters 38 – 42. Proverbs 30:18 – 33 tells us this list is, "too wonderful" to comprehend. Oh, what a God we have – our Creator! There are too many attributes to give here, so please look up the rest of them.

Read All of Job 38
Job 38:3 – 11

*Gird up now thy loins like a man; for I will demand of thee, and answer thou me.
Where wast thou (Job) when I laid the foundations of the earth?
Who hath laid the measures thereof, if thou knowest? Whereupon are the foundations thereof fastened?
When the morning stars sang together, and all the sons of God shouted for joy?
Or Who shut up the sea with doors,
When I made the cloud the garment thereof, and thick darkness a swaddling band for it (the sea),
And brake up for it (the sea) My decreed place, and set bars and doors,
And said, Hitherto shalt thou come, but no further: and here shall thy proud waves be stayed?*

Job 38:12, 13, 16, 17a

*Hast thou commanded the morning since thy days; and caused the dayspring to know his place;
That it might take hold of the ends of the earth, that the wicked might be shaken out of it?
Hast thou entered into the springs of the sea? or hast thou walked in the search of the depth?
Have the gates of death been opened unto thee?*

Read the rest of Job 38:18 – 41, and then Proverbs 30:18 – 33, given below, for a great blessing and knowledge from God Himself.

Proverbs 30:18 - 33

There be <u>three things</u> which are <u>too wonderful for me</u>, yea, <u>4</u> which I know not:
The way of an <u>eagle</u> in the air; the way of a <u>serpent</u> upon a rock; the way of a ship <u>in the midst of the sea</u>; and <u>the way of a man with a maid</u>.
Such is the way of an <u>adulterous woman</u>; she eateth, and wipeth her mouth, and saith, I have done no wickedness.

For <u>three things</u> the earth is disquieted, and for <u>4</u> which it cannot bear:
For a <u>servant</u> when he reigneth; and a <u>fool</u> when he is filled with meat;
For an odious <u>woman</u> when she is married; and an <u>handmaid</u> that is heir to her mistress.

There be <u>4 things</u> which are little upon the earth, but they are exceeding wise:
The <u>ants</u> are a people not strong, yet they prepare their meat in the summer;
The <u>conies</u> are but a feeble folk, yet make they their houses in the rocks;
The <u>locusts</u> have no king, yet go they forth all of them by bands;
The <u>spider</u> taketh hold with her hands, and is in kings 'palaces.

There be <u>three things</u> which go well, yea, <u>4</u>
are comely in going:
A <u>lion</u> which is strongest among beasts, and turneth not away for any;
A <u>greyhound</u>; an he goat also; and a king, against whom there is no rising up.
If thou hast done foolishly in lifting up thyself, or if thou hast thought evil, lay thine hand upon thy mouth.

Surely the <u>churning</u> of milk bringeth forth butter,
and the <u>wringing</u> of the nose bringeth forth blood:
so the <u>forcing</u> of wrath bringeth forth strife.

MAY 10

3 KINDS OF "buts"
The "good," the "bad," the "ugly"

I formerly thought Proverbs 12 was the "but" chapter but No, No, No! – The "buts" reside in many more than one chapter. They mainly start with Chapter 10 and continue through Chapter 15, with many more sprinkled throughout all of Proverbs. In these six chapters of Proverbs, we can heed the message: obtain wisdom and understanding, which begins with the fear (awe) of the Lord – our Master Creator! *The fear of the Lord is the beginning of wisdom: and the knowledge of the holy is understanding* (Proverbs 9:10). Read these few "teasers" and then consider adding a "chapter a day" of Proverbs, to your daily scheduled reading. Try this for a least a year and watch how God will change your life.

Wisdom and the Fear of God as Contrasted with Folly and Sin
My selection from Proverbs 10:1 - 32
1. The Proverbs of Solomon.
A wise son maketh a glad father, but the foolish son is the heaviness of his mother.
2. Treasures of wickedness profit nothing, but righteousness delivereth from death.
5. He that gathereth in summer is a wise son, but he that sleepeth in harvest is a son that causeth shame.
11. The mouth of a righteous man is a well of life, but violence covereth the mouth of the wicked.
13. In the lips of him that hath understanding, wisdom if found; but a rod is for the back of him that is void of understanding
19. In the multitude of words there lacketh not sin, but he that refraineth his lips is wise
29. The way of the Lord is strength to the upright, but destruction shall be to the workers of iniquity
32. The lips of the righteous know what is acceptable, but the mouth of the wicked speaketh perverseness

(Look it up and highlight your own choices)

MAY 11

THE ROCK

My youngest grandchild used to bring small rocks whenever she would come home from being outside. Rocks are everywhere so they weren't unusual or special, she just liked them. I understand because I like them too. But now both we both restrain ourselves and limit how many we bring home. However, when we get together, we still stack our rocks and call them our "Ebenezers" – as evidence we are thankful for all the help from God. (see I Samuel 7:12). **THE ROCK** is different – See below and find out how.

He is <u>OUR ROCK</u>! This ROCK is <u>JESUS</u>!

<u>II Samuel 22:2 - 3</u>
And he said, the Lord is my Rock, and my fortress, and my deliverer; The God of my Rock; in Him will I trust: He is my shield, and the horn of my salvation, my high tower, and my refuge, my saviour; Thou savest me from violence.

<u>Psalms 92:15</u>
To shew that the Lord is upright: He is my rock, and there is no unrighteousness in Him.

<u>II Samuel 22:32, 47</u>
For who is God, save the Lord? and who is a Rock, save our God? The Lord liveth; and blessed be my Rock; and exalted be the God of the Rock of my salvation.

<u>Psalms 40:2</u>
He brought me up also out of an horrible pit, out of the miry clay, and set my feet upon a Rock, and established my goings.

<u>Psalms 61:2</u>
From the end of the earth will I cry unto Thee, when my heart is overwhelmed: lead me to the Rock that is higher than I.

MAY 12

WEARY to REST

As our world is weary and poor, we are called to rest in the Lord. "*I will give you rest*" (Exodus 33:14). Think back to the time of Exodus, yes, they also were promised the gift of rest from God. This is nothing new. Whatever you are feeling, He feels your emotion and can give you rest. Because of Him, we can show others this rest for the soul through Christ in our lives. We are His children and His followers, and like Him we must dare to suffer, <u>then conquer</u>, as we claim His Rest. He is the only cure for all the ills in this world. Let Him give you rest.

Exodus 33:14
And He (God) said, My presence shall go with thee, and I will give thee rest.

Proverbs 3:11, 12
My son, despise not the chastening of the Lord; neither be weary of his correction: For whom the Lord loveth he correcteth; even as a father the son in whom he delighteth

Jeremiah 6:16
Thus saith the Lord, Stand ye in the ways, and see, and ask for the old paths, where is the good way, and walk therein, and ye shall find rest for your souls. But they said, We will not walk therein.

Galatians 6:9
And let us not be weary in well doing: for in due season we shall reap, if we faint not.

Psalms 37:7a
Rest in the Lord, and wait patiently for him: fret not thyself because of him who prospereth in his way, because of the man who bringeth wicked devices to pass.

MAY 13

A LATE BLOOMER

Yes, me! At this my 80th year, I feel I have not accomplished much for Christ. I understand common regrets, but God has since revealed to me that the accomplishments of my own efforts and will are not my goal, but instead what He has done throughout my life including things I may not even know of. Now He is allowing me to search my memory and take a different route – His. Join me, and as we go: we will put on paper, the precious things He has stored in our hearts, and share them with others. Oh, to read them again and again, even if only for our own peace and joy.

John 6:28, 29
What shall we do, that we might work the works of God? Jesus answered and said unto them, <u>This is the work of God, that ye believe on Him Whom He hath sent</u>.

Deuteronomy 17:19
It shall be with him, and he shall read therein all the days of his life: that he may learn to fear the Lord his God, to keep all the words of this law and these statutes, to do them:

Joshua 1:8a, 9b
This book of the law shall not depart out of thy mouth; but thou shalt meditate therein day and night, that thou mayest observe to do according to all that is written therein: . . . Be strong and of a good courage; be not afraid, neither be thou dismayed: for the Lord thy God is with thee whithersoever thou goest.

II Timothy 3:15, 16
And that from a child thou hast known the holy scriptures, which are able to make thee wise unto salvation through faith which is in Christ Jesus.

MAY 14

"to the faithful" in CHRIST JESUS

Ephesians is written "to the faithful in Christ Jesus." When coming to verse 3, I wanted to know more of the intended meaning than just skipping over it. So, with my Scofield Study Bible (almost word by word) I received a deeper understanding: by recognizing the key words "spiritual blessings" and "heavenly places." These describe our position in grace as a believer and a child of God.

Ephesians 1:1b-6
. . . to the faithful in Christ Jesus: Grace be to you, and peace, from God our Father, and from the Lord Jesus Christ. Blessed be the God and Father of our Lord Jesus Christ, Who hath blessed us with <u>all spiritual blessings</u> in <u>heavenly places in Christ</u>: According as He hath chosen us in Him before the foundation of the world, that we should be holy and without blame before Him in love: Having predestinated us unto the adoption of children by Jesus Christ to Himself, according to the good pleasure of His will, To the praise of the glory of His grace, wherein He hath made us accepted in the Beloved.

II Peter 1:4
Whereby are given unto us exceeding great and precious promises: that by these ye might be partakers of the divine nature, having escaped the corruption that is in the world through lust.

I John 5:13
These things have I written unto you that believe on the name of the Son of God; that ye may <u>know</u> that ye have eternal life, and that ye may <u>believe</u> on the Name of the Son of God.

John 17:17 -- 19
Sanctify them through Thy truth: Thy word is truth.
As Thou hast sent Me into the world, even so have I also sent them into the world.
And for their sakes I sanctify myself, that they also might be sanctified through the truth.

MAY 15

AFRAID? AFRAID OF WHAT?

In China, leading up to World War II, many Christian Missionaries were martyred for their faith in Jesus Christ. We now hear of thousands of Christians being killed, (even beheaded) around the world, especially in the Middle East. I recently read a story about E. H. Hamilton, one such Missionary in China. After hearing of others being killed, he wrote this poem below before he, too, was captured and killed for his faith. This poem became a source of encouragement and strength for the other missionaries about to suffer the same fate. With deep gratitude, we must reflect on the cost of past and present sacrifices that have been endured on our behalf so we can have the privilege of knowing Jesus Christ as our Savior.

What about today? Would we be willing to have such courage and "not be afraid"?

"Afraid? Of What?"
By E. H. Hamilton

Afraid? Of What? To feel the spirit's glad release?
To pass from pain to perfect peace, The strife and strain of life to cease?
Afraid? Of What?

Afraid? Of What? Afraid to see the Savior's face To hear His welcome,
and to trace The glory gleam from wounds of grace?
Afraid? Of What?

Afraid? Of What? A flash, a crash, a pierced heart; Darkness, light,
O Heaven's art! A wound of His a counterpart?
Afraid? Of What?

Afraid? Of What? To do by death what life could not –
Baptized with blood a stony plot, Till souls shall blossom from the spot?
Afraid? Of What?

MAY 16

BE CALM, BE QUIET

Agitation is an emotion we all understand and carry deep down that can bubble up all too often without much warning - so destructive of the present good. If we replace our power of agitation with God's power; we can become calm and still. We need help – His help to exercise the discipline to turn to God for His power to stay calm and face up to our quick human responses by having God's presence within us. <u>Calmness with God is trusting Him</u>. He will destroy the destructive power over the evil of being "agitated." We can learn to be calm by trusting that God is in us.

Psalms 107:28 - 30
Then they cry unto the Lord in their trouble, and He bringeth them out of their distresses. He maketh the storm a calm, so that the waves thereof are still. Then are they glad because they be quiet; so He bringeth them unto their desired haven.

Ecclesiastes 9:17, 18
The words of wise men are heard in quiet more than the cry of him that ruleth among fools. Wisdom is better than weapons of war: but one sinner destroyeth much good.

Isaiah 32:17
And the work of righteousness shall be peace; and the effect of righteousness quietness and assurance forever.

Acts 19:36
Seeing then that these things cannot be spoken against, ye ought to be quiet, and to do nothing rashly

I Peter 3:4
But let it be the hidden man of the heart, in that which is not corruptible, even the ornament of a meek and quiet spirit, which is in the sight of God of great price.

MAY 17

MY OWN WAY

Often, we ask what other people think before we make a decision. We hope their opinions agree with what we want. There is a better way because our ways are not God's ways.

Isaiah 55:8, 9
For My thoughts are not your thoughts, neither are your ways My ways, saith the Lord. For as the heavens are higher than the earth, so are My ways higher than your ways,

Romans 3:16 - 18
Destruction and misery are in their ways: And the way of peace have they not known: There is no fear of God before their eyes.

Think of God and give up <u>self</u> - **MY OWN WAY**! Leave more and more choices to Him by keeping your eyes and soul ever open to Him. Live in the rapture of <u>His Kingdom</u>, where self is dead; and not bound to this earth.

Psalms 18:30
As for God, His way is perfect: the Word of the Lord is tried: He is a buckler to all those that trust in Him.

Proverbs 12:15
The way of a fool is right in his own eyes: but he that hearkeneth unto counsel is wise.

Proverbs 14:12
There is a way that seemeth right unto a man, but the end thereof are the ways of death.

Proverbs 19:3
The foolishness of man perverteth his way: and his heart fretteth against the Lord.

Jeremiah 23:12
Wherefore their way shall be unto them as slippery ways in the darkness: they shall be driven on, and fall therein:

MAY 18

NAKEDNESS/CLOTHED

We don't hear many conversations about nakedness. Usually, it is a very private matter. But in the movies, it is exploited or sometimes depicted in a manner of humiliation and torture. Also, in the movies, it seems that nakedness is so tantalizing and exciting to see that causes society to call it X-rated. Even Adam and Eve were stunned and ashamed when they realized they were naked after they disobeyed God, by eating the fruit from the tree they were told by God not to eat. This is the first recording of Nakedness. Motive and attitude is the actual crime against God when we sin.

Isaiah 61:10
I will greatly rejoice in the Lord, my soul shall be joyful in my God; for He hath <u>clothed</u> me with <u>the garments of salvation</u>, He hath <u>covered</u> me with <u>the robe of righteousness</u>, as a bridegroom decketh himself with ornaments, and as a bride adorneth herself with her jewels.

Genesis 2:24, 25
Therefore shall a man leave his father and his mother, and shall cleave unto his wife: and they shall be one flesh. And <u>they were both naked, the man and his wife, and were not ashamed.</u>

Genesis 3:10, 11, 21
And he (Adam) said, I heard Thy voice in the garden, and I was afraid, because I was naked; and I hid myself. And He (God) said, Who told thee that thou wast naked? Hast thou eaten of the tree, whereof I commanded thee that thou shouldest not eat? Unto Adam also and to his wife did <u>the Lord God</u> make coats of skins, and <u>clothed them</u>.

I Peter 5:5b
Yea, all of you be subject one to another, and be <u>clothed with humility</u>: for God resisteth the proud, and giveth grace to the humble.

MAY 19

CLEAN, CLEAN, CLEAN

A Clean House
A Clean Body
A Clean Car
Etc., Etc., Etc.
All down to the last detail!

Cleanliness can be fanatical or be the foundation for processes, schedules, and inspections. Yes, cleanliness is good because it helps us to take care of what God has given us. However, there is a more important cleansing (metaphorically) that cost God the sacrifice of His Dear Son. Read below and see our need and God's answer – Once for all!

Psalms 19:9, 12
The fear of the Lord is clean, enduring for ever: the judgments of the Lord are true and righteous altogether. Who can understand his errors? cleanse Thou me from secret faults.

Psalms 51:2, 7, 10
Wash me throughly from mine iniquity, and cleanse me from my sin. Purge me with hyssop, and I shall be clean: wash me, and I shall be whiter than snow. Create in me a clean heart, O God; and renew a right spirit within me.

Psalms 119:9 - 11
Wherewithal shall a young man cleanse his way? by taking heed thereto according to Thy word. With my whole heart have I sought Thee: O let me not wander from Thy commandments. <u>*Thy word have I hid in mine heart, that I might not sin against Thee.*</u>

Proverbs 16:2, 4
All the ways of a man are clean in his own eyes; but the Lord weigheth the spirits. The Lord hath made all things for Himself: yea, even the wicked for the day of evil.

MAY 20

I JOHN 1:7, 8, 9, 10

Even a child can understand the plain language of these verses, although many adults miss the message, sometimes intentionally. All our lives we are faced with "either/or" propositions, but this is the most important one we must know. The consequences of choosing the wrong way *"makes God a liar"* ** to us. I'm confident if anyone has meditated on this truth they would admit we have all sinned. What a merciful, loving God we have; *"He is faithful and just to <u>forgive</u> us our sins, and to <u>cleanse</u> us from all unrighteousness."* *

I John 1:7, 8, 9, 10

But if we walk in the Light, as He is in the light, we have fellowship one with another, and the blood of Jesus Christ His Son cleanseth us from all sin. If we say that we have no sin, we deceive ourselves, and the Truth is not in us. If we confess our sins, *<u>He is faithful and just to forgive us our sins</u>, <u>and to cleanse us from all unrighteousness</u>. If we say that we have not sinned, ** <u>we make Him a liar</u>, and His word is not in us

Romans 3:23, 24

For all have sinned, and come short of the glory of God; Being justified freely by His grace through the redemption that is in Christ Jesus:

Ephesians 6:11, 12

Put on the whole armour of God, that ye may be able to stand against the wiles of the devil. For we wrestle not against flesh and blood, but against principalities, against powers, against the rulers of the darkness of this world, against spiritual wickedness in high places.

MAY 21

THOU KNOWEST ME

God's presence is with me at all times (omnipresent), everywhere I go! Let me remember this truth. Let me not forget, the wonder knowing You go with me everywhere. **"Marvelous are Thy works; and that my soul knoweth right well."** ** To read this Psalm below, every day would make me a different person. I would want to be close to God, my Creator, and wholly desire to stay by His side.

Psalms 139:1-14, 17

O Lord, Thou hast searched me, and known me.
Thou knowest my down-sitting and mine uprising,
Thou understandest my thought afar off.
Thou compassest my path and my lying down,
and art acquainted with all my ways.
For there is not a word in my tongue,
but, lo, O Lord, Thou knowest it altogether.
Thou hast beset me behind and before,
and laid Thine hand upon me.
Such knowledge is too wonderful for me;
it is high, I cannot attain unto it.
Whither shall I go from Thy Spirit?
or whither shall I flee from Thy presence?
If I ascend up into heaven, Thou art there:
if I make my bed in hell, behold, Thou art there.
If I take the wings of the morning,
and dwell in the uttermost parts of the sea;
Even there shall Thy hand lead me,
and Thy right hand shall hold me.
If I say, Surely the darkness shall cover me;
even the night shall be light about me.
Yea, the darkness hideth not from Thee;
but the night shineth as the day:
the darkness and the light are both alike to Thee.
For thou hast possessed my reins:
Thou hast covered me in my mother's womb.
<u>*I will praise Thee; for I am fearfully and wonderfully made:*</u>
**<u>*marvellous are Thy works; and that my soul knoweth right well.*</u>
How precious also are Thy thoughts unto me, O God! *how great is the sum of them!*

MAY 22

SAVE THE CHILDREN

When we see a plea for money on television for a non-profit organization, we are shown very sad children or animals in need - to touch our hearts. This brings to my mind a higher calling. The Scriptures have much to say about the matter of children. Christ even scolded His disciples to let the little children come to Him and to forbid them not.

Mark 10:13 – 16
And they brought young children to Him, that He should touch them: and His disciples rebuked those that brought them. But when Jesus saw it, He was much displeased, and said unto them, Suffer the little children to come unto Me, and forbid them not: for of such is the kingdom of God.
Verily I say unto you, Whosoever shall not receive the kingdom of God as a little child, he shall not enter therein. And He took them up in His arms, put His hands upon them, and blessed them.

God loves children so much He uses the example of a child to portray how we need to come to Him (how do you see little children?). As His children, God shows us unconditional love, mercy, grace, forgiveness, and patience. Look at these verses showing how important children are to God.

Matthew 18:4, 5, 10
Whosoever therefore shall humble himself as this little child, the same is greatest in the kingdom of heaven. And whoso shall receive one such little child in My name receiveth Me. Take heed that ye despise not one of these little ones; for I say unto you, That in heaven <u>their angels</u> do always behold the face of My Father which is in heaven.

Galatians 3:26
For ye are all the children of God <u>by faith in Christ Jesus</u>.

MAY 23

SCRIPTUAL KNOWLEDGE

While reading *The Autobiography of George Muller*,* I found the plans he and his brother devised together through prayer - a call to realize "unscriptural practices" in the "religious societies" of their day. Thereby, they could not remain united with them. Thus, "By the Blessing of God," they established an "institution" and many orphanages to spread the true Gospel at home and abroad, starting in 1834. Now, their Journey continues on, via the book by Muller. Who could have thought, more than 100 years later his Journal would still available for our reading and touching lives? He wrote of their complete life of faith, waiting on God to answer their prayers for needs, and not having to ask for anything from unbelievers. Here are some of the Scriptures that spurred them on to this long-lasting endeavor.

Psalms 34:8, 9
O taste and see that the Lord is good: blessed is the man that trusteth in Him. O fear the Lord, ye His saints: for there is no want to them that fear Him.

Psalms 118:8
It is better to trust in the Lord than to put confidence in man.

Zechariah 4:6b
Not by might, nor by power, but by My spirit, saith the Lord of hosts.

Romans 13:8
Owe no man any thing, but to love one another: for he that loveth another hath fulfilled the law.

Philippians 4:19
But my God shall supply all your need according to His riches in glory by Christ Jesus.

* *The Autobiography of George Muller*; by Whitaker House, Kensington, PA

MAY 24

A QUIET SPIRIT and LIFE

By this time, we all know of the Bible verse:
Psalms 46:10a
Be still, and know that I am God:

I see this framed above my kitchen sink every day. It is a thrill and reminder of knowing, I believe and have confidence in Him. He is God – my God! I do not need to fret or be obnoxious, because He has commanded me to "be still." He loves a peaceful and quiet spirit - what the world misunderstands. They may think we are aloof or uninterested. Not so! It is the knowing a quiet spirit does not cause strife, but brings peace. Check it out below.

Ecclesiastes 4:6
Better is an handful with quietness, than both the hands full with travail and vexation of spirit.

Lamentations 3:26
It is good that a man should both hope and quietly wait for the salvation of the Lord.

Acts 19:36
Seeing then that these things cannot be spoken against, ye ought to be quiet, and to do nothing rashly.

I Thessalonians 4:11, 12
And that ye study to be quiet, and to do your own business, and to work with your own hands, as we commanded you; That ye may walk honestly toward them that are without, and that ye may have lack of nothing.

I Peter 3:4b
. . . the ornament of a meek and quiet spirit, which is in the sight of God of great price.

MAY 25

WHAT WE SHOULD HATE

We should hate what God hates.
As we read before, Proverbs 16 **gives us a whole list of things God hates.** This is good to review of our list concerning our behavior and life style. But there is more to go along with these; WHAT <u>WE</u> SHOULD HATE (our sin). Take a look and ask the Lord to help at all times, to be aware of His Ever Presence, to guide us on our way. He will lead us to life eternal.

Psalms 101:3 – 7 (King David's determination)
I will set no wicked thing before mine eyes: I hate the work of them that turn aside; it shall not cleave to me. A froward heart shall depart from me: I will not know a wicked person. Whoso privily slandereth his neighbour, him will I cut off: him that hath an high look and a proud heart will not I suffer. Mine eyes shall be upon the faithful of the land, that they may dwell with me: he that walketh in a perfect way, he shall serve me. He that worketh deceit shall not dwell within my house: he that telleth lies shall not tarry in my sight.

Psalms 119:104
Through Thy precepts I get understanding: therefore I hate every false way.

Psalms 139:19 - 22
Surely Thou wilt slay the wicked, O God: depart from me therefore, ye bloody men. For they speak against Thee wickedly, and Thine enemies take Thy name in vain. Do not I hate them, O Lord, that hate Thee? and am not I grieved with those that rise up against Thee? I hate them with perfect hatred: I count them mine enemies.

Proverbs 8:13
The fear of the Lord is to hate evil: pride, and arrogancy, and the evil way, and the froward mouth, do I hate.

Zechariah 8:17
And let none of you imagine evil in your hearts against his neighbour; and love no false oath: for all these are things that I hate, saith the Lord.

MY HELP

Just recently I was curious enough to research the **hymn** "**Come Thou Fount,**" by R. Robinson (1735-1790). The meaning of the phrase, "*Here I raise my Ebenezer, Hither by Thy help I'm come,*" has baffled me as I sang it in church for years not knowing what "my Ebenezer" meant. I kept wondering how I could raise **"my Ebenezer"** for all the help I have received from God all these years. So now I know. The lyrics are based on the scriptural passage, when Samuel was praising God for victory over the enemy at **Ebenezer.** Samuel took **a** stone and set it up and named it **Ebenezer**, saying; "*Hitherto hath the Lord helped us*" (I Samuel 7:12). By my stone stacking, I am raising "**my Ebenezer**" to praise God for His help; putting rock on rock or stone on stone whenever or wherever I desire. Like I mentioned before, my granddaughter, Amelia, and I stack rocks together, and call them our "**Ebenezers,**" just like Samuel did to thank God for His help in days of old.

Psalms 121:1 – 8
*I will lift up mine eyes unto the hills,
from whence cometh my help.
My help cometh from the Lord,
which made heaven and earth.
He will not suffer thy foot to be moved:
He that keepeth thee will not slumber.
Behold, He that keepeth Israel
shall neither slumber nor sleep.
The Lord is thy keeper:
the Lord is thy shade upon thy right hand.
The sun shall not smite thee by day,
nor the moon by night.
The Lord shall preserve thee from all evil:
He shall preserve thy soul.
The Lord shall preserve thy going out and thy coming in
from this time forth, and even for evermore.*

MAY 27

SPARROWS, CHICKENS and EAGLES

"Free as a bird," "Birds of a feather flock together," "For the birds" These are all phrases we have heard, used, and know. The Bible also uses characteristics of the fowls of the air, created by God, to compare some of their qualities, to teach to us symbols of His care, and to give instructions.

I am unaware of man trying to mate and "improve" one kind of bird with another as they have done so openly with flowers, fruits, vegetables, dogs, and cats, etc. Birds are still free to sing the songs given to them by God, to sing His praises we enjoy also. God knows each one of us as He knows each sparrow. What a picture! His eye is on the sparrow according to scripture, "**ye are of more value than many Sparrows**" (Matthew 10:29 – 31b).

Deuteronomy 14:11 - 20
Of all clean birds ye shall eat. But these are they of which ye shall not eat: the eagle, and the ossifrage, and the ospray, And the glede, and the kite, and the vulture after his kind, And every raven after his kind, And the owl, and the night hawk, and the cuckow, and the hawk after his kind, The little owl, and the great owl, and the swan, And the pelican, and the gier eagle, and the cormorant, And the stork, and the heron after her kind, and the lapwing, and the bat. And every creeping thing that flieth is unclean unto you: they shall not be eaten. But of all clean fowls ye may eat.

Job 39:27 - 29
Doth the eagle mount up at thy command, and make her nest on high? She dwelleth and abideth on the rock, upon the crag of the rock, and the strong place. From thence she seeketh the prey, and her eyes behold afar off.

Isaiah 40:31
But they that wait upon the Lord shall renew their strength; they shall mount up with wings as eagles; they shall run, and not be weary; and they shall walk, and not faint.

MAY 28

REMEMBER MEMORIAL DAY
coming soon

I just finished reading *In the Presence Of My Enemies*, by Howard and Phyllis Rutledge in 1973. I was so moved by this tribute for Memorial Day, I recommend it to all.

I like non-fiction books written in the past more than the latest and greatest novels. This true story is deeply touching because it tells how so many have suffered for our freedoms. Howard tells of the time he and others spent in a prison camp in North Vietnam and how they coped and helped each other by remembering the Lord. They tried to remember all the scriptures and songs they learned in the past, even back to childhood, to give them hope, strength, and perseverance to survive (see Nehemiah 4:14). These, scriptures, memories, and songs brought back their sanity during times of torture, loneliness, distress, etc. Remember to thank God for all of our "defenders of peace," and honor them.

Psalms 119:49, 50, 52 – 55a
Remember the word unto Thy servant, upon which Thou hast caused me to hope. This is my comfort in my affliction: for Thy word hath quickened me. I remembered . . . and have comforted myself. Horror hath taken hold upon me because of the wicked . . . Thy statutes have been my songs in the house of my pilgrimage (distress). I have remembered Thy name, O Lord, in the night

Nehemiah 4:14b
. . . Be not ye afraid of them: remember the Lord, which is great and terrible, and fight for your brethren, your sons, and your daughters, your wives, and your houses.

MAY 29

WOE

When you hear the word "WOE," does it give you pause? It does me! Woe and Whoa sound alike and both give a warning of danger, a command to stop an action, or consequences of an act. Two phrases come to my mind - "Woe is me," and the command for a horse stop - "Whoa." We are wise to be aware of how God uses the word "WOE" in Scripture to open our eyes to our behavior and avoid being hypocrites.

Heed His warnings.

Proverbs 23:29, 30a
Who hath woe? who hath sorrow? who hath contentions? who hath babbling? who hath wounds without cause? who hath redness of eyes? They that tarry long at the wine;

Isaiah 6:5
Then said I, Woe is me! for I am undone; because I am a man of unclean lips, and I dwell in the midst of a people of unclean lips: for mine eyes have seen the King, the Lord of hosts.

Isaiah 29:15
Woe unto them that seek deep to hide their counsel from the Lord, and their works are in the dark, and they say, Who seeth us? and Who knoweth us?

Isaiah 30:1
Woe to the rebellious children, saith the Lord, that take counsel, but not of Me; and that cover with a covering, but not of My spirit, that they may add sin to sin:

Matthew 18:7
Woe unto the world because of offences! for it must needs be that offences come; but woe to that man by whom the offence cometh!

MAY 30

FREEDOM, In Remembrance

As a little girl in school I loved singing, **"My Country 'Tis Of Thee."** Although many years have passed since I heard it sung, I still know the words to the first and last verses. Perhaps now, this patriotic song is not "politically correct" but I am so thankful for the "ring" of freedom in my heart.

"MY COUNTRY 'TIS OF THEE"
By Frances Scott Key (1779-1843)

My country, 'tis of thee, sweet land of liberty,
Of thee I sing:
Land where my fathers died, Land of the pilgrims' pride,
From ev'ry mountain side <u>*Let freedom ring*</u>*!*

Let music swell the breeze, And ring from all the trees
Sweet freedom's song:
Let mortal tongues awake, Let all that breath partake;
Let rocks their silence break, The sound prolong

Our fathers; God, to Thee, Author of liberty,
To Thee we sing:
Long may our land be bright with freedom's holy light;
Protect us by Thy might, Great God, our King!

In school, we seldom if ever, sang the last stanza where the word God was mentioned but through my Christian heritage, I learned this land is a gift from God and have been so thankful to have been born here.

O how I wish children today could learn and sing this song at school. Freedom and Liberty are straight from God's hand of mercy. Let us not forget what a history this county has! Let us not lose what God has given us!

MEMORIAL DAY

MAY 30^(TH)

Lest we Forget!

Editor's Note:
The actual date for Memorial Day will change each year, but always celebrated on the last Monday in May.

MAY 31
"THIS WORLD IS NOT MY HOME"

This is one of the songs that calm my heart over and over whenever I get disturbed by the daily news, or the events of the world; and remember to sing it. You can't help but look forward to that day when we will see Jesus and His Kingdom comes!

Here are the words for two verses and the <u>Chorus</u>!

"THIS WORLD IS NOT MY HOME"
by E. & A. Bhebe

This world is not my home, I'm just a-passin' through,
My treasures are laid up somewhere beyond the blue.
The angels beckon me from heaven's open door
And I can't feel at home in this world anymore.

Chorus
O Lord, you know I have no friend like You.
If heaven's not my home then Lord what will I do?
The angels beckon me from heaven's open door
And I can't feel at home in this world anymore.

Just over in glory land we'll live eternally.
The saints on every hand are shouting Victory.
Their songs of sweetest Praise drift back from Heaven's shore.
And I can't feel at home in this world anymore.

Chorus
O Lord, you know I have no friend like You.
If heaven's not my home then Lord what will I do?
The angels beckon me from heaven's open door
And I can't feel at home in this world anymore.

JUNE

CONNECT THE DOTS

Job 28:28
And unto man He said, Behold, the fear of the Lord, that is wisdom; and to depart from evil is understanding.

JUNE 1

POLLYANNA'S "GLAD GAME"

We have all heard the negative connotations of being a "Pollyanna," by thinking of such a person who is foolishly over optimistic, excessively happy, or someone who denies reality. This was not the intention of the author, Eleanor Portor (1868-1920) in her famous book, *Pollyanna*, written in 1912. Her main message was to teach us the child-like faith of rejoicing in all things; not as an escape from reality, but from a faith in God, trusting Him in all of life's ups and downs. She called this the **GLAD GAME**, and credited her father for teaching her the importance for us to "rejoice," "be glad," "shout for joy," etc. Since God put these phrases in the Bible (more than 800 times) they must be something important for us to do. Below are just a few to review and to renew your child-like faith by rejoicing in God. Through all the ups and downs of life – give thanks in all things, and BE GLAD!

Psalms 9:2
I will be glad and rejoice in Thee: I will sing praise to Thy name, O Thou most High.

Psalms 35:27
Let them shout for joy, and be glad, that favour My righteous cause: yea, let them say continually, Let the Lord be magnified, which hath pleasure in the prosperity of His servant.

Psalms 40:16
Let all those that seek Thee rejoice and be glad in Thee: let such as love Thy salvation say continually, The Lord be magnified.

Psalms 64:10
The righteous shall be glad in the Lord, and shall trust in Him; and all the upright in heart shall glory.

JUNE 2

I AM SO GLAD!

This project of a 365-day journal has been so good for me because I have to search my brain for thoughts for each day. Without the Holy Spirit reminding me I would be "speechless" and in this case "wordless." It is a wonderful thing that we have been given a memory to look back and to be able to draw out the great lessons God has taught us and is still teaching us every day. Below is a song that I learned over 70 years ago which reminded me of "gladness." The title is "Jesus Loves Even Me," and in my hymnal, it does not show that it is copyrighted, so it might be hard to find. I hope you remember it too. If you can find the music, try to learn it and teach it to your children.

"JESUS LOVES EVEN ME"
by Philip P. Bliss (1838-1876)

I am so glad that our Father in Heaven
Tells of His love in the Book He has giv'n;
Wonderful things in the Bible I see:
This is the dearest that Jesus loves me.

Chorus
I am so glad that Jesus loves me,
Jesus loves me, Jesus loves me;
I am so glad that Jesus loves me,
Jesus loves me, Jesus loves even me.

Though I forget Him and wander away,
Still He doth love me whenever I stray;
Back to His dear loving arms would I flee,
When I remember that Jesus loves me.

Oh, if there's only one song I can sing,
When in His beauty I see the great King
This shall my song in eternity be:
Oh, what a wonder that Jesus loves me.

JUNE 3

SEPARATED?

The idea of being "separated" from worldly desires, is rarely spoken of today in Christian circles because it might be offensive to somebody and turn them off; or we might be considered aloof, self-righteous, or hypocritical. But if we believe God's Word and His commands. How can we ignore what is written?

<u>II Corinthians 6:17</u>
Wherefore <u>come out from among them, and be ye separate</u>, saith the Lord, and touch not the unclean thing; and I will receive you,

This is not a new command because we can even find it in the Old Testament, given to His chosen people. So, what about the world? For us, once we believe, we are to be set apart for His service. Separate, from the things of this world that cause us to be trapped and led away from God's love to us - be it people, places, or things.

<u>II Corinthians 6:17, 18:</u>
Wherefore come out from among them, and be ye separate, saith the Lord, and touch not the unclean thing; and I will receive you, And will be a Father unto you, and ye shall be My sons and daughters, saith the Lord Almighty.

<u>Matthew 25:31, 32</u>
When the Son of man shall come in His glory, and all the holy angels with Him, then shall He sit upon the throne of His glory: And before Him shall be gathered all nations: and He shall separate them one from another, as a shepherd divideth his sheep from the goats:

<u>Romans 8:35, 39</u>
Who shall separate us from the love of Christ? shall tribulation, or distress, or persecution, or famine, or nakedness, or peril, or sword? Nor height, nor depth, nor any other creature, shall be able to separate us from the love of God, which is in Christ Jesus our Lord.

JUNE 4

GOD IN THE FLESH

God in the flesh - His Incarnation.

This is the embodiment of God in the human form of Jesus – God's only begotten Son. No other human can be "God with Us," though some have tried to deceive us. This is what gives us full confidence in God's Word. We can completely believe Him. However, even our faith to believe in Him comes from God. Jesus taught us He and the Father are One! Jesus is God in the flesh and there is no denying it. He said in John 8:24: *I said therefore unto you, that ye shall die in your sins: for if ye <u>believe not</u> that I am He, ye shall die in your sins.*

He lived and then died on the cross for us and was resurrected, that we may also have eternal life with Him. He is the God of our Salvation! All of Scripture testifies of Him!   **Believe! Believe! Believe!**

John 20:24 – 29, 31

But Thomas, one of the twelve, called Didymus, was not with them when Jesus came. The other disciples therefore said unto him, We have <u>seen</u> the Lord. But he said unto them, Except I shall <u>see</u> in His hands the print of the nails, and put my finger into the print of the nails, and thrust my hand into his side, I will not believe.

And after eight days again His disciples were within, and Thomas with them: then came Jesus, the doors being shut, and stood in the midst, and said, Peace be unto you. Then saith He to Thomas, Reach hither thy finger, and behold My hands; and reach hither thy hand, and thrust it into My side: and be not faithless, but believing. And Thomas answered and said unto Him, My Lord and my God. Jesus saith unto him, Thomas, because thou hast <u>seen</u> Me, thou hast believed: blessed are they that have not seen, and yet have believed. But these are written, that ye might believe that Jesus is the Christ, the Son of God; and that believing ye might have life through His name.

JUNE 5

COME UNTO ME

In my computer room, I have a picture of hands – the hands inviting anyone to COME. You have probably seen the same picture if you have been to a Christian book store. It is very compelling and was painted to resemble the hands of Christ biding us to come to Him. We all have many needs that Jesus wants to help us with and He wants to carry our burdens in exchange for His burden, which is light.

Matthew 11:28 - 30
Come unto Me, all ye that labour and are heavy laden, and I will give you rest. Take My yoke upon you, and learn of Me; for I am meek and lowly in heart: and ye shall find rest unto your souls. For My yoke is easy, and <u>*My burden is light*</u>*.*

Nothing can shake you when you place yourself in the hands of God.

Psalms 55:22
Cast thy burden upon the Lord, and He shall sustain thee: He shall never suffer the righteous to be moved.

Mark 10:14, 15
But when Jesus saw it, He was much displeased, and said unto them, Suffer the little children to come unto Me, and forbid them not: for of such is the kingdom of God. Verily I say unto you, Whosoever shall not receive the kingdom of God as a little child, he shall not enter therein.

John 6:37
All that the Father giveth Me shall come to Me; and him that cometh to Me I will in no wise cast out.

Hebrews 7:25
Wherefore He is able also to save them to the uttermost that come unto God by Him, seeing He ever liveth to make intercession for them.

JUNE 6

LEARN HOW TO TALK TO YOURSELF

Talking to your self isn't all bad!
King David in the Bible did so in Psalms 42:1 – 6

As the hart panteth after the water brooks, so panteth my soul after Thee, O God. My soul thirsteth for God, for the living God: when shall I come and appear before God? My tears have been my meat day and night, while they continually say unto me, Where is thy God? <u>When I remember</u> these things, I pour out my soul in me: for I had gone with the multitude, I went with them to the house of God, with the voice of joy and praise, with a multitude that kept holyday. Why art thou cast down, O my soul? and why art thou disquieted in me? hope thou in God: for I shall yet praise Him for the help of His countenance. O my God, my soul is cast down within therefore <u>will I remember</u> Thee.

Keep on reading the rest of Psalms 42, below! This idea of <u>talking to yourself</u> and <u>not letting yourself talk to you,</u> was explained to me in D. Martyn Lloyd-Jones' book, *Spiritual Depression.** Most of our unhappiness in life is due to the fact that we are listening (passively) to ourselves instead of talking (boldly) to ourselves.

Psalms 42:7 - 11

Deep calleth unto deep at the noise of Thy waterspouts: all Thy waves and Thy billows are gone over me. Yet the Lord will command His loving-kindness in the daytime, and in the night His song shall be with me, and my prayer unto the God of my life. I will say unto God my rock, Why hast Thou forgotten me? why go I mourning because of the oppression of the enemy? As with a sword in my bones, mine enemies reproach me; while they say daily unto me, Where is thy God? Why art thou cast down, O my soul? and why art thou disquieted within me? **Hope thou in God:** *for I shall yet praise Him, Who is the health of my countenance,*
*and **my God.***

* D. Martyn Lloyd-Jones' book, *Spiritual Depression* - Wm. B. Eerdmans Publishing, 1965

JUNE 7

THE "NOTEBOOK" HABIT

Your journal, or whatever you want to call it – **just do it**!
I guess I've been doing this somewhat without giving it a thought or name. Mine has been all the notes I've accumulated over the years I've made when reading, listening to my pastors, my personal studies, the under linings in my Bible, etc. Until recently, all these notes were kept in boxes and packed away or scattered around. I did keep them and moved them with me as we moved from place to place. Now I know that it would have been better if I would have put or pasted, all of the above in journals.

As I reviewed my notes, I can see how and what God has taught me over the years. He has been so good, kind, and faithful for giving me so many good teachers of the faith through His servants and pastors. I thank God for all of them. My childhood was spent in Nebraska, and then after my marriage, God has moved us many times and we found His people everywhere He sent us. We consider ourselves as "pilgrims" in this world. He has never failed us.

Psalms 119:11, 15, 16
Thy word have I hid in mine heart, that I might not sin against Thee. I will meditate in Thy precepts, and have respect unto Thy ways. I will delight myself in Thy statutes: I will not forget Thy word.

II Corinthians 4:3, 4
But if our gospel be hid, it is hid to them that are lost: in whom the god of this world hath blinded the minds of them which believe not, lest the light of the glorious gospel of Christ, Who is the image of God, should shine unto them.

Colossians 3:2, 3, 4
Set your affection on things above, not on things on the earth. For ye are dead, and your life is hid with Christ in God. When Christ, Who is our life, shall appear, then shall ye also appear with Him in glory.

JUNE 8

JOY IN THE LORD

My cousin's name is Joy!
What a reminder it would be daily to remember how we should live our life – in the Joy of the Lord! I Know of another person whose name is Joy and her friends call her Joyful. That's the name I would like to be known for because it implies a great love toward God and man. However, I fall short of having joy in my heart enough – not to be called Joyful. Thinking back again to my childhood I remember the Sunday School chorus:

> I have the joy, joy, joy, joy down in my heart.
> Where? Down in my Heart. Where? Down in my Heart.
> I HAVE THE JOY, JOY, JOY, JOY DOWN IN MY HEART
> Down in my heart to <u>stay</u>.

Until now, I forgot all about this <u>Chorus</u>, until one day, my husband and I sang it in our car to our 3 youngest grandchildren. It should not be that hard to remember to "be Joyful." I will rejoice! Scripture tells us how.

<u>Psalms 35:9</u>
And my soul shall be joyful in the Lord: it shall rejoice in His salvation.

<u>Acts 2:28</u>
Thou hast made known to me the ways of life; Thou shalt make me full of joy with Thy countenance.

<u>Romans 5:11</u>
And not only so, but we also joy in God through our Lord Jesus Christ, by Whom we have now received the atonement.

<u>Romans 15:13</u>
Now the God of hope fill you with all joy and peace in believing, that ye may abound in hope, through the power of the Holy Ghost.

JUNE 9

A RAINY DAY

Can you imagine our world without rain? It is the one thing we cannot live without physically. We need water. When rain spoils our plans, we get upset and have to make changes. When our crops need watering, we count it a blessing. Sounds like we are a little fickle and selfish. When there is a flood, right away we say, "Why God, so much rain at one time?" I've been in a flash flood in Colorado, and from experience I saw fear and we prayed and asked God to keep us safe, Thank God, He did! This might be the benefit some people need to remember - Who is in control? Many verses in the Old Testament give examples of God's dealings with man with rain and His power. Very interesting! Give thanks to Him in all things.

Isaiah 55:10, 11
For as the rain cometh down, and the snow from heaven, and returneth not thither, but watereth the earth, and maketh it bring forth and bud, that it may give seed to the sower, and bread to the eater: So shall My word be that goeth forth out of My mouth: it shall not return unto me void, but it shall accomplish that which I please, and it shall prosper in the thing whereto I sent it.

Jeremiah 14:22
Are there any among the vanities of the Gentiles that can cause rain? or can the heavens give showers? art not Thou He, O Lord our God? Therefore, we will wait upon Thee: for Thou hast made all these things.

James 15:17, 18
Elias was a man subject to like passions as we are, and he prayed earnestly that it might not rain: and it rained not on the earth by the space of three years and six months. And he prayed again, and the heaven gave rain, and the earth brought forth her fruit.

JUNE 10

LORD, I WAS JUST THINKING ABOUT YOU

This can be surprising! Just out of the blue a blessing from the Lord enters into our minds!
Who are You, O God? How can I think of things so high? It is only because of Your love toward us and Your gift of Your Spirit within, that we can know You, and learn of You, and be reminded of the deep things about You!

I Corinthians 2:9 - 12
But as it is written, Eye hath not seen, nor ear heard, neither have entered into the heart of man, the things which God hath prepared for them that love Him. But God hath revealed them unto us by His Spirit: for the Spirit searcheth all things, yea, the deep things of God. For what man knoweth the things of a man, save the spirit of man which is in him? Even so the things of God knoweth no man, but the <u>Spirit of God</u>. Now we have received, not the spirit of the world, but the Spirit which is of God; <u>that we might know the things that are freely given to us of God</u>.

Ecclesiastes 8:17
Then I beheld all the work of God, that a man cannot find out the work that is done under the sun: because though a man labour to seek it out, yet he shall not find it; yea further; though a wise man think to know it, yet shall he not be able to find it.

Proverbs 23:7
For as he thinketh in his heart, so is he:

Psalms 139:17
How precious also are thy thoughts unto me, O God! how great is the sum of them!

Matthew 5:17, 18
Think not that I (Jesus) am come to destroy the law, or the prophets: I am not come to destroy, but to fulfil. For verily I say unto you, Till heaven and earth pass, one jot or one tittle shall in no wise pass from the law, till all be fulfilled.

JUNE 11

NO ONE'S LOOKING

Know that the devil is the source of all temptations and there is a certain mindset in us that tells us, if it doesn't hurt anyone but "me," I can do it? No one's looking! Do you believe that it is possible for a person to have both a private and a public character? Should they be the same or are they very different from each other? Are we Believers or Make-Believers? Yes, as believers, do we have some fear of being persecuted by the world. But as a child of God we must choose who to follow – God or man.

Test it out – a "Believer" or a "Make-Believer"? Do you put your character into compartments? If so, the compartments will soon merge together and you will lose sight of which one is important to you. With the help of the Holy Spirit, desire to please God and develop the life He would have in you live in private, in public, and with friends. Be consistent. Be faithful to the Lord. Don't be tossed TO and FRO – Stand Firm!

Psalms 10:11,
He hath said in his heart, God hath forgotten: He hideth His face; He will never see it.

Psalms 14:2
The Lord looked down from heaven upon the children of men, to see if there were any that did understand, and seek God.

Psalms 64:5, 10
They encourage themselves in an evil matter: they commune of laying snares privily; they say, Who shall see them? The righteous shall be glad in the Lord, and shall trust in Him;

Jeremiah 23:23, 24
Am I a God at hand, saith the Lord, and not a God afar off? Can any hide himself in secret places that I shall not see him? saith the Lord. Do not I fill heaven and earth? saith the Lord.

JUNE 12

TEARS

There are so many reasons for tears – both physical and emotional. Tears of Joy of course are our favorite, but other times, be it with a blessing or a sorrow we can feel the comforting hand of God with us. Physically, tears have a purpose to lubricate and clean the surface between the eyeball and eyelid. If we don't have them we learn how important they are and get a remedy to replace them. Emotionally they can relieve tension and grief. Another moment of tears, are tears of love in:

<u>John 11:33 – 36</u>
When Jesus therefore saw her weeping, and the Jews also weeping which came with her, He groaned in the spirit, and was troubled, And said, Where have ye laid him (Lazarus)? They said unto Him, Lord, come and see. <u>Jesus wept</u>. Then said the Jews, Behold how He loved him!

<u>Kings 20:5</u>
*Thus saith the Lord, the God of David thy father,
I have heard thy prayer, I have seen thy tears: behold, I will heal thee:*

<u>Job 16:20</u>
My friends scorn me: but mine eye poureth out tears unto God.

<u>Psalms 6:6, 7</u>
I am weary with my groaning; all the night make I my bed to swim; I water my couch with my tears. Mine eye is consumed because of grief . . .

<u>Psalm 56:8</u>
Thou tellest my wanderingss: put Thou my tears into Thy bottle: are they not in Thy book?

<u>Psalms 126:5</u>
They that sow in tears shall reap in joy.

JUNE 13

FRET NOT

We use the word fret occasionally so we ought to know what it means, but It would pay you to look it up again in a dictionary to get the whole meaning for our use. Not a pretty sight or attribute, is it? <u>The Bible does not use the word "fret" often</u> but when it does, we get the picture. It interrupts our peace with God and shows a discontentment toward Him. We are not to compare our circumstances with how God treats others or be concerned or even think that God is unfair with His dealings towards us. Fretting is a direct path to jealousy.

Review these few verses below, and know God is God and deals with us individually with His knowing what is best for us to bring us to Himself. Instead of "looking at others," look unto God – "the author and finisher of our faith." You cannot look at two things at the same time.

<u>Proverbs 24:19, 20</u>
<u>Fret not thyself</u> because of evil men, neither be thou envious at the wicked; For there shall be no reward to the evil man; the candle of the wicked shall be put out.

<u>Psalms 37:1, 2</u>
<u>Fret not thyself</u> because of evildoers, neither be thou envious against the workers of iniquity. For they shall soon be cut down like the grass, and wither as the green herb.

<u>Proverbs 24:19, 20</u>
<u>Fret not thyself</u> because of evil men, neither be thou envious at the wicked; For there shall be no reward to the evil man; the candle of the wicked shall be put out.

<u>Proverbs 19:3</u>
The foolishness of man perverteth his way: and <u>his heart fretteth against the Lord</u>.

JUNE 14

JOHN 6:37 – On the Wall!

This Bible verse was on the wall of Bemis Park Baptist Church in Omaha, Nebraska; where I was born spiritually, and grew up in the Lord, and married my high school sweetheart.

You couldn't miss it – week after week, it was right behind the choir loft and the Pastor's pulpit. Even now when I look at our wedding pictures – it is there. What a blessing it has been after all these 60 years of marriage God has given us.

> . . . *"him that cometh to Me I will in no wise cast out."*

This promise from God I have carried with me all of my life. What a blessing and privilege to hold on to. God is so good!

John 6:37
All that the Father giveth Me shall come to Me; and <u>him that cometh to Me I will in no wise cast out</u>.

John 10:10, 28 - 30
The thief cometh not, but for to steal, and to kill, and to destroy: I am come that they might have life, and that they might have it more abundantly. And I give unto them eternal life; and they shall never perish, neither shall any man pluck them out of My hand. My Father, which gave them Me, is greater than all; and no man is able to pluck them out of My Father's hand. I and My Father are one.

Matthew 7:13, 14
Enter ye in at the strait gate: for wide is the gate, and broad is the way, that leadeth to destruction, and many there be which go in there at: Because strait is the gate, and narrow is the way, which leadeth unto life, and few there be that find it.

JUNE 15

HE FIRST LOVED ME

When you think back, there are abundances of "firsts" in our lives but none can compare with the **First Love** we find in:

I John 4:19
We love Him, because He first loved us.

Such a little verse says it all! "**He *first loved us.***" Can you imagine? The God of all creation loved us way before we knew Him. This is so unbelievable that it takes faith to believe in such a glorious statement. If we don't believe it we are calling God a liar - how can anyone do that knowingly? God even takes away our unbelief and replaces it with the gift of faith. How wonderful is that! As you read below, see for yourself how important and wide spread His great love is toward us.

Acts 13:46
Then Paul and Barnabas waxed bold, and said, It was necessary that the word of God should first have been spoken to you (Jews): but seeing ye put it from you, and judge yourselves unworthy of everlasting life, lo, we turn to the Gentiles.

Acts 26:23
That Christ should suffer, and that He should be the first that should rise from the dead, and should shew light unto the people, and to the Gentiles.

Romans 2:10, 11
But glory, honour, and peace, to every man that worketh good, to the Jew first, and also to the Gentile: For there is no respect of persons with God.

Ephesians 6:2, 3
Honour thy father and mother; (which is the first commandment with promise;) That it may be well with thee, and thou mayest live long on the earth.

JUNE 16

LISTEN, HEAR, OBEY

Trying to remember all that I have learned and believe has always given me unrest and struggles. Now what I am learning – stop trying so hard to remember everything. It is the Holy Spirit that is in charge to bring me these promptings in every situation as I need them. It is up to me to trust Him and listen for His still small voice from within me, and then to hear and respond willingly with my obedience.

John 14:26
But the Comforter, which is the Holy Ghost, whom the Father will send in My name, He shall teach you all things, and bring all things to your remembrance, whatsoever I have said unto you.

It is not faith to run ahead of Him or want to see the end from the beginning. But faith is to trust and obey God's promptings. Believe!

Psalms 139:7
*Whither shall I go from **Thy spirit**? or whither shall I flee from Thy presence*

I Corinthians 2:9, 10, 13
*But as it is written, Eye hath not seen, nor ear heard, neither have entered into the heart of man, the things which God hath prepared for them that love Him. But God hath revealed them unto us **by His Spirit**: for the Spirit searcheth all things, yea, the deep things of God. Which things also we speak, not in the words which man's wisdom teacheth, but which the Holy Ghost teacheth; comparing spiritual things with spiritual.*

John 14:16, 17
*And I (Jesus) will pray the Father, and He shall give you another Comforter, that He may abide with you for ever; Even the Spirit of Truth; Whom the world cannot receive, because it seeth Him not, neither knoweth Him: but ye know Him; for **He dwelleth with you, and shall be in you**.*

JUNE 17

CARRY A SONG
AS YOU GO ALONG

Matthew 26:30
And when they had sung an hymn they went out into the mount of Olives.

The Book of Psalms is full of songs and I'm sure Jesus and His disciples sang many of them by heart as they went about. Just try to imagine them singing together. But their last song together at the Last Supper had to be one of agony for Christ. He knew what was about to happen. We also should be able to sing or carry a song of praise in our hearts no matter what lies ahead. Even though we don't know the future we know God knows. And we can have the confidence that it is part of His plan for us individually and is for our good and His honor and glory. This is what we call faith.

Psalms 7:17
*I will praise the Lord according to his righteousness:
and will sing praise to the name of the Lord most high.*

Psalms 40:3
And he hath put a new song in my mouth, even praise unto our God: many shall see it, and fear, and shall trust in the Lord.

Psalms 96:1, 2
O sing unto the Lord a new song: sing unto the Lord, all the earth. Sing unto the Lord, bless his name; shew forth his salvation from day to day.

Ephesians 5:19 - 21
Speaking to yourselves in psalms and hymns and spiritual songs, singing and making melody in your heart to the Lord; Giving thanks always for all things unto God and the Father in the name of our Lord Jesus Christ; Submitting yourselves one to another in the fear of God.

JUNE 18

A LIST MAKER

Maybe it's because I am so forgetful, I admit, I am a LIST maker. I see all around the house lists either on scrap paper or in little pocket notebooks. They are not very organized so they are quite useless unless I happen to stumble upon them. I find thoughts and things I want to do, books I want to read, places I want to go, people I should call, birthdays to remember, groceries to buy, etc. They go on and on. Even this is a list! But there is one list that needs to be included on everyone's list: **Psalms 103**

Bless the Lord, O my soul: and all that is within me, bless His Holy Name. Bless the Lord, O my soul, and forget not all His benefits:
Continue Psalms 103, to the end

(verse 3) Who forgiveth all thine iniquities; Who healeth all thy diseases; Who redeemeth thy life from destruction; Who crowneth thee with lovingkindness and tender mercies; Who satisfieth thy mouth with good things; so that thy youth is renewed like the eagle's. The Lord executeth righteousness and judgment for all that are oppressed. He made known His ways unto Moses, His acts unto the children of Israel. The Lord is merciful and gracious, slow to anger, and plenteous in mercy. He will not always chide: neither will He keep his anger forever. He hath not dealt with us after our sins; nor rewarded us according to our iniquities. For as the heaven is high above the earth, so great is His mercy toward them that fear Him. As far as the east is from the west, Like as a father pitieth his children, so the Lord pitieth them that fear Him. For he knoweth our frame; He remembereth that we are dust. As for man, his days are as grass: as a flower of the field, so he flourisheth. For the wind passeth over it, and it is gone; and the place thereof shall know it no more. (17) But the mercy of the Lord is from everlasting to everlasting upon them that fear Him, and His righteousness unto children's children; . . . continue on your own (18 – 22)!
You will be blessed!

JUNE 19

JESUS IS WORSHIPPED

We are to do likewise. – Worship Jesus!
Not only did people worship God in the Old Testament, it was also the trinity that was given to them that they worshipped, as recorded in Genesis 1:1, 2, 3.

In the beginning <u>God</u> created the heaven and the earth.
And the earth was without form, and void; and darkness was upon the face of the deep. <u>And the Spirit of God</u> moved upon the face of the waters. And God said, Let there be light: and there was light.

But straight forward it is the command in the New Testament, that we are to worship <u>God</u> through <u>Jesus Christ, our Lord</u>, as <u>His Spirit</u> moves us. Many worshipped Him in person, and are examples to us.

John 1:1 - 4
In the beginning was the Word, and <u>the Word was with God</u>, and the Word was God. The same was in the beginning with God. All things were made by Him; and without Him was not anything made that was made. In Him was Life; and the Life was the Light of men.

Psalms 40:16
Let all those that seek Thee rejoice and be glad in Thee: let such as love Thy salvation say continually, The Lord be magnified.

Matthew 2:11
And when they were come into the house, they saw the young child with Mary His mother, and fell down, and worshipped Him: . . .

Matthew 28:9
And as they went to tell His disciples, behold, Jesus met them, saying, All hail. And they came and held Him by the feet, and worshipped Him.

JUNE 20

D. L. MOODY'S BEST FRIEND

Of course, you guessed it – Jesus was Moody's best friend.
You probably also know that he was the founder of the Moody Bible Institute in Chicago, Illinois, which bears his name. If not, look him up on the Internet. Very interesting! Today, his school is being pressured by the cares of this world, just like many other Christian schools around the country that are being asked to "get with it" and change with the times. Pray for the faculties and students of this generation, that they may hold fast to the Word of God, as friends of our Lord Jesus Christ.

James 4:4
... know ye not that the friendship of the world is enmity with God? whosoever therefore will be a friend of the world is the enemy of God.

And Jesus can and should be our best friend too He is "everywhere present," He is our "guide" . . . But most of all He is our Savior (John 3:16)! Only **BELIEVE**

John 3:17
For God sent not His Son into the world to condemn the world; but that the world through Him might be saved.

John 15:13
Greater love hath no man than this that a man lay down his life for his friends.

Psalms 73:24, 25
Thou shalt guide me with Thy counsel, and afterward receive me to glory. Whom have I in heaven but Thee? and there is none upon earth that I desire beside Thee.

JUNE 21

GOD OF ALL COMFORT
By Hannah Whithall Smith

This is one of my favorite books because it encourages me to remember who I am in Jesus Christ. But most importantly, Who He is to me. It was written long ago, but the copy I have was printed by Moody Press (uncopyrighted), 1956, edition, ISBN # 0-8024-0018-3. If you can, find it, get it, and read it.

Forget "I," "me," "my," and forget how "I feel." Rather, replace "I," etc., for Jesus; "He," "Him," and "His." We must ask ourselves, not "am I good"? But "is He (God) good"? Therefore, keep your eyes off "self" and "the self-life" and keep your eyes on the Lord both inwardly and outwardly.

We can only see the thing we look at, so while we are looking at ourselves, we simply cannot "behold God." We grow to be like what we look at. We cannot see self and God at the same time.

Hannah Smith's final conclusion and chapter is, "God is enough."

Psalms 18:2, 3
The Lord is my rock, and my fortress, and my deliverer; my God, my strength, in Whom I will trust; my buckler, and the horn of my salvation, and my high tower. I will call upon the Lord, who is worthy to be praised: so shall I be saved from mine enemies.

Philippians 4: 7
And the peace of God, which passeth all understanding, shall keep your hearts and minds through Christ Jesus.

II Corinthians 3:5
Not that we are sufficient of ourselves to think anything as of ourselves; but our sufficiency is of God;

JUNE 22

HOLY GROUND

Have you ever thought that wherever you step you are stepping on HOLY GROUND? Never forget wherever God is, it is a Holy Place. As His children, He is always in us and will never leave us or forsake us – no matter where we take Him. This ought to make us mindful of where we go, what we say, what we see, and who we meet. My Mother taught us when she was the superintendent of our Sunday School.

>"OH, BE CAREFUL LITTLE EYES WHAT YOU SEE"
>Oh, be careful little eyes what you see.
>Oh, be careful little ears what you hear.
>There's a Father up above looking down in tender love
>Oh, be careful little eyes what you see.
>
>Oh, be careful little mouth what you say.
>Oh, be careful little mouth what you say.
>There's a Father up above looking down in tender love
>Oh, be careful little mouth what you say.
>
>FINALE
>Oh, be careful little eyes, ears, mouth, hands, feet
>What you see, hear, say, do, and go
>Oh, be careful little eyes, ears, mouth, hands, feet
>What you see, hear, say, do, and go
>There's a Father up above looking down in tender love
>So be careful little feet where you go.

We are simply to come to God as a little child, asking forgiveness and become one of His own. "KIS" – Keep it simple, but grow up and become mature in Him.

<u>Exodus 3:5</u>
And he (Moses) said, Here am I. And He (God) said, Draw not nigh hither: put off thy shoes from off thy feet, for the place whereon thou standest is Holy Ground.

JUNE 23

TO SEE JESUS
(**Zacchaeus** – Luke 19:1 - 10)

Whatever it takes . . . to see JESUS!

What can I say? Read about Zacchaeus and what lengths he was willing to go to see Jesus! He is one of my favorite people in the Bible, because he was a little man and had to think differently to see Jesus. He didn't care about his reputation or anything else. He wanted to see JESUS!

Luke 19:1 - 10

And Jesus entered and passed through Jericho. And, behold, there was a man named Zacchaeus, which was the chief among the publicans, and he was rich. And he sought to see Jesus Who He was; and could not for the press, because he was little of stature. And he ran before, and climbed up into a sycomore tree to see Him: for He was to pass that way. And when Jesus came to the place, He (Jesus) looked up, and saw him, and said unto him, Zacchaeus, make haste, and come down; for today I must abide at thy house. <u>*And he (Zacchaeus) made haste, and came down, and received Him (Jesus) joyfully*</u>*. And when they saw it, they all murmured, saying, That He was gone to be guest with a man that is a sinner. And Zacchaeus stood, and said unto the Lord; Behold, Lord, the half of my goods I give to the poor; and if I have taken anything from any man by false accusation, I restore him fourfold. And Jesus said unto him, This day is salvation come to this house, forsomuch as he also is a son of Abraham.*

<u>*For the Son of man is come to seek and to save that which was lost.*</u>

JUNE 24

PRAY GOD'S PROMISES for
ALL THE CHILDREN OF THE WORLD

Scripture has a lot to say about children, all the children.

First and foremost, pray that the Children of the World will come to know about God, and His only begotten Son, Jesus Christ. You are probably thinking that that is a mighty big and broad prayer so shouldn't we be more specific? That will come later after God shows you special needs. Who is praying for the children around the world? Those we don't even know about and certainly those we have heard about that are suffering because they are Christians. These are evil times. Be concerned enough to pray that God in His providence, will touch their lives in His own way and time. We at least can do what we are able, and that is to pray.

"Jesus loves the little Children"

Jesus loves the little Children. All the Children of the world,
Red and Yellow, Black and White,
They are precious in His sight,
Jesus loves the little Children of the world.

Jesus died for all the Children. All the Children of the world,
Red and Yellow, Black and White,
They are precious in His sight,
Jesus died for all the Children of the world

Matthew 18: 1 – 3
At the same time came the disciples unto Jesus, saying, Who is the greatest in the kingdom of heaven? And Jesus called a little child unto Him, and set him in the midst of them, And said, Verily I say unto you, Except ye be converted, and become as little children, ye shall not enter into the kingdom of heaven.

JUNE 25

GOD WITH US

Instead of me telling this great truth in my own words, read it for yourself straight from God's Word below. You can see, Jesus had quite a journey here on earth that Isaiah prophesied about, long before His birth.

<u>Isaiah 7:14</u>
Therefore the Lord Himself shall give you a sign; Behold, a virgin shall conceive, and bear a son, and shall call His name Immanuel (<u>God with us</u>).

After much time passed, an angel of the Lord appeared to Joseph in a dream telling him not to fear to take Mary as his wife

<u>Matthew 1:18 - 25</u>
Now the birth of Jesus Christ was on this wise: When as His mother Mary was espoused to Joseph, before they came together, she was found with Child of the Holy Ghost. Then Joseph her husband, being a just man, and not willing to make her a public example, was minded to put her away privily. But while he thought on these things, behold, the angel of the Lord appeared unto him in a dream, saying, Joseph, thou son of David, fear not to take unto thee Mary thy wife: for that which is conceived in her is of the Holy Ghost. And she shall bring forth a Son, and thou shalt call His Name Jesus: for He shall save His people from their sins. <u>Now all this was done, that it might be fulfilled which was spoken of the Lord by the prophet (Isaiah), saying, Behold, a virgin shall be with Child, and shall bring forth a Son, and they shall call His Name Emmanuel</u>, which being interpreted is, <u>God with us</u>. Then Joseph being raised from sleep did as the angel of the Lord had bidden him, and took unto him his wife: And knew her not till she had brought forth her firstborn Son: and he called His name JESUS.

How comforting is this? **<u>God with Us</u>**! Keep on learning how miraculous it was - His coming to earth and that even now He will dwell in our hearts by His Spirit.

JUNE 26

CONNECT THE DOTS

(God's Wisdom)

After retiring from my job, I knew I needed a "hobby" to keep me busy; so, I went back to drawing and painting. I turned to "dot" painting like the Aborigines have mastered. They paint their wisdom and stories of their history handed down to them from generation to generation.

So, I thought, I could do that style too. Now, instead of "worldly wisdom" I would share God's wisdom by adding His Word to every painting. His word is more important than my paintings or words. Now instead of painting I desired to write and review what God has taught me. I asked for <u>His</u> inspiration His wisdom, from His Word! The "dot" painting taught me patience, and "stick-to-it-tive-ness" to finish a tedious painting. With this same desire I am persevering, and learning the art of "Connecting the Dots" of my spiritual life. With the help of the Holy Spirit, I am reviewing notes from books I read, scriptures I underlined in several of my own Bibles, notes from pastors I listened to, etc. I recognize that I have been on this journey all along, but now this is a renewed and revived experience with God – to see again and apply His Wisdom.

Proverbs 4:5 – 7
Get wisdom, get understanding: forget it not; neither decline from the words of My mouth. Forsake her (wisdom) not, and she shall preserve thee: love her, and she shall keep thee. Wisdom is the principal thing; therefore get wisdom: and with all thy getting get understanding.

I Corinthians 1:30, 31
But of Him are ye in Christ Jesus, <u>who of God</u> is made unto us wisdom, and righteousness, and sanctification, and redemption: That, according as it is written, He that glorieth, let him glory in the Lord.

JUNE 27

DISCOURAGEMENT

Discouragement is to be resisted just like any other sin. It is all from our old nature and temptations from Satan to take our eyes off Jesus. Resist and repent and forget the past and "go for the mark."

<u>Philippians 3:13, 14</u>
. . . but this one thing I do, forgetting those things which are behind, and reaching forth unto those things which are before, I press toward the mark for the prize of the high calling of God in Christ Jesus.

The scripture below describes how Israel was discouraged as well as the consequences of their actions and their deliverance. This example is a foretaste of the picture of how <u>Jesus delivered us on His cross</u>. We also pay such a price when we cause or hang on to our discouragements. Repent and ask forgiveness.

<u>Numbers 21:4- 9</u>
And they journeyed from mount Hor by the way of the Red sea, to compass the land of Edom: and the soul of the people was much discouraged because of the way. And the people spake against God, and against Moses, Wherefore have ye brought us up out of Egypt to die in the wilderness? for there is no bread, neither is there any water; and our soul loatheth this light bread. And the Lord sent fiery serpents among the people, and they bit the people; and much people of Israel died. Therefore the people came to Moses, and said, We have sinned, for we have spoken against the Lord, and against thee; pray unto the Lord, that He take away the serpents from us. And Moses prayed for the people. And the Lord said unto Moses, Make thee a fiery serpent, and <u>set it upon a pole: and it shall come to pass, that every one that is bitten, when he looketh upon it, shall live</u>. And Moses made a serpent of brass, and put it upon a pole, and it came to pass, that if a serpent had bitten any man, when he beheld the serpent of brass, he lived.

JUNE 28

SOME OF MY DAD'S FAVORITE VERSES

The most important thing I learned from my parents was to believe and love God's Word. They led me to love Jesus too, and at an early age I accepted Him as MY Savior. Then as I became older I personally had the desire to know Jesus better. That's when all my studying and learning began and what a blessing it has been all these years. Through joys and a few sorrows, He has been my guide. So, when I found these verses listed in front of my father's Bible, I made a list and I want to share some of it with you.

John 1:12, 13
But as many as received Him, to them gave he power to become the sons of God, even to them that believe on His name: Which were born, not of blood, nor of the will of the flesh, nor of the will of man, but of God.

John 3:7
Marvel not that I said unto thee, Ye must be born again.

John 10:9, 10
I am the door: by Me if any man enter in, he shall be saved, and shall go in and out, and find pasture. The thief cometh not, but for to steal, and to kill, and to destroy: I am come that they might have life, and that they might have it more abundantly.

John 14:6
*Jesus saith unto him, I am the Way, the Truth, and the Life:
no man cometh unto the Father, but by Me.*

I Peter 2:24
For Christ also hath once suffered for sins, the just for the unjust that He might bring us to God, being put to death in the flesh, but quickened by the Spirit:

JUNE 29

A RANSOMED SOUL

Looking again at the Scriptures that my Dad left behind in his Bible, it is a sure thing that if anybody looked at them, they would know how to come to God through faith in His Son, Jesus Christ. I am one of those "Ransomed Souls." Below are more of the verses listed that my Dad left behind.

<u>Ezekiel 18:20</u>
The soul that sinneth, it shall die. The son shall not bear the iniquity of the father, neither shall the father bear the iniquity of the son: the righteousness of the righteous shall be upon him, and the wickedness of the wicked shall be upon him.

<u>Romans 3:20</u>
Therefore by the deeds of the law there shall no flesh be justified in His sight: for by the law is the knowledge of sin.

<u>II Corinthians 5:21</u>
For He hath made Him to be sin for us, Who knew no sin; that we might be made the righteousness of God in Him.

<u>Hebrews 9:27</u>
And as it is appointed unto men once to die, but after this the judgment:

<u>Hebrews 11:6</u>
But without faith it is impossible to please Him: for he that cometh to God must believe that He is, and that He is a rewarder of them that diligently seek Him.

<u>Psalms 62:5-7</u>
My soul, wait thou only upon God; for my expectation is from Him. He only is my rock and my salvation: He is my defence; I shall not be moved. In God is my salvation and my glory: the rock of my strength, and my refuge, is in God.

JUNE 30

I LOVE THE LORD

How can you not Love the Lord? How can we reject so great a salvation? Day after day He even gives us the breath we breathe that we cannot live without. The first breath of Adam came from God Himself, our Creator. Then after disobedience came into the world, God gave His only begotten Son to die in our place to pay the debt of our sins. What a gift of love, if we only receive it.

Matthew 22:37
Jesus said unto him, Thou shalt love the Lord thy God with all thy heart, and with all thy soul, and with all thy mind.
This is the first and great commandment.

Romans 6:23
For the wages of sin is death; but the gift of God is eternal life through Jesus Christ our Lord.

Ephesians 3:19
And to know the love of Christ, which passeth knowledge, that ye might be filled with all the fulness of God.

I Peter 1:8, 9
Whom having not seen, ye love; in Whom, though now ye see Him not, yet believing, ye rejoice with joy unspeakable and full of glory: Receiving the end of your faith, even the salvation of your souls.

I John 4:19
We love Him, because He first loved us.

Psalms 18:1, 2
I will love thee, O Lord, my strength. The Lord is my rock, and my fortress, and my deliverer; my God, my strength, in whom I will trust; my buckler, and the horn of my salvation, and my high tower.

JULY

TESTED BY FIRE

I Peter 1:7
That the trial of your faith, being much more precious than of gold that perisheth, though it be tried with fire, might be found unto praise and honour and glory at the appearing of Jesus Christ:

JULY 1

DWJWD

Most of us have heard about WWJD, and what these four letters stand for. WWJD – What Would Jesus Do? I even have the book written in 1896, *In His Steps,* by Charles M. Sheldon, with the revised version written by his great-grandson, Dr. Garrett W. Sheldon, in 1993, *What Would Jesus Do*. What I would like to suggest for us today, is to go one step farther. DWJWD! Do What Jesus Would Do! – DWJWD.

Often times, we know "what Jesus would do," but we choose not to do it. Other times we don't know what He would DO. So, we must know Him better. Of course, we need help to DO - super-natural help. For this reason, Jesus said He would not leave us comfortless, but would ask His Father to send us His Holy Spirit. You can read about His actual arrival in the book of Acts! Today, listen for, and DO His promptings. Trust and depend on Him all day along, day by day!

Proverbs 3:27a
Withhold not good from them to whom it is due, when it is in the power of thine hand to do it.

Acts 10:38
God anointed Jesus of Nazareth with the Holy Ghost and with power: Who went about doing good . . .

Philippians 2:13
For it is God which worketh in you both to will and to do of His good pleasure.

Galatians 6:10b
. . . Let us DO good to all men

JULY 2

THE THRONE ROOM

Imagine King Solomon's throne room, as the Bible describes in I Kings 10:18-20 - the richest and finest throne in the world; much less the Throne Room of God. We can come instantly into His Throne Room just as if He is our "dear Daddy" - "**Abba Father.**" As God's children we have this privilege, of coming to Him in prayer instantly, no matter when or where we are. He listens, He hears, He answers. Also, God has given to us Jesus Christ as our Savior, mediator, and advocate. We don't have to come into God's presence alone or afraid, but boldly - Into His Holy of Holies. Christ knows all about us; our thoughts, and all that we are going through, and receives us with open arms. Just think of that! Desire to <u>bow</u> before Him with honor and praise.

Hebrews 4:14 - 16
Seeing then that we have a Great High Priest, that is passed into the heavens, Jesus the Son of God, let us hold fast our profession. For we have not an High Priest which cannot be touched with the feeling of our infirmities; but was in all points tempted like as we are, yet without sin. Let us therefore come <u>boldly unto the throne of grace</u>; that we may obtain mercy, and find grace to help in time of need.

Psalms 89:14, 15
Justice and judgment are the habitation of Thy Throne: mercy and truth shall go before Thy face. Blessed is the people that know the joyful sound: they shall walk, O Lord, in the light of Thy countenance.

Psalms 45:6, 7
Thy Throne, O God, is for ever and ever: the sceptre of Thy kingdom is a right sceptre. Thou lovest righteousness, and hatest wickedness: therefore God, thy God, hath anointed thee with the oil of gladness above thy fellows.

JULY 3

INEQUALITY The state of being unequal

Inequality is the "buzz word" of the day; the cry we hear around the world. The dictionary calls inequality a "condition" that refers to, not being equal in social or economic status. No surprise here. We are not all equal. Perfect equality is impossible. General equality only exists in arithmetic, i.e. one plus one equals two! We are not all equal for many reasons: physical qualities and aptitudes; as well as greed, jealousy, prejudice, age covetousness, hatred, discrimination, laziness, etc. Inequality can be related to our sins that we don't want to admit. We can see over and over again the influence of governments hoping to solve social problems by making more and more laws! God, our creator has <u>individual</u> plans for each of us, so <u>we cannot all be the same</u>. Know the TRUTH! Think of "INEQUALITY" as an individual heart problem and not a social one! The only place we can find true equality is in the heart of God.

I Samuel 2:7 - 8:
The Lord maketh poor, and maketh rich: He bringeth low, and lifteth up. He raiseth up the poor out of the dust, and lifteth up the beggar from the dunghill, to set them among princes, and to make them inherit the throne of glory: for the pillars of the earth are the Lord 's, and He hath set the world upon them.

Acts 10:34b, 35
Of a truth I perceive that God is no respecter of persons: But in every nation he that feareth Him, and worketh righteousness, is accepted with Him.

Romans 2:11
For there is no respect of persons with God.

John 13:34
A new commandment I give unto you, That ye love one another; as I have loved you, that ye also love one another.

JULY 4

NEW LIFE and LIVE

We have the desire (given to us by God) to live! See Psalms 34:12. We see much sorrow and trials in this world, but also some happiness, joy, peace and calm. Christ said He came that we *"might have life more abundantly,"* (John 10:10); (plentiful supply, fullness to overflowing). As we compare the lives of men before and after Christ's coming – in bondage of sin, or freedom in Christ – now, we face our choice - here and now! Choose God's gift of eternal life!

Deuteronomy 31:26, 27
Take this book of the law, and put it in the side of the ark of the covenant of the Lord your God, that it may be there for a witness against thee. For I know thy rebellion, and thy stiff neck: behold, while I (Moses) am yet alive with you this day, ye have been rebellious against the Lord; and how much more after my death?

Proverbs 21:21
He that followeth after righteousness and mercy findeth life, righteousness, and honour.

Jeremiah 21:8b
Thus saith the Lord; Behold, I set before you the way of life, and the way of death (choose life).

John 3:16
For God so loved the world, that He gave His only begotten Son, that <u>whosoever</u> *(*put your name here*) believeth in Him (Jesus Christ) should not perish, but have everlasting life*

John 3:36
He that believeth on the Son (Jesus Christ) hath everlasting life: and he that believeth not the Son shall not see life; but the wrath of God abideth on him.

JULY 5

ALL

"All" is an inclusive little word. We could imagine things all day long and still could not think of everything. Anything that can be seen or touched are all temporal and will pass away, so don't get too worn out "counting" them. True, these are all blessings, but soon they will fade away or wear out. Concentrate instead on the unseen things from above that come down from our heavenly Father. "All" these spiritual blessings will last forever and are also too numerous to count. But don't give up trying, because searching the scriptures helps us understand how great a loving and "good" God we have. A giver of blessings - even the air we breathe and ALL His daily care.

Proverbs 22:2, 4
The rich and poor meet together: the Lord is the maker of them all. By humility and the fear of the Lord are riches, and honour, and life.

Luke 20:38
For He is not a God of the dead, but of the living: for all live unto Him.

Romans 3:23, 24
For all have sinned, and come short of the glory of God; Being justified freely by His grace through the redemption that is in Christ Jesus:

II Corinthians 5:15
And that He died for all, that they which live should not henceforth live unto themselves, but unto Him which died for them, and rose again.

I Timothy 2:6
Who gave Himself a ransom for all, to be testified in due time.

JULY 6

JOY TO GIVE

You have been blessed! Give away this Joy to others
". . . freely ye have received, freely give," (Matthew 10:8) everywhere you go. The Book of Psalms is full of joy! For our example.

Psalms 16:11
Thou wilt shew me the path of life: in Thy presence is fulness of joy; at Thy right hand there are pleasures for evermore.

This is passing on our joy through giving our love, joy, laughter, and peace. These gifts are all contagious and can be spread around the world. We may not understand how this is possible but God is able, through His Holy Spirit, and His desire is for us to spread His love. These are God-currents that change lives. Look, "love," and see Him in all people because He created each of us in His own image. We are all in need His love and His gift of Salvation.

Nehemiah 8:10
Then he (Nehemiah) said unto them, Go your way, eat the fat, and drink the sweet, and send portions unto them for whom nothing is prepared: for this day is holy unto our Lord:
neither be ye sorry; for the joy of the Lord is your strength.

Psalms 51:12, 13
Restore unto me the joy of Thy salvation; and uphold me with Thy free spirit. Then will I teach transgressors Thy ways; and sinners shall be converted unto Thee.

Jeremiah 15:16
Thy words were found, and I (Jeremiah) did eat them; and Thy word was unto me the joy and rejoicing of mine heart: for I am called by Thy Name, O Lord God of hosts.

Romans 15:13
Now the God of hope fill you with all joy and peace in believing, that ye may abound in hope,
through the power of the Holy Ghost.

JULY 7

LEARN SOMETHING NEW TODAY

All our learning and skills come from God as seen in Exodus 31:3 – 11. This pretty much covers it all how God taught man for His service. Early on, He taught them manual skills, intellectual knowledge, artistic talents, and wisdom. This training was used to build a place to worship Him. Whether be it temporal or spiritual, there is much to learn. We must keep growing and using what we learn to honor Him.

<u>Ecclesiastes 12:12 - 14</u>
. . . by these, my son, be admonished: of making many books there is no end; and much study is a weariness of the flesh. Let us hear the <u>conclusion</u> of the whole matter: Fear God, and keep His commandments: for this is the whole duty of man. For God shall bring every work into judgment, with every secret thing, whether it be good, or whether it be evil.

Be wise in the choosing of what you put in your mind and life. Don't waste your time on something that is unprofitable to you and others. Paul wrote to Timothy this important advice giving us pause, for us to remember today:

<u>II Timothy 2:15 - 17</u>
*Study to shew thyself approved unto God, a workman that needeth not to be ashamed, rightly dividing the Word of Truth. But <u>shun profane and vain babblings</u>: for they will
increase unto more ungodliness. And their word will eat as doth a canker:*

I have always been familiar with and even memorized verse **15**; but not verses **16** and **17**; I will count them today as something new for me. They never penetrated my heart before, but the warning is as important, as what I desire to study. Be discerning! We are never too young or old to heed.

JULY 8

"FAITH IS THE VICTORY"

Consider the words of this hymn. This rousing song we can sing and pray with thankful hearts, over and over. When you believe, agree with the words, and make it your battle song, you can say; "<u>O glorious victory that overcomes the world.</u>" Without faith, we cannot believe God and accept His love to us.

<u>Mark 11:22</u>
And Jesus answering saith unto them, Have faith in God.

"FAITH IS THE VICTORY"
by John H. Yates (1837-1900) and Ira D. Sankey (1840-1908)

Encamped along the hills of light, Ye Christian soldiers, rise,
And press the battle ere the night Shall veil the glow skies.
Against the foe in vales below Let all our strength be hurled;
Faith is the victory, we know That overcomes the world.

<u>Chorus</u>
Faith is the victory!
Faith is the victory!
O glorious victory
That overcomes the world.

His banner over us is love, Our sword the Word of God;
We tread the road the saints above With shouts of triumph trod.
By faith they like a whirl-wind's breath Swept on o'er every field;
The faith by which they conquered death Is still our shinning shield.

To him that overcomes the foe White raiment shall be giv'n;
Before the angels he shall know His name confessed in heaven.
Then onward from the hills of light, Our hearts with love aflame;
We'll vanquish all the hosts of night In Jesus' conq'ring Name.

JULY 9

KISS

We know what KISS means:
"Keep It Simple Sweetie!"

Our opinions are fleeting, since the words we speak fly away so soon after they are said; and are insignificant compared to the TRUTHS of God's Words. Just as Jesus did, say what you mean and mean what you say. Dwell and meditate on what Jesus says in His WORD! Let it change your life!

Matthew 5:37
But let your communication be, Yea, yea; Nay, nay: for whatsoever is more than these cometh of evil.

Matthew 6:13
And lead us not into temptation, but deliver us from evil: For Thine is the kingdom, and the power, and the glory, forever. Amen.

Matthew 6:33, 34
But seek ye first the kingdom of God, and His righteousness; and all these things shall be added unto you. Take therefore no thought for the morrow: for the morrow shall take thought for the things of itself. Sufficient unto the day is the evil thereof.

Mark 4:19
And the cares of this world, and the deceitfulness of riches, and the lusts of other things entering in, choke the Word, and it becometh unfruitful.

Luke 12:31, 32
But rather seek ye the kingdom of God; and all these things shall be added unto you. Fear not, little flock; for it is your Father's good pleasure to give you the kingdom.

JULY 10

COMPASSION

When I read or hear the word compassion, I think of lonely, sad, poor, helpless people with lives of despair. There are so many people suffering, it seems overwhelming with nothing I can do to make a difference. So, instead, I try to keep the trials of this world out of my mind. <u>I should know better</u>! Where would I be if God had this same attitude? We all have problems and troubles in our lives and we may think we are smart and strong enough to handle whatever comes. However, God loves using people to help others for His purposes; thereby showing His love and compassion through us, as we support one another. We are not to ignore the people along our pathway where we find ourselves. He has put us where we are right now for a purpose, so let's look around and be aware of what we can do to help when needed.

We are all in need of a "Savior."

Matthew 9:36a
But when He (Jesus) saw the multitudes, He was moved with compassion on them . . .

Zechariah 7:9
Thus speaketh the Lord of hosts, saying, Execute true judgment, and shew mercy and compassions every man to his brother:

II Chronicles 30:9b
. . . for the Lord your God is gracious and merciful, and will not turn away His face from you, if ye return unto Him.

Psalms 111:4
He hath made His wonderful works to be remembered: the Lord is gracious and full of compassion.

Psalms 145:9
The Lord is good to all: and His tender mercies are over all His works.

JULY 11

"COUNT YOUR BLESSINGS"

We are often tempted to count the "blessings" of others leading us to unhappiness and discontentment. Covetousness and jealousy are harsh words for this attitude, but right on. Either word we choose, our eyes are opened to the truth - telling God we are unhappy with all the blessings He gives to us personally, and He does not know what is best for us. This leads to blaming God for our circumstances, and our discontentment leads to bitterness. Snap out of this it! Start counting <u>your</u> blessings from God.

Remember, when you are tempted, please sing this song with me!

"COUNT YOUR BLESSINGS"
by Johnson Oatman, Jr. (1856-1922)

When upon life's billows you are tempest tossed,
When you are discouraged, thinking all is lost,
Count your many blessings – name them one by one,
And it will surprise you what the Lord hath done.

Chorus
Count your blessings name them one by one;
Count your blessings see what God hath done;
Count your blessings, name them one by one.
Count your many blessings see what God hath done.

When you look at others with their lands and gold,
Think that Christ has promised you His wealth untold;
Count you many blessing – money cannot buy
Your reward in heaven nor your home on high.

So amid the conflict, whether great or small,
Do not be discouraged - God is over all;
Count your many blessings – angels will attend,
Help and comfort give you to your journey's end.

JULY 12

BE HONEST WITH YOURSELF

There is much information and truth about ourselves and our honest relationship with God in the New Testament books of First, Second, and Third John. Read, read, and re-read! We read but we do not practice the truth or walk in the Light. We say we have no sin and deceive ourselves, and by doing so, we call God a liar. Even though we don't want to do this, we may not be aware of our actions toward God. By repetitively reading these three books, we can become sensitive to how we are living and then can know if we are living in the light of God's Word or are walking in darkness. Here scripture is presented clearly and plainly for our easy understanding - God's gift of faith, open to everyone. We need to be honest with ourselves and believe God's Word.

I John 1:6 - 10
If we say that we have fellowship with Him, and walk in darkness, we lie, and do not the truth: But if we walk in the Light, as He is in the Light, we have fellowship one with another, and the blood of Jesus Christ His Son cleanseth us from all sin. If we say that we have no sin, we deceive ourselves, and the Truth is not in us. If we confess our sins, He is faithful and just to forgive us our sins, and to cleanse us from all unrighteousness. If we say that we have not sinned, we make Him a liar, and His word is not in us.

I John 2:9 - 12
He that saith he is in the Light, and hateth his brother, is in darkness even until now. He that loveth his brother abideth in the Light, and there is none occasion of stumbling in him. But he that hateth his brother is in darkness, and walketh in darkness, and knoweth not whither he goeth, because that darkness hath blinded his eyes. I write unto you, little children, because your sins are forgiven you for His Name's sake.

Keep on reading I, II, III JOHN

JULY 13

SMILE

Be conscious of the facial expressions (or countenance) you display – they tell others a lot about you. Our faces show our attitudes within our heart and our innermost feelings (unless you go around with a poker face). We can give the greatest gift of a Smile to anyone in passing. It doesn't even cost a thing. A smile will instantly change any negative vibes between you and the one you "flash" it to.

Desire to show the love and joy God gives you to share. Think of it, you may give someone their only smile of the day. Start smiling today and see if you can feel the joy from God in your own heart. Often you will receive a smile in return as you see happiness in someone else. Smiling can be contagious.

<u>Numbers 6:25, 26</u>
The Lord make His face shine upon thee, and be gracious unto thee: The Lord lift up His countenance upon thee, and give thee peace.

<u>Psalms 34:5</u>
They looked unto Him, and were lightened: and their faces were not ashamed.

<u>Psalms 42:11</u>
Why art thou cast down, O my soul? and why art thou disquieted within me? hope thou in God: for I shall yet praise Him, Who is the health of my countenance, and my God.

<u>Acts 2:28</u>
*Thou hast made known to me the ways of life;
Thou shalt make me full of joy with Thy countenance.*

JULY 14

NEVER BE "BENT OUT OF SHAPE"

Being "Bent Out of Shape" is the quickest way to discourage yourself and others. We all know what it means to be "out of shape" physically, but we ignore the mental attitude of being "bent out of shape." A negative attitude may come upon us so fast it seems we just can't help it. No, no, no! We need to recognize it as a temptation and accept the promise that God has prepared for us a way to overcome.

I Corinthians 10:13

There hath no temptation taken you but such as is common to man: but God is faithful, Who will not suffer you to be tempted above that ye are able; but will with the temptation also make a way to escape, that ye may be able to bear it.

Let me tell you of my recent "bent out of shape" spell. During yesterday's typing my computer went haywire and I didn't handle this very well. I learned how quickly reactions can happen, and how ugly the attitude of being "Bent Out of Shape" is. There are two sides to the coin of "offense." One being offended by the Word of God and to those giving out the message; and the other as believers, taking "offence" whenever our feelings are attacked.

Matthew 15:10 - 12

And He (Jesus) called the multitude, and said unto them, Hear, and understand: Not that which goeth into the mouth defileth a man; but <u>that which cometh out of the mouth</u>, this defileth a man. Then came His disciples, and said unto Him, Knowest Thou that the Pharisees were offended, after they heard this saying?

Philippians 1:10

That ye may approve things that are excellent; that ye may be sincere and without offence till the day of Christ;

JULY 15

BORED? WAKE UP CURIOSITY

The Bible does not use these words of our day; "bored" and "curiosity." We have to think deeper to find instructions to help us with this problem. There is as always, a right way and a wrong way to live because we have both the old and new nature battling within us. To stay on track, we need to be cautious to keep Christ as central in waking up our curiosity. Paul describes this in his book to the Romans (Gentiles).

Romans 7:15 - 20
For that which I do I allow not: for what I would, that do I not; but what I hate, that do I. If then I do that which I would not, I consent unto the law that it is good. Now then it is no more I that do it, but sin that dwelleth in me. For I know that in me (that is, in my flesh,) dwelleth no good thing: for to will is present with me; but how to perform that which is good I find not. For the good that I would I do not: but the evil which I would not, that I do. Now if I do that I would not, it is no more I that do it, but sin that dwelleth in me.

Sounds a little confusing until you put yourself into this place. Wonderfully, Paul has explained this universal problem. We all want to do the right thing and when we get bored or tempted, we seem to do wrong things. But here Paul gives us hope with deliverance!

Romans 7:21 -25
I find then a law, that, when I would do good, evil is present with me. For I delight in the law of God after the inward man: But I see another law in my members, warring against the law of my mind, and bringing me into captivity to the law of sin which is in my members. O wretched man that I am! Who shall deliver me from the body of this death? I thank God through Jesus Christ our Lord. So then with the mind I myself serve the law of God; but with the flesh the law of sin.

JULY 16

ABOMINATIONS

So that we can be on the same wave length, here are some meanings of the word "abominations."

- To detest; abhor, intense dislike of a thing
- An intense disgust for someone
- A hateful and detestable action
- A loathing of something
- An idol in place of God Himself

These very strong, descriptive words, are found in Scripture many times. We need to learn and know about these things, so we can avoid them, but not ignore them. They are offensive to our loving God. It is a good thing God is so merciful toward us and forgives when we fail – as we ask Him. Below are just a few "abominations" listed, but it would make a good study to learn more of what God's Word has to say.

Leviticus 18:30
Therefore, shall ye keep Mine ordinance, that ye commit not any one of these abominable customs, which were committed before you, and that ye defile not yourselves therein: I am the Lord your God.

Proverbs 11:20
They that are of a froward heart are abomination to the Lord: but such as are upright in their way are His delight.

Proverbs 6:16 - 19
These six things doth the Lord hate: yea, seven are an abomination unto Him: A proud look, a lying tongue, and hands that shed innocent blood, An heart that deviseth wicked imaginations, feet that be swift in running to mischief, A false witness that speaketh lies, and he that soweth discord among brethren.

JULY 17

THE NAME OF JESUS

As we have learned, there is power in the Name of Jesus. Say it often, say it prayerfully and say it with joy. The book *He Shall Be Called*, written by Robert J. Morgan (copyright, 2005); describes 150 names given to Jesus and their meanings. There is no other name that is above the Name of Jesus for our salvation.

<u>Acts 4:12;</u>
Neither is there salvation in any other: for there is none other name under heaven given among men, whereby we must be saved.

Whether in immediate need or just thinking about Him, call out to Him and He will show you His love, tenderness and care.

<u>Jeremiah 33:3</u>
Call unto Me, and I will answer thee, and shew thee great and mighty things, which thou knowest not.

Say Jesus' Name when being tempted; just as He used scripture when in the "wilderness" being tempted by Satan.

<u>Matthew 4:10, 11</u>
Then saith Jesus unto him, Get thee hence, Satan: for it is written, Thou shalt worship the Lord thy God, and Him only shalt thou serve. <u>Then the devil leaveth Him</u>, and, behold, angels came and ministered unto Him.

Whenever you are lonely, just call out His Name and all your thoughts will dwell upon Him, and His presence will surround you if you will let it. Jesus Christ is tender and all powerful and He wants you to call on Him.

<u>Romans 10:8</u>
But what saith it? The Word is nigh thee, even in thy mouth, and in thy heart: that is, the Word of faith, which we preach;

JULY 18

LIAR, LIAR, LIAR

There are so many lies today from so many sources! From the very beginning, Satan lied and tempted Eve in the Garden of Eden.

<u>Genesis 3:1</u>
Now the serpent was more subtle than any beast of the field which the Lord God had made. And he said unto the woman (Eve), Yea, hath God said, Ye shall not eat of every tree of the garden?

The world is so bold even God is called a Liar. God warned us of this in:

<u>Romans 3:3, 4a</u>
For what if some did not believe? Shall their unbelief make the faith of God without effect? God forbid: yea let God be true, but every man a liar . . .

Lying is so rampant, I had an "epiphany" to <u>compile</u> a book of **10,000 TRUTHS** from **God's Word,** that I had studied over the years. Truths I can review and stand on as my sure foundation as I get bombarded with all the un-truths around me. This book was not in place of daily study **in** the whole Bible, but a quick reference of what I learned for encouragement. Catch yourself next time you are tempted to lie. Don't let lies just slip out of your mouth as if they have no consequence.

<u>Proverbs 17:4</u>
A wicked doer giveth heed to false lips; and a liar giveth ear to a naughty tongue.

<u>John 8:44a, b</u>
Ye are of your father the devil, and the lusts of your father ye will do. He was a murderer from the beginning, and abode not in the truth, because there is no truth in him. When he speaketh a lie, he speaketh of his own:

JULY 19

PERSEVERVANCE

Many, many times I have failed to persevere. Now, here I am learning about this; yet another gift of grace from God – Perseverance. *Charles Haddon Spurgeon, "The Prince of Preachers"* of the late 1800's, is quoted as saying; *"By perseverance the snail reached the ark."* Now that's endurance! What a sight that would be, but it illustrates no matter how long a challenge takes – Persevere!

Joshua 1:9
Have not I commanded thee? Be strong and of a good courage; be not afraid, neither be thou dismayed: for the Lord thy God is with thee whithersoever thou goest.

Psalms 19:14
Let the words of my mouth, and the meditation of my heart, be acceptable in Thy sight, O Lord, my strength, and my Redeemer.

Proverbs 3:5 - 8
Trust in the Lord with all thine heart; and lean not unto thine own understanding. In all thy ways acknowledge Him, and He shall direct thy paths. Be not wise in thine own eyes: fear the Lord, and depart from evil. It shall be health to thy navel, and marrow to thy bones.

John 8:31, 32
Then said Jesus to those Jews which believed on Him, If ye continue in My word, then are ye My disciples indeed; and ye shall know the truth, and the truth shall make you free.

Romans 2:7, 8
To them who by patient continuance in well doing seek for glory and honour and immortality, eternal life: But unto them that are contentious, do not obey the truth, but obey unrighteousness, indignation and wrath

JULY 20

BE FLEXIBLE - CHANGEABLE

Paul is a good example for us in the lesson of being flexible. He was sensitive to the guidance of God and several times God sent him in a different direction that he desired to go. First, in Acts 16:6 – 10: Paul wanted to go to Asia, and no reason was given to him (just forbidden) for the change in plans.

Now when they had gone throughout Phrygia and the region of Galatia, and were forbidden of the Holy Ghost to preach the Word in Asia,

Then in Acts 22:25, Paul was in Jerusalem in prison for preaching the gospel and was facing the plan to *"examine him by scourging and a possible death."* He had to be flexible to go from freedom to prison (many times in his life time).

I particularly like the comfort and promise God gave to Paul while he was in prison, possibly facing death, in:

Acts 23:10, 11
And when there arose a great dissension, the chief captain, fearing lest Paul should have been pulled in pieces of them, commanded the soldiers to go down, and to take him by force from among them, and to bring him into the castle. And the night following the <u>Lord stood by him</u>, and said, Be of good cheer, Paul: for as thou hast testified of Me in Jerusalem, so must thou bear witness also at Rome.

We may not have to face extreme circumstances to be "flexible" but there are many instances where every day people have been changed by being "flexible"; especially when they received God's plan through Christ in their lives.

John 3:30
He must increase, but I must decrease.

JULY 21

KEEP THE FIRE BURNING WITHIN

To "keep the fire burning within," we must first trust with thanksgiving how we came to this desire. Then with God's Word we see our part and then God's work within our heart. Many verses keep us on this goal – to honor, worship, praise our Lord, and share His love with others. This is a day by day renewal and obeying what God has in place for us to do. Remain on "fire" for God!

Fear of what other people will say quickly puts out the "Fire." This should not be.

Hebrews 12:28, 29
Wherefore we receiving a kingdom which cannot be moved, let us have grace, whereby we may serve God acceptably with reverence and godly fear: For our God is a consuming fire.

Psalms 66:10, 12
For Thou, O God, hast proved us: Thou hast tried us, as silver is tried. Thou hast caused men to ride over our heads; we went through fire and through water: but Thou broughtest us out into a wealthy place.

Jeremiah 23:29a
Is not My Word like as a fire? saith the Lord;

Acts 2:3, 4a
And there appeared unto them cloven tongues like as of fire, and it sat upon each of them. And they were all filled with the Holy Ghost,

I Corinthians 3:11, 13
For other foundation can no man lay than that is laid, which is Jesus Christ. Every man's work shall be made manifest: for the day shall declare it, because it shall be revealed by fire;
and the fire shall try every man's work of what sort it is.

JULY 22

MUCH MORES

The biblical phrase "Much More" intrigued me enough to open up my *Cruden's Complete Concordance* to see there are 18 "much mores" listed. Cruden was born in 1701, and kept track of words without a computer! Still used today, this treasure and can be found in many libraries of preachers. This Concordance contains 220,000 references and had some inaccuracies in the original edition, but have since been corrected. My volume was copyrighted in 1930, by The John C. Winston Company. The 18 "much more" phrases describe the condition of the human heart, <u>be it good or bad</u>. Here are a few of them.

<u>Romans 5:8 – 11</u>.
But God commendeth His love toward us, in that, while we were yet sinners, Christ died for us. <u>Much more</u> then, being now justified by His blood, we shall be saved from wrath through Him. For if, when we were enemies, we were reconciled to God by the death of His Son, <u>much more</u>, being reconciled, we shall be <u>saved by His life</u>. And not only so, but we also joy in God through our Lord Jesus Christ, by Whom we have <u>now received the atonement</u>.

<u>Exodus 36:5</u>
And they spake unto Moses, saying, The people bring <u>much more</u> than enough for the service of the work, which the Lord commanded to make.

<u>Matthew 6:30</u>
Wherefore, if God so clothe the grass of the field, which today is, and tomorrow is cast into the oven, shall He not <u>much more</u> clothe you, O ye of little faith?

<u>II Corinthians 3:9</u>
For if the ministration of condemnation be glory, <u>much more</u> doth the ministration of righteousness exceed in glory.

JULY 23

FAILURES are STEPPING STONES to Success

There are lessons to be learned all our lives. Some work out successfully and some are failures. These are the ones we learn the most from (so "they" say). As "they" say, "failures are stepping stones"; but who among us likes that walk? However, reality often contradicts these "words of wisdom." Paul had a different point of view that came from the very heart of God.

<u>II Corinthians 12:8 - 10</u>
For this <u>thing</u>, I besought the Lord thrice, that it might depart from me. And He said unto me, My grace is sufficient for thee: for My strength is made perfect in weakness. Most gladly therefore will I rather glory in my <u>infirmities</u>, that the power of Christ may rest upon me. Therefore, I take pleasure in infirmities, in reproaches, in necessities, in persecutions, in distresses for Christ's sake: for when I am weak, then am I strong.

Again, I like to stack rocks with my youngest granddaughter to thank God for all His help. Perhaps now we should also think of rocks as stepping stones God places before us. However, the stones would have to be much bigger than the ones we stack. Our failures also seem so big to us. This is where God comes in with His help, to guide us on to where He wants to take us; our journey together. Trust Him and enjoy the walk!

<u>Job 11:14 – 18a</u>
If iniquity (failure) be in thine hand, put it far away, and let not wickedness dwell in thy tabernacles. For then shalt thou lift up thy face without spot; yea, thou shalt be stedfast, and shalt not fear: Because thou shalt <u>forget thy misery</u>, and <u>remember it as waters that pass away</u>: And thine age shall be clearer than the noonday; thou shalt shine forth, thou shalt be as the morning. And thou shalt be secure, because <u>there is hope</u>. . .

JULY 24

READING THROUGH THE BIBLE

So far in this book, there has been a lot of scripture. I hope you have the desire to "read through the Bible" on your own. What is stopping you? You do not need to read it in one year! What's the hurry? Bible reading is for your learning and longing to know God better and know what He has in store for you as His dear child. Persevere! Don't give up! Ask the Holy Spirit within you, to give you assistance. The Bible is a living Word and will feed you when you are in need and hungry.

On a personal note; my husband and I have been reading *Thru the Bible*, with J. Vernon McGee (5 Volumes). We began over a couple of years ago now, because he goes verse by verse sharing knowledge and insight of his many years of experiences of schooling; studying, and pastorates. We have learned so much from him, just like sitting down with him as our Pastor – oh, the wisdom God has given him throughout the whole Bible.

<u>John 5:39</u>
Search the scriptures; for in them ye think ye have eternal life: and they are they which testify of Me.

<u>Romans 15:4</u>
For whatsoever things were written aforetime were written for our learning, that we through patience and comfort of the scriptures might have hope.

<u>II Timothy 3:16</u>
All scripture is given by inspiration of God, and is profitable for doctrine, for reproof, for correction, for instruction in righteousness:

<u>I Peter 2:2, 3</u>
As newborn babes, desire the sincere milk of the word, that ye may grow thereby: If so be ye have tasted that the Lord is gracious.

JULY 25

FLATTERY

Recognize Flattery for what it is worth!

In reading the Scriptures below, I reaffirmed the meaning of the word. I see a difference between honest compliments that are meant for encouragement, and flattery. The Bible has much to say against flattery, and the words used in the dictionary doesn't say anything good about it either: . . . *"excessive compliments excessive and often in<u>sin</u>cerely, to win favor."* That's pretty clear. It is <u>insincere praise</u>. It is lying, and that has been taught to us clearly as sinning.

<u>Psalms 5:9</u>
For there is no faithfulness in their mouth; their inward part is very wickedness; their throat is an open sepulchre; they flatter with their tongue.

<u>Psalms 12:2</u>
They speak vanity every one with his neighbour: with flattering lips and with a double heart do they speak.

<u>Psalms 36:2, 3</u>
For he flattereth himself in his own eyes, until his iniquity be found to be hateful. The words of his mouth are iniquity and deceit: he hath left off to be wise, and to do good.

<u>Psalms 78:36</u>
Nevertheless they did flatter him with their mouth, and they lied unto him with their tongues.

<u>Proverbs 20:19</u>
He that goeth about as a talebearer revealeth secrets: therefore meddle not with him that flattereth with his lips.

<u>I Thessalonians 2:5</u>
For neither at any time used we flattering words, as ye know, nor a cloke of covetousness; God is witness:

JULY 26

EXCUSES, EXCUSES, EXCUSES

Excuses, excuses, excuses, are usually followed with a "<u>but, because of</u> . . .," or blaming someone else. "<u>But</u>" never on oneself. I know this because I became an expert with the "<u>but</u>" word. It implies doubts or "I can't." Read this quote from "Yoda," of Star Wars fame! **"Do or Do Not! There is not TRY"** Stop and think about that – how true it is! Either/Or! When we "do not," we usually rationalize with excuses and drive it away. We think of all kinds of reasons! The Bible says that there is the one deadly argument that we try to excuse ourselves from - knowing the true God. We even make up one false argument to excuse the heathen who have never heard or maybe never will learn about Jesus. Take a look. There is no excuse especially for those that have heard – there is one true God.

Romans 1:20, 22 - 25
For the invisible things of Him from the creation of the world are clearly seen, being understood by the things that are made, even His eternal power and Godhead; so that <u>they are without excuse</u>: . . . Professing themselves to be wise, they became fools, And changed the glory of the uncorruptible God into an image made like to corruptible man, and to birds, and four-footed beasts, and creeping things. Wherefore God also gave them up to uncleanness through the lusts of their own hearts, to dishonour their own bodies between themselves: Who changed the truth of God into a lie, and worshipped and served the creature more than the <u>Creator</u>, <u>Who</u> is blessed forever. Amen.

Romans 2:14 – 16
For when the Gentiles (heathen), which have not the law, <u>do by nature</u> the things contained in the law, these, having not the law, are a law unto themselves: Which shew <u>the work of the law written in their hearts</u>, their <u>conscience also bearing witness</u>, and their thoughts the mean while <u>accusing</u> or else <u>excusing</u> <u>one another</u>; In the day when God shall judge the secrets of men by Jesus Christ according to my gospel.

JULY 27

BACKSLIDING
Slipping away from God

Backsliding is not a pretty word and is rarely used in the normal conversations. Backsliding is primarily found in the Old Testament describing the inconsistent obedience of God's chosen people. In the New Testament, backsliding is used as a gradual slipping away from what fallen believers had learned from Jesus Christ and the apostles. God deals with this falling away with much displeasure. Even with punishment attached to backsliding, the good news is in God's mercy. He gives us a promise for pardon of sin in the person of Jesus Christ.

<u>II Corinthians 11:3</u>
But I fear, lest by any means, as the serpent beguiled Eve through his subtilty, so your minds should be corrupted from the simplicity that is in Christ.

<u>Galatians 3:1, 3</u>
O foolish Galatians, who hath bewitched you, that ye should not obey the truth, before whose eyes Jesus Christ hath been evidently set forth, crucified among you?...Are ye so foolish? having begun in the Spirit, are ye now made perfect by the flesh?

<u>Galatians 5:1</u>
Stand fast therefore in the liberty wherewith Christ hath made us free, and be not entangled again with the yoke of bondage.

<u>Jeremiah 2:19</u>
Thine own wickedness shall correct thee, and thy backslidings shall reprove thee: know therefore and see that it is an evil thing and bitter, that thou hast forsaken the Lord thy God, and that My fear is not in thee, saith the Lord God of hosts.

JULY 28

EXPECTANT ATTITUDE

Keep an expectant attitude of "good" and not evil.
This takes our faith in God, and His promise in Jeremiah 29:11 – 13: *For I know the thoughts that I think toward you, saith the Lord, thoughts of peace, and not of evil, to give you an <u>expected</u> end. Then shall ye call upon Me, and ye shall go and pray unto Me, and I will hearken unto you. And ye shall seek Me, and find Me, when ye shall search for Me with all your heart.*

"Expectant Faith" refers to the "good and perfect gifts" - "gifts of peace, that come from God alone." He is always working for our good and knows what lies ahead. As His child, be joyful in all things and expect great things are happening for our good from our Heavenly Father. Learn from the lessons of Joseph in the Old Testament. After all he went through, he kept the faith, and in the end, he could say:

<u>Genesis 50:20</u>
But as for you (Joseph's brothers), ye thought evil against me; but <u>God meant it unto good</u>, to bring to pass, as it is this day, to save much people alive.

No matter what, in good times or trials, keep your eyes on the promise - "God is good." This is not a "Pollyanna" attitude or feeling, but a matter of faith in God, our Heavenly Father!

<u>Job 2:10b</u>
What? shall we receive good at the hand of God, and shall we not receive evil? In all this did not Job sin with his lips.

<u>Matthew 7:11</u>
If ye then, being evil, know how to give good gifts unto your children, how much more shall your Father which is in heaven give good things to them that ask Him?

JULY 29

HUMBLE YOURSELF

An arrogant person cannot fake or pretend true humility. Others may be fooled, but God knows. Be true to yourself and examine your motives. Arrogance is the preferred "front" of our day, but God is aware and has harsh words for the proud, and He gives grace to the humble. The Scriptures below, tell the humble truth!

James 4:6
But He giveth more grace. Wherefore He saith, God resisteth the proud, but giveth grace unto the humble.

Psalms 10:17
Lord, Thou hast heard the desire of the humble: Thou wilt prepare their heart, Thou wilt cause Thine ear to hear:

Isaiah 57:15
For thus saith the High and Lofty One that inhabiteth eternity, whose Name is Holy; I dwell in the high and holy place, with Him also that is of a contrite and humble spirit, to revive the spirit of the humble, and to revive the heart of the contrite ones.

Matthew 23:5 - 7
But all their works they do for to be seen of men: they make broad their phylacteries, and enlarge the borders of their garments, And love the uppermost rooms at feasts, and the chief seats in the synagogues, And greetings in the markets, and to be called of men, Rabbi, Rabbi.

Matthew 23:10 - 12
Neither be ye called masters: for One is your Master, even Christ. But he that is greatest among you shall be your servant. And whosoever shall exalt himself shall be abased; and he that shall humble himself shall be exalted.

JULY 30

A LIST OF ATTITUDES TO REMEMBER

We can deliberately choose to "put on" these attitudes with the help and guidance of the Holy Spirit that lives within us; to bring honor to God and joy to others. This takes both our will and practice; and listening to the promptings of God's Spirit to guide our feelings and responses throughout our day.

"godliness"	Faithful	Patience	Strengthen-Others
A quiet life	Flexible	Peaceable	Study
Affection	Forgiveness	Perseverance	Sufficiency of-God
Availability	Gladness	Practice by Doing	Surrender
Be a Blessing	Helpful	Prayer- Believing	Tenderhearted
Be Christ Like	Honest	Purpose with Passion	Thoughtfulness
Be Kind	Joyful	Reconciliation	Trust and Obey
Be of Good Courage	Kind Words	Rejoicing	Trust Christ
Be Still	Kindness	Rest in ME	Unafraid
Be Strong	Lift up Spirits	Righteousness	Wait and- Endure
Be Taught	Listen	Security	Wisdom
Be Thankful	Look Up	Seeking	Words of -Wisdom
Believe	LOVE	Service	Yesterday- Today- Forever
Calmness	LOVE the LORD	Shining Light	
Channel of - Blessings	Meditate on - truth	Singing Heart	
Cheerfulness	Moderation	Smile	**Choose - Your**
Compassionate	Disciplined	Stand Fast	**Choice for Today!**
Contentment	Encouraging	Strength-Today	
Disciplined	Never Fear		
Encouraging	Opportunities-		

<u>On your own</u> . . .
Today's Scripture reading should be from your Bible:
I Corinthians 13 *"The Love Chapter"*
and add I Colossians 3:12 – 17

JULY 31

"HAST THOU SEEN?"
Poem

I am closing out this month of July with an old, old hymn with very special words. As mentioned before, I have received rich blessings from the many hymns learned in the past. But this one, "HAST THOU SEEN?," I just found pasted in the back of an old used hymn book in my book case, and wanted to share it. I have never heard it sung but the author is believed to be Narayan Vaman Tilak who lived in (Urda), Pakistan – long ago. I could not find the circumstances or date of his writing, but this hymn gives us such passionate questions we all need to answer during our life time. As you read it below, ask yourself these questions.

"HAST THOU SEEN?"
by Narayan Vaman Tilak who lived in (Urda), Pakistan

Hast thou ever seen the Lord, Christ the Crucified?
Hast thou seen those wounded hands? Hast thou seen His side?
Hast thou seen the cruel thorns, woven for a crown?
Hast thou, hast thou seen His blood, Dropping, dropping down?

Hast thou seen thyself in them? They that hurt Him so?
Hast thou seen the sinner who caused his Saviour's woe?
Hast thou seen how dark the night was which Calv'ry wore?
Hast thou seen a loneliness such as Jesus bore?

Hast thou seen how He, to save, Suffers thus and dies?
Hast thou seen on whom He looks with His loving eyes?
Hast thou ever, ever seen Love that was like this?
Hast thou given up thy life wholly to be His?

AUGUST

BOXED IN

Romans 12:1, 2

I beseech you therefore, brethren, by the mercies of God, that ye present your bodies a living sacrifice, holy, acceptable unto God, which is your reasonable service. And be not <u>conformed</u> to this world: but <u>be ye transformed by the renewing of your mind</u>, that ye may prove what is that good, and acceptable, and perfect, will of God.

AUGUST 1

I HAVE ARRIVED!

Think again!

Do you really believe, "you have arrived"; either socially or spiritually? Sure, you may be successful in your own view, and the view of many others but we are not to compare ourselves with anyone. Paul, in the Bible warns us:

<u>Romans 12:3</u>
For I say, through the grace given unto me, to every man that is among you, not to think of himself more highly than he ought to think; but to think soberly, according as God hath dealt to every man the measure of faith.

If anyone could say "they have arrived," it would be Paul. He was <u>a Hebrew of the Hebrews</u>, and he gives us a synopsis (Philippians 3:5, 6) of all that he had accomplished before he became a follower of Christ on the road to Damascus; so we can understand his unique perspective.

<u>I Corinthians 10:12, 13</u>
Wherefore let him that thinketh he standeth take heed lest he fall. There hath no temptation taken you but such as is common to man: but God is faithful, who will not suffer you to be tempted above that ye are able; but will with the temptation also make a way to escape, that ye may be able to bear it.

<u>Philippians 3:4 – 8</u>
Though I might also have confidence in the flesh. If any other man thinketh that he hath whereof he might trust in the flesh, I (Paul) more: Circumcised the eighth day, of the stock of Israel, of the tribe of Benjamin, <u>an Hebrew of the Hebrews</u>; as touching the law, a Pharisee; Concerning zeal, persecuting the church; touching the righteousness which is in the law, blameless. But what things were gain to me, those I counted loss for Christ. Yea doubtless, and I count all things but loss for the excellency of the knowledge of Christ

AUGUST 2

PROVERBS 22 and PROVERBS 23

These two chapters in Proverbs, makes a list to educate us on how we should live to honor God in our daily lives. These two chapters provide great insight, so I am using **excerpts** from them for **two** days. Paul, in many of his letters in the New Testament, refers to how we should live; by using the word "conversation." We use this word for what we say, but we know we communicate through our actions too. **Look these up for extra study.**

EPHESIANS 2:3; 4:22 – HEBREWS 13:5,7 – I PETER 1:15

Proverbs 22
A good name is rather to be chosen than great riches, and loving favour rather than silver and gold. The rich and poor meet together: the Lord is the maker of them all. A prudent man foreseeth the evil, and hideth himself: . . . By humility and the fear of the Lord are riches, and honour, and life. Train up a child in the way he should go: and when he is old, he will not depart from it. The rich ruleth over the poor, and the borrower is servant to the lender. Cast out the scorner, and contention shall go out; The eyes of the Lord preserve knowledge, and He overthroweth the words of the transgressor . . . Foolishness is bound in the heart of a child; but the rod of correction shall drive it far from him. Bow down thine ear, and hear the words of the wise, and apply thine heart unto My knowledge. That thy trust may be in the Lord, . . . That I might make thee know the certainty of the words of truth; Rob not the poor, because he is poor: For the Lord will plead their cause, and spoil the soul of those that spoiled them. Make no friendship with an angry man; and with a furious man thou shalt not go: Lest thou learn his ways,

AUGUST 3

PROVERBS 22 and <u>PROVERBS 23</u>

Also see: EPHESIANS 2:3; 4:22 – HEBREWS 13:5,7 – I PETER 1:15

<u>Proverbs 23</u>

Labour not to be rich: cease from thine own wisdom. Wilt thou set thine eyes upon that which is not? for riches certainly make themselves wings; they fly away as an eagle toward heaven. Eat thou not the bread of him that hath an evil eye, neither desire thou his dainty meats: For as he thinketh in his heart, so is he: Eat and drink, saith he to thee; but his heart is not with thee. Speak not in the ears of a fool: for he will despise the wisdom of thy words. Apply thine heart unto instruction, and thine ears to the words of knowledge. Withhold not correction from the child: for if thou beatest him with the rod, he shall not die. Thou shalt beat him with the rod, and shalt deliver his soul from hell. Let not thine heart envy sinners: but be thou in the fear of the Lord all the day long. Hear thou, my son, and be wise, and guide thine heart in the way. Be not among winebibbers; among riotous eaters of flesh: For the drunkard and the glutton shall come to poverty: and drowsiness shall clothe a man with rags. Hearken unto thy father that begat thee, and despise not thy mother when she is old. The father of the righteous shall greatly rejoice: and he that begetteth a wise child shall have joy of him. Thy father and thy mother shall be glad, and she that bare thee shall rejoice.
<u>*My son, give Me thine heart, and let thine eyes observe My ways.*</u>

AUGUST 4

"STANDING ON THE PROMISES"

The hymn speaks of my own heart-felt message. I am very happy to sing it now. The author and composer, Russell Kelso Carter (1849-1928), in his 79 years, accomplished many different endeavors. His **"Standing On the Promises Of God"** enabled him to be a sheep herder, a Methodist minister, publisher of text books, and even a physician in Baltimore. Please read (or sing along with me) and believe.

"STANDING ON THE PROMISES"
by R. Kelso Carter (1849-1928)

Standing on the promises of Christ my King,
Thru eternal ages let His praises ring,
Glory in the highest I will shout and sing,
Standing on the promises of God.

Chorus
Standing, standing, Standing on the promises
of God my Savior;
Standing, standing, Standing,
I'm standing on the promises of God

Standing on the promises that cannot fail,
When the howling storms of doubt and fear assail,
By the living Word of God I shall prevail
Standing on the promises of God

Standing on the promises of Christ the Lord,
Bound to Him eternally by love's strong cord,
Overcoming daily with the Spirit's sword,
Standing on the promises

Standing on the promises I cannot fall,
Listening every moment to the Spirit's call,
Resting in my Savior as my all in all,
Standing on the promises of God.

AUGUST 5

DO I REALLY BELIEVE?
Or, DO I JUST SAY I BELIEVE?

Through the years, I have had to personally answer THESE questions for myself. As every trial comes my way, I am reminded and need again to confirm – Yes, I really believe - God! To reinforce this, I even have a small collection of "Promise" books (by various compilers), written for quick references to promises needed at a moment's notice. The promise that comforts me most and comes to my mind quickly is:

Hebrews 13:5b
. . . for He hath said, I will never leave thee, nor forsake thee.

Hebrews 13:6, 8
So that we may boldly say, The Lord is my helper, and I will not fear what man shall do unto me. Jesus Christ the same yesterday, and to day, and for ever.

The "BEATITUDES." are scriptural treasures to help us stay aligned with the will of God. A good way to apply these truths to our lives is to face how we are, and then receive the Blessings and Promises from God, Himself. "BE – Attitudes."

Matthew 5:2 – 12a
And He (Jesus) opened His mouth, and taught them, saying, Blessed are the poor in spirit . . . Blessed are they that mourn: . . . Blessed are the meek: . . . Blessed are they which do hunger and thirst after righteousness: . . . Blessed are the merciful: for they shall obtain mercy. . . . Blessed are the pure in heart: . . . Blessed are the peacemakers: . . . Blessed are they which are persecuted for righteousness' sake: . . . Blessed are ye, when men shall revile you, and persecute you, . . . Rejoice, and be exceeding glad: for great is your reward in heaven:

AUGUST 6

ENDURE

As the Lord that endured for us, we also must endure with the hope He gives us, to endure till the end. We are told trials are blessings, and our endurance will be rewarded. If we believe Jesus, taking Him at His word, we trust His promises.

Matthew 5:11, 12
Blessed are ye, when men shall revile you, and persecute you, and shall say all manner of evil against you falsely, for My sake. Rejoice, and be exceeding glad: for great is your reward in heaven: for so persecuted they the prophets which were before you.

So, we see the negative turns into positive when we believe God's promises. It is His love and mercy for us that gives us this endurance.

Joshua 4:24
That all the people of the earth might know the hand of the Lord, that it is mighty: that ye might fear (awe) the Lord your God for ever.

Psalms 9:7, 8a
But the Lord shall endure for ever: He hath prepared His throne for judgment. And He shall judge the world in righteousness,

Psalms 37:28
For the Lord loveth judgment, and <u>forsaketh not His saints</u>; <u>they are preserved for ever</u>: but the seed of the wicked shall be cut off.

Psalms 126:5
They that sow in tears shall reap in joy.

Luke 6:23a
Rejoice ye in that day, and leap for joy: for, behold, your reward is great in heaven. . .

AUGUST 7

IMPETUOUS

There are many adjectives describing impetuous actions or emotions: impulsive; judgmental, hasty, sudden abruptness, lack of a sense of responsibility. The most dangerous is, the lack of proper regard for consequences of an action or thought against someone; and this should make us pause.

As for the idea of sudden energy or action, I sometimes feel I'm not impetuous enough. I may hesitate too long to make some important decisions. I have come to the conclusion there must be a "happy medium." We must have an awareness of our responsibilities and possible consequences.

Romans 2:1, 3
Therefore, thou art inexcusable, O man, whosoever thou art that judgest: for wherein thou judgest another, thou condemnest thyself; for thou that judgest doest the same things. And thinkest thou this, O man, that judgest them which do such things, and doest the same, that thou shalt escape the judgment of God?

Romans 12:16 - 19
Be not wise in your own conceits. Recompense to no man evil for evil. Provide things honest in the sight of all men. If it be possible, as much as lieth in you, live peaceably with all men. Dearly beloved, avenge not yourselves, but rather give place unto wrath: for it is written, Vengeance is mine; I will repay, saith the Lord

II Corinthians 11:29, 30
Who is weak, and I am not weak? who is offended, and I burn not? If I must needs glory, I will glory of the things which concern mine infirmities.

AUGUST 8

TRUTH HURTS

If we receive a true criticism of our actions or behavior, it does hurt. None of us like to be reminded of our weak areas. If this truth is spoken in love, we must distinguish between; if truth hurts, our "feelings" are hurt; or if in fact, the truth has been spoken to help us see where we can benefit or better ourselves. Don't be touchy, but hear! Don't take offense but take it to heart and gain from the words of correction. Truth doesn't always come from other people or ones we love, but can come from the most important source – the Bible. These Truths are life changing and can affect our eternity. Truth hurts when we leave our comfort zone to either change our life-style or change a deep-rooted lie we may be harboring.

Genesis 32:10a
I am not worthy of the least of all the mercies, and of all the truth, which Thou hast shewed unto Thy servant;

Psalms 85:10
Mercy and truth are met together; righteousness and peace have kissed each other.

Romans 2:8, 9
But unto them that are contentious, and do not obey the truth, but obey unrighteousness, indignation and wrath, Tribulation and anguish, upon every soul of man that doeth evil, of the Jew first, and also of the Gentile.

I Thessalonians 5:14
Now we exhort you, brethren, warn them that are unruly, comfort the feebleminded, support the weak, be patient toward all men.

AUGUST 9

ACROSS OUR PATH

Stray dogs or cats have touched many-a-heart when one finds an animal crossing his path; and then takes that animal home with him. Today we want to think about the people, events, places we go, etc., that cross our path. We can give or take, depending on the situation, but be open to the giving of kindness, and hope. Even a simple smile can cheer up someone. A friendly smile will brighten your day. Give smiles away "freely"; they cost you nothing but kindness. Be mindful of the people or things that cross your pathway today. Be calm and know that God is directing your path. Follow Him, our Guide, right beside us.

Psalms 32:8
I will instruct thee and teach thee in the way which thou shalt go: I will guide thee with Mine eye.

Hosea 14:9
Who is wise, and he shall understand these things? prudent, and he shall know them? for the ways of the Lord are right, and the just shall walk in them: but the transgressors shall fall therein.

Colossians 3:12 - 14
Put on therefore, as the elect of God, holy and beloved, bowels of mercies, kindness, humbleness of mind, meekness, longsuffering; Forbearing one another, and forgiving one another, if any man have a quarrel against any: even as Christ forgave you, so also do ye. And above all these things put on charity, which is the bond of perfectness.

AUGUST 10

GENTLENESS

Gentleness first comes from the Hand of God:
He gives us the desire to show gentleness as an <u>unselfish</u> act of kindness to one another - even to our pets, other animals and the plants in our gardens. Instinctively we know when gentleness is required. God gives us a choice, but, in our selfishness, we do not always choose His path. Most of us know this verse, Ephesians 4:32, by heart, because we need this reminder, for help from God.

Ephesians 4:32
And be ye kind one to another, tenderhearted, forgiving one another, even as God for Christ's sake hath forgiven you.

Psalms 18:35
Thou hast also given me the shield of Thy salvation: and Thy right hand hath holden me up, and Thy gentleness hath made me great.

I Corinthians 4:20, 21
For the kingdom of God is not in word, but in power. What will ye? shall I come unto you with a rod, or in love, and in the spirit of meekness (gentleness)?

Galatians 5:22, 23
But the fruit of the Spirit is love, joy, peace, longsuffering, gentleness, goodness, faith, meekness, temperance: against such there is no law.

Galatians 6:1
Brethren, if a man be overtaken in a fault, ye which are spiritual, restore such an one in the spirit of meekness (gentleness); considering thyself, lest thou also be tempted.

AUGUST 11

MY SHEEP HEAR MY VOICE

John 10:27, 28
<u>My sheep hear My voice</u>, and I know them, and they follow Me: And I give unto them eternal life; and they shall never perish, neither shall any man pluck them out of My hand.

By faith, this is the promise we can stand on firmly. We may not hear an audible voice, but we know in our hearts by the Holy Spirit, this is "<u>soooooo</u>" true. The phrase *"and they follow Me,"* describes the response of His sheep. Are we following Him today?

John 10:1 - 4
Verily, verily, I say unto you, He that entereth not by the Door into the sheepfold, but climbeth up some other way, the same is a thief and a robber. But he that entereth in by the door is thesShepherd of the sheep. To him the porter openeth; and <u>the sheep hear His voice: and He calleth His own sheep by name</u>, and <u>leadeth</u> them out. And when He putteth forth His own sheep, He goeth before them, and <u>the sheep follow Him</u>: for <u>they know His voice</u>.

John 10:11, 14, 15
I am the Good Shepherd: the Good Shepherd giveth His life for the sheep. <u>I am the Good Shepherd</u>, and know My sheep, and am known of Mine. As the Father knoweth Me, even so know I the Father: and I lay down My life for the sheep.

Isaiah 40:11
He shall feed His flock like a shepherd: He shall gather the lambs with His arm, and carry them in His bosom, and shall gently lead those that are with young.

AUGUST 12

THE EVER-LIVING ONE

As you read the words of this hymn, meditate on these thoughts and the wonder of God's grace.

"MY FAITH HAS FOUND A RESTING PLACE"
by Lidie H. Edmunds (19th century)

My faith has found a resting place –
Not in device nor creed:
I trust the Ever-living One –
His wounds for me shall plead

Chorus
I need no other argument,
I need no other plea;
It is enough that Jesus died,
And that He died for me.

Enough for me that Jesus saves –
This ends my fear and doubt;
A sinful soul I come to Him –
He'll never cast me out.

My heart is leaning on the Word –
The written Word of God:
Salvation by my Savior's name –
Salvation thru His blood.

My great Physician heals the sick,
The lost He came to save;
For me His precious blood He shed,
For me His life He gave.

Revelation 1:18
I am He that liveth, and was dead; and, behold, I am alive for evermore, Amen; and have the keys of hell and of death

I Thessalonians 4:13
For if we believe that Jesus died and rose again, even so them also which sleep in Jesus will God bring with Him.

AUGUST 13

CEDARS OF LEBANON

Psalms 104:16
The trees of <u>the Lord</u> are full of sap; <u>the cedars of Lebanon, which He hath planted</u>; . . .

When I read this phrase, "the cedars of Lebanon, which <u>He (God) hath planted</u>"; I found some pictures on the Internet. Because in the pictures, they appear as pretty scrubby looking trees, I continued in the Bible for information about what was so special about them, and how these trees were used. Scripture refers to the Cedars of Lebanon as aromatic, durable wood. They were used for building in the "Iron Age" of Israel. These trees could attain a height of 100 feet, with trunks six feet in diameter and produce cones that grew on top of the branch. David used these Cedars in building his palace, (II Samuel 5:11); as did Solomon in the construction of <u>a palace</u> for himself and **"an house to the Name of the Lord my God"**; (I Kings 7:1 – 3, and II Chronicles 2:1 – 10). Highly praised as a mighty tree, the Cedars of Lebanon were used for many building projects through decades.

Then, the Bible compares the whole story of this special **tree** (in Ezekiel 17). with **Pharaoh, King of Egypt** (in Ezekiel 31). God, Himself has shown us His wrath as an example of His power, and what He did to the **tree** (humbled it); as well as He did to the other (the **Pharaoh** - cut him off). Very interesting!

Ezekiel 17:24
<u>And all the trees of the field shall know that I the Lord have brought down the high tree</u>, have <u>exalted the low tree</u>, have dried up the green tree, and have made the dry tree to flourish: I the Lord have spoken and have done it.

Ezekiel 31:1b, 2, 3, 7, 10 – 12
1. . . . the Lord came unto me (Ezekiel), saying,
2. . . . <u>speak unto Pharaoh king of Egypt, and to his multitude</u>; Whom art thou like in thy greatness?
3. Behold, the Assyrian was a cedar in Lebanon with fair branches, and with a shadowing shroud, and of an high stature; and his top was among the thick boughs.
7. Thus was <u>he fair in his greatness</u>, in the length of his branches: for his root was by great waters

10. Therefore thus saith the Lord God; <u>Because thou hast lifted up thyself in height</u>, and he hath shot up his top among the thick boughs, <u>and his heart is lifted up in his height</u>;

11. I have therefore delivered him into the hand of the mighty one of the heathen; he shall surely deal with him: <u>I have driven him out for his wickedness</u>.

12. And strangers, the terrible of the nations, have <u>cut him off</u>, and have left him: upon the mountains and in all the valleys his branches are fallen, and his boughs are broken by all the rivers of the land; and all the people of the earth are gone down from his shadow, and have left him.

AUGUST 14

KINGDOM LIVING

Whose kingdom you are living in? If we desire the Kingdom of God we must <u>believe</u> in God's way through Jesus Christ, His Son. <u>Accept</u> Him as your as Savior and repent by turning your life around to <u>follow</u> Him. Then, we are a part of God's Kingdom here on earth and for all eternity. **How wonderful is that?**

Psalms 103:19
The Lord hath prepared His throne in the heavens; and His kingdom ruleth over all.

Psalms 145:11 - 13
They shall speak of the glory of Thy kingdom, and talk of Thy power; To make known to the sons of men His mighty acts, and the glorious majesty of His kingdom. Thy kingdom is an everlasting kingdom, and Thy dominion endureth throughout all generations.

Matthew 4:17
From that time Jesus began to preach, and to say, <u>Repent</u>: for the kingdom of heaven is at hand.

Matthew 7:21
Not every one that saith unto Me, Lord, Lord, shall enter into the kingdom of heaven; but he that doeth the will of My Father which is in heaven.

John 3:3, 6, 7
Verily, verily, I (Jesus) say unto thee, Except a man be born again, he cannot see the kingdom of God. That which is born of the flesh is flesh; and that which is born of the Spirit is spirit. Marvel not that I said unto thee, <u>Ye must be born again</u>.

AUGUST 15

CHRIST, WHO IS OUR LIFE, OUR CREATOR

John 14:6
Jesus saith unto him, I am the Way, the Truth, and the Life: no man cometh unto the Father, but by Me.

John 1:1 - 4
In the beginning was the Word, and the Word was with God, and the Word was God. The same was in the beginning with God. All things were made by Him; and without Him was not any thing made that was made. In Him was life; and the life was the light of men.

These are two of the many foundations of the Christian life. They are forever truths, we know by faith to hold on to – no matter what! Continue to search the scriptures for other facts and promises God has given us for confidence and direction on our way.

Proverbs 3:5 – 7
Trust in the Lord with all thine heart; and lean not unto thine own understanding. In all thy ways acknowledge Him, and He shall direct thy paths. Be not wise in thine own eyes: fear the Lord, and depart from evil.

Colossians 3:1 - 4
If ye then be risen with Christ, seek those things which are above, where Christ sitteth on the right hand of God.
Set your affection on things above, not on things on the earth. For ye are dead, and your life is hid with Christ in God.
When Christ, Who is our life, shall appear, then shall ye also appear with Him in glory.

Hebrews 10:12 - 14
But this Man (Jesus), after He had offered One sacrifice for sins forever, sat down on the right hand of God; From henceforth expecting till His enemies be made His footstool. For by One offering He hath perfected for ever them that are sanctified.

AUGUST 16

BE ONE OF GOD'S HAPPY, JOYFUL PEOPLE

There is often confusion between happiness and joy. We know when we are happy and especially when we are unhappy. But happiness seems to be a daily goal we often cannot achieve unless circumstances line up with what we want. This kind of "happiness" flees quickly. That's why we continually demand to be coddled, and entertained, and most of all to have our own way – all a form of selfishness. The Bible has a better way of defining "happy and joyful people". For example, the queen of Sheba visited King Solomon and recognized the connection between happiness and wisdom, as recorded in I Kings 10:7 – 10. Look and see more wisdom from God's Word.

<u>Psalms 35:9</u>
And my soul shall be joyful in the Lord: it shall rejoice in His salvation.

<u>Proverbs 16:20b</u>
. . . and whoso trusteth in the Lord, happy is he.

<u>Ecclesiastes 7:14</u>
In the day of prosperity be joyful, but in the day of adversity consider: God also hath set the one over against the other, to the end that man should find nothing after Him.

<u>Isaiah 61:10a</u>
I will greatly rejoice in the Lord, my soul shall be joyful in my God; for He hath clothed me with the garments of salvation, He hath covered me with the robe of righteousness,

<u>Colossians 1:11, 12</u>
Strengthened with all might, according to His glorious power, unto all patience and longsuffering <u>with joyfulness</u>; <u>Giving thanks unto the Father</u>, which hath made us meet to be partakers of the inheritance of the saints in light:

AUGUST 17

WHERE DID I COME FROM?

We often hear stories, about children asking "where did I came from?" Sometimes silly answers are given – about a stork, or even found under a rock, etc. The reasoning for these "falsehoods" is the child is too young to understand the real truth. A cute story (lie) is easier to tell to shut down the conversation. God didn't leave us in the dark. He told us that He knew us in the womb, and would never forget us even if a mother would. O how wonderful! God also shared His life with us by giving us His Dear Son Jesus Christ; with a purpose for us to live, to glorify Him and have life eternal.

Job 14:1, 5
Man that is born of a woman is of few days, and full of trouble.
Seeing his days are determined, the number of his months are with Thee,
Thou hast appointed his bounds that he cannot pass;

Psalms 139:13 - 17
Thou hast possessed my reins: Thou hast covered me in my mother's womb.
I will praise Thee; for I am fearfully and wonderfully made:
marvellous are Thy works; and that my soul knoweth right well.
My substance was not hid from Thee,
when I was made in secret, and curiously wrought in the lowest parts of the earth.
Thine eyes did see my substance, yet being unperfect;
and in Thy book all my members were written, which in continuance were fashioned,
when as yet there was none of them.
How precious also are Thy thoughts unto me, O God!
how great is the sum of them!

Isaiah 49:15
Can a woman forget her sucking child, that she should not have compassion on the son of her womb? Yea, they may forget, yet will I not forget thee.

AUGUST 18

HE KNEW NO SIN

God sent His only begotten Son down to earth to dwell among us. This is His way to deliver us <u>all</u> from the sin of the human race. We have <u>all</u> fallen short of the glory of God by our disobedience against Him and we need a Savior.

Romans 5:19 - 21

For as by one man's (Adam) disobedience many were made sinners, so by the obedience of One (Jesus Christ) shall many be made righteous. Moreover the law entered, that the offence might abound. But where sin abounded, <u>grace did much more abound</u>: That as sin hath reigned unto death, even so might grace reign through righteousness unto eternal life by Jesus Christ our Lord.

Because there is no other acceptable sacrifice, God sent the man/God – Jesus, who knew no sin. God laid <u>all</u> sins, past, present and future on Him, on the cross; to pay our debt and redeem the whole world - <u>Whosoever</u> believeth on Him!

I Peter 1:18 - 20

Forasmuch as ye know that ye were not <u>redeemed</u> with corruptible things, as silver and gold, from your vain conversation received by tradition from your fathers; But <u>with the precious blood of Christ</u>, as of a lamb without blemish and without spot: Who verily was foreordained before the foundation of the world, but was manifest in these last times for you . . .

I Peter 2:21, 22

*For even hereunto were ye called: because Christ also suffered for us, leaving us an example, that ye should follow His steps:
Who did no sin, neither was guile found in His mouth:*

AUGUST 19

ANYONE CAN BE KIND
You would think so! Everyone should know how, and would be kind to others.

We are taught at home and school to be kind and not bully anyone. Scripture has much to say about kindness.

Ephesians 4:32,
And be ye kind one to another, tenderhearted, forgiving one another, even as God for Christ's sake hath forgiven you.

Kindness is not a "should be," but a <u>command</u> given to us in GOD'S Word, to "hear and do."

Luke 6:35
But love ye your enemies, and do good, and lend, hoping for nothing again; and your reward shall be great, and ye shall be the children of the Highest: <u>for He is kind</u> unto the unthankful and to the evil.

Ephesians 4:25, 27, 29
Wherefore putting away lying, speak every man truth with his neighbour: for we are members one of another. Neither give place to the devil. Let no corrupt communication proceed out of your mouth, but that which is good to the use of edifying, that it may minister grace unto the hearers.

Colossians 3:12
Put on therefore, as the elect of God, holy and beloved . . . kindness, humbleness of mind, meekness, longsuffering;

II Peter 1:7
And to godliness brotherly kindness; and to brotherly kindness charity.

AUGUST 20

CHRISTIAN/non-CHRISTIAN
God Gives Us the Choice

<u>Joshua 24:15</u>
And if it seem evil unto you to serve the Lord, <u>choose you this day whom ye will serve</u>; whether the gods which your fathers served that were on the other side of the flood, or the gods of the Amorites, in whose land ye dwell: <u>but as for me and my house, we will serve the Lord.</u>

All the derivatives of "choose" often come to mind. Our choosing never ends; moment by moment we are bombarded by our own thoughts - the good, the bad, the ugly. These thoughts can lead us to places we should or should not go. But thank God, He has given us, as believing Christians, His Holy Spirit to help us choose the good. Don't be fooled; our minds can be Satan's playground depending on our thought patterns. He is out to destroy us.

<u>I Peter 5:8 - 11</u>
Be sober, be vigilant; because your adversary the devil, as a roaring lion, walketh about, seeking whom he may devour: Whom resist stedfast in the faith, knowing that the same afflictions are accomplished in your brethren that are in the world. But the God of all grace, who hath called us unto His eternal glory by Christ Jesus, after that ye have suffered a while, make you perfect, stablish, strengthen, settle you. To Him be glory and dominion for ever and ever. Amen.

<u>Romans 13:13, 14</u>
Let us walk honestly, as in the day; not in rioting and drunkenness, not in chambering and wantonness, not in strife and envying. But <u>put ye on the Lord Jesus Christ</u>, and make not provision for the flesh, to fulfil the lusts thereof.

AUGUST 21

POWERFUL, MIGHTY, IS OUR GOD
With Loving Kindness

God's loving kindness comforts us; but demonstrations of God's power may frighten us. We love God's loving kindness bringing us through rough times but when He uses His power to defeat sin (and He will use it); we see His judgment protecting His holiness; for He cannot look upon sin. He is coming again to defeat evil forever.

I Peter 3:22
Who is gone into heaven, and is on the <u>right hand of God</u>; angels and authorities and powers being made subject unto Him.

I Peter 5:6
Humble yourselves therefore under <u>the mighty hand of God</u>, that He may exalt you in due time:

Psalms 75:8
For in the <u>hand of the Lord</u> there is a cup, and the wine is red; it is full of mixture; and He poureth out of the same: but the dregs thereof, all the wicked of the earth shall wring them out, and drink them.

Isaiah 5:25
. . . For all this His anger is not turned away, <u>but His hand is stretched out still</u>.

Isaiah 59:1, 2
Behold, <u>the Lord's hand</u> is not shortened, that it cannot save; neither His ear heavy, that it cannot hear: But your iniquities have separated between you and your God, and your sins have hid His face from you, that He will not hear.

AUGUST 22

DIGGING FOR DIAMONDS

Digging for diamonds was once on my "Bucket List." I thought we could go to the diamond field in Arkansas, dig, and find my treasure. But now I am older and wiser, this dream has passed. When we were in Israel, we did "dig" for pottery, but found some shards that we couldn't keep <u>if</u> they were "so big." Now I have had my fill of digging for earthly treasure. I am on a more exciting dig in the Scriptures: full of Spiritual gems and promises. God will also use <u>some physical jewels</u> in His New Jerusalem; - <u>a must read</u> (Revelation 21:10 – 23). Some of these gems I recognize or have heard of, and others are new to me, but very valuable! Let me continue to share a couple of my finds to inspire you to go on your own personal "dig."

<u>Job 28:12 - 18</u>
But where shall wisdom be found? and where is the place of understanding? Man knoweth not the price thereof; neither is it found in the land of the living. The depth saith, It is not in me: and the sea saith, It is not with me. It cannot be gotten for gold, neither shall silver be weighed for the price thereof. It cannot be valued with the gold of Ophir, with the precious onyx, or the sapphire. The gold and the crystal cannot equal it: and the exchange of it shall not be for jewels of fine gold. No mention shall be made of coral, or of pearls: for <u>the price of wisdom</u> is above rubies.

<u>Isaiah 61:10</u>
I will greatly rejoice in the Lord, my soul shall be joyful in my God; for He hath clothed me with the garments of salvation, He hath covered me with the robe of righteousness, as a bridegroom decketh himself with ornaments, and as a bride adorneth herself with her jewels.

AUGUST 23

KNOW YOUR HEART

Matthew 5:8
Blessed are the pure in heart: for they shall see God.

You may ask, how do we become "Pure in Heart," when scripture tells us our heart is deceitful and wicked. The hope and cure, is given to us in the book of Jeremiah. The Lord knows the intentions of our heart. Read below and see what God sees in the heart of man.

Jeremiah 17:7, 9, 10
Blessed is the man that trusteth in the Lord, and whose hope the Lord is. <u>The heart is deceitful above all things, and desperately wicked: who can know it?</u> I the Lord search the heart, I try the reins, even to give every man according to his ways, and according to the fruit of his doings.

I Samuel 16:7a, c
But the Lord said unto Samuel, Look not on his countenance, or on the height of his stature . . . for the Lord seeth not as man seeth; for man looketh on the outward appearance, <u>but the Lord looketh on the heart.</u>

Matthew 7:3
And why beholdest thou the mote that is in thy brother's eye, but considerest not the beam that is in thine own eye?

Ephesians 5:15 - 17
See then that ye walk circumspectly, not as fools, but as wise, redeeming the time, because the days are evil. Wherefore be ye not unwise, but understanding what <u>the will of the Lord</u> is.

I Thessalonians 5:15b - 19
. . . follow that which is good, both among yourselves, and to all men. Rejoice evermore. Pray without ceasing. In everything give thanks: for this is <u>the will of God in Christ Jesus</u> concerning you. Quench not the Spirit.

AUGUST 24

FOLLOW ME

Psalms 119:35 - 37
Make me to go in the path of Thy commandments; for therein do I delight. Incline my heart unto Thy testimonies, and not to covetousness. Turn away mine eyes from beholding vanity; and quicken Thou me in Thy way.

We have probably never heard an audible voice from God, but we hear His promptings through His Holy Spirit within our hearts. He may never require us to leave our home or country, but He gives us opportunities daily to follow Him in words and deeds. We often put off the little things He asks us to do for Him. As a procrastinator, this is my tendency. The Bible records other excuses given to Christ from people He called to follow Him.

Psalms 122:1
I was glad when they said unto me, Let us go into the house of the Lord.

Luke 9:23
And He said to them <u>all</u>, If any man will come after Me, let him deny himself, and take up his cross daily, and follow Me.

EXCUSES
Luke 9:59 – 62
And He said unto another, Follow me. But he said, Lord, suffer me first to go and bury my father. Jesus said unto him, Let the dead bury their dead: but go thou and preach the kingdom of God.

And another also said, Lord, I will follow Thee; but let me first go bid them farewell, which are at home at my house. And Jesus said unto him, No man, having put his hand to the plough, and <u>looking back, is fit for the kingdom of God.</u>

AUGUST 25

"WHAT WONDEROUS LOVE IS THIS"

This song is a beautiful old folk hymn. A favorite piece proclaiming God's love to us. Remember Jesus was "hung" in our place:

<u>Deuteronomy 21:22, 23a</u>
And if a man have committed a sin worthy of death, and he be to be put to death, and thou hang him on a tree. . . (for he that is hanged is accursed of God)

"WHAT WONDEROUS LOVE IS THIS"
An American Folk Hymn (Author unknown)

What wonderous love is this, O my soul! O my soul!
What wondrous love is this, O my soul!
What wondrous love is this that caused the Lord of bliss,
<u>*To bear the dreadful curse for my soul, for my soul,*</u>
<u>*To bear the dreadful curse for my soul, for my soul.*</u>

When I was sinking down, sinking down, sinking down,
When I was sinking down, sinking down, sinking down,
When I was sinking down, beneath God's righteous frown,
<u>*Christ laid aside His crown for my soul, for my soul.*</u>
<u>*Christ laid aside His crown for my soul, for my soul.*</u>

To God and to the Lamb I will sing, I will sing.
To God and to the Lamb I will sing, I will sing.
To God and to the Lamb Who is the great 'I Am,'
<u>*While millions join the theme, I will sing, I will sing.*</u>
<u>*While millions join the theme, I will sing, I will sing.*</u>

And when from death I'm free, I'll sing on, I'll sing on,
And when from death I'm free, I'll sing on, I'll sing on,
And when from death I'm free, I'll sing and joyful be,
<u>*And thro' eternity I'll sing on, I'll sing on,*</u>
<u>*And thro' eternity I'll sing on, I'll sing on.*</u>

AUGUST 26

SELF - DECEPTION

As we analyze ourselves, there is often no middle ground. We either see ourselves positively or negatively, with a danger of coming to a conclusion either way. We do, however, have the instruction in:

Romans 12:3
For I say, through the grace given unto me, to every man that is among you, not to think of himself more highly than he ought to think; but to think soberly, according as God hath dealt to every man the measure of faith.

Yes, there is a danger and warning of how we observe ourselves, giving us insight of how we should view ourselves.

I Corinthians 3:18 - 20
Let no man deceive himself. If any man among you seemeth to be wise in this world, let him become a fool, that he may be wise. For the wisdom of this world is foolishness with God. For it is written, He taketh the wise in their own craftiness. And again, the Lord knoweth the thoughts of the wise, that they are vain.

II Corinthians 13:5
Examine yourselves, whether ye be in the faith; prove your own selves. Know ye not your own selves, how that Jesus Christ is in you, except ye be reprobates?

Colossians 3:2 - 4
Set your affection on things above, not on things on the earth. For ye are <u>dead</u>, and <u>your life is hid with Christ in God</u>. When Christ, Who is our life, shall appear, then shall ye also appear with Him in glory.

I John 1:10
If we say that we have not sinned, we make Him a liar, and His word is not in us.

AUGUST 27

PEACE WITH GOD

Everywhere you look, the world cries out for PEACE. Everyone is looking in the wrong direction – man's perception. We should be looking for the Prince of Peace instead of the false peace found here on earth. How is worldly wisdom working for us? Not so good!

<u>Psalms 4:8</u>
I will both lay me down in peace, and sleep: for Thou, Lord, only makest me dwell in safety.

<u>Isaiah 26:3</u>
Thou wilt keep him in perfect peace, whose mind is stayed on Thee: because he trusteth in Thee.

<u>John 14:1, 27</u>
Let not your heart be troubled: ye believe in God, believe also in me. Peace I leave with you, My peace I give unto you: not as the world giveth, give I unto you. Let not your heart be troubled, neither let it be afraid.

<u>John 16:33</u>
These things I have spoken unto you, that in Me ye might have peace. In the world ye shall have tribulation: but be of good cheer; I have overcome the world.

<u>Romans 5:1, 2</u>
Therefore being justified by faith, we have <u>peace with God</u> through our Lord Jesus Christ: By Whom also we have access by faith into this grace wherein we stand, and rejoice in hope of the glory of God.

<u>Philippians 4:7</u>
And the peace of God, which passeth all understanding, shall keep your hearts and minds through Christ Jesus.

<u>Colossians 3:15</u>
And let the peace of God rule in your hearts, to the which also ye are called in one body; and be ye thankful.

AUGUST 28

O LORD OUR GOD

There are so many verses in the Bible dedicated to teaching us the attributes and power of God, and the nature of God and His Son, Jesus Christ, our Savior.

Psalms 8:1 - 4

<u>O Lord our Lord</u>, how excellent is Thy name in all the earth! Who hast set Thy glory above the heavens. Out of the mouth of babes and sucklings hast Thou ordained strength because of Thine enemies, that Thou mightest still the enemy and the avenger. When I consider Thy heavens, the work of Thy fingers, the moon and the stars, which Thou hast ordained; What is man, that thou art mindful of him? and the son of man, that Thou visitest him?

<u>We have no excuse</u> in not knowing who God is. We cannot know all about Him until He comes again and we see Him fact to face; but God's Word gives us ample information to stand in awe, and to love, honor, and praise Him.

Luke 4:16 – 22a

*And He (Jesus) came to Nazareth, where He had been brought up: and, as His custom was, He went into the synagogue on the sabbath day, and stood up for to read. And there was delivered unto Him the book of the prophet Esaias. And when He had opened the book, He found the place where it was written, The Spirit of the Lord is upon Me, because He hath anointed Me to preach the gospel to the poor; He hath sent Me to heal the brokenhearted, to preach deliverance to the captives, and recovering of sight to the blind, to set at liberty them that are bruised, To preach the acceptable year of the Lord.
And He closed the book, and He gave it again to the minister, and sat down. And the eyes of all them that were in the synagogue were fastened on Him. And He began to say unto them, <u>This day is this scripture</u> (Isaiah 61:1, 2) <u>fulfilled in your ears</u>. And all bare Him witness . . .*

John 1:9 - 14

That was the true Light, which lighteth every man that cometh into the world. He was in the world, and the world was made by Him, and the world knew Him not. He came unto His own, and His own received Him not. But as many as received Him, to them gave He power <u>to become the sons of God</u>, even to them that believe on His name: which were born, not of blood, nor of the will of the flesh, nor of the will of man, but of God. And the Word was made flesh, and dwelt among us, (and we beheld His glory, the glory as of the Only Begotten of the Father), full of grace and truth.

<u>John 8:27 – 30, 32</u>
They understood not that He spake to them of the Father. Then said Jesus unto them, When ye have lifted up the Son of Man, then shall ye know that I am He, and that I do nothing of Myself; but as My Father hath taught Me, I speak these things. And He that sent Me is with Me: the Father hath not left Me alone; for I do always those
things that please Him. <u>As He spake these words, many believed on Him</u>. And ye shall know the truth, and the truth shall make you free.

<u>John 17: 17, 18; 21 – 23</u>
Sanctify them through Thy truth: Thy word is truth. As Thou hast sent Me into the world, even so have I also sent them into the world. That they all may be one; as Thou, Father, art in Me, and I in Thee, that they also may be one in Us: that the world may believe that Thou hast sent Me. And the glory which Thou gavest Me I have given them; that they may be one, even as We are One: I in them, and Thou in Me, that they may be made perfect in one; and that the world may know that Thou hast sent Me, and hast loved them, as Thou hast loved Me.

AUGUST 29

JESUS' PARABLES and MIRACLES

Like Jesus' disciples, you may be asking this same question: Why did Jesus speak to the multitudes in parables? He answered by explaining that some will hear, understand, and follow Him while some others will only hear. Not all will be converted because some of the people's hearts were "<u>waxed gross.</u>" These are not my words but a quote. I can imagine that you would never even think the word "<u>gross</u>" could be in the Bible.

<u>Matthew 13:10, 11; 13 - 15</u>
And the disciples came, and said unto Him, Why speakest Thou unto them in parables? He answered and said unto them, Because it is given unto you to know the mysteries of the kingdom of heaven, but to them it is not given.

Therefore speak I to them in parables: because they seeing see not; and hearing they hear not, neither do they understand. And in them is fulfilled the prophecy of Esaias, which saith, By hearing ye shall hear, and shall not understand; and seeing ye shall see, and shall not perceive: For this people's heart is <u>waxed gross</u>, and their ears are dull of hearing, and their eyes they have closed; lest at any time they should see with their eyes, and hear with their ears, and should understand with their heart, and should be converted, and I should heal them.

<u>Matthew 13:16, 17</u>
But blessed are your eyes, for they see: and your ears, for they hear. For verily I say unto you, that many prophets and righteous men have desired to see those things which ye see, and have not seen them; and to hear those things which ye hear, and have not heard them.

<u>I Corinthians 4:1</u>
Let a man so account of us, as of the ministers of Christ, and stewards of the <u>mysteries</u> of God.

AUGUST 30

FORGIVEN

Forgiveness is a two - way street! Well, maybe more of a continuum by following Christ's example of forgiveness. When we are forgiven through our Savior, we in turn must also forgive others who have offended us, no matter how big or small the transgression. We are not to retaliate but forgive.

Mark 2:7
Why doth this Man (Jesus) thus speak blasphemies? who can forgive sins but God only?

Luke 23:34a
Then said Jesus, Father, forgive them; for they know not what they do.

Romans 12:19
Dearly beloved, avenge not yourselves, but rather give place unto wrath: for it is written, Vengeance is Mine; I will repay, saith the Lord.

Hebrews 10: 31
It is a fearful thing to fall into the hands of the living God.

Psalms 85:2
Thou hast forgiven the iniquity of Thy people, Thou hast covered all their sin. Selah.

Psalms 32:1
Blessed is he whose transgression is forgiven, whose sin is covered.

Romans 4:7
Saying, Blessed are they whose iniquities are forgiven, and whose sins are covered.

I John 2:12
I write unto you, little children, because your sins are forgiven you for His Name's sake.

AUGUST 31

LEANING ON JESUS

Let this subject, <u>leaning on Jesus</u>, be our daily goal. Our sour pride (I can do this myself) keeps us from living this way until we face troubled times; then we rush to His arms.

"LEANING ON THE EVERLASTING ARMS"
by Elisha A. Hoffman (1839-1929)
and A. J. Showalter (1858-1924)

<u>Chorus</u>
Leaning on Jesus, leaning on Jesus,
safe and secure from all alarms;
leaning on Jesus, leaning on Jesus,
I'm leaning on the everlasting arms.

That's just the chorus of this encouraging song.
Now for the **three verses**:

What a fellowship, what a joy divine,
Leaning on the everlasting arms;
What a blessedness, what a peace is mine,
Leaning on the everlasting arms.

O how sweet to walk in this pilgrim way,
Leaning on the everlasting arms.
O how bright the path grows from day to day,
Leaning on the everlasting arms.

What have I to dread, what have I to fear,
Leaning on the everlasting arms.
I have blessed peace with my Lord so near,
Leaning on the everlasting arms.

SEPTEMBER

BOLD SPIRIT

II Timothy 1:7
For God has not given us a spirit of fear, but of power and of love and of a sound mind.

SEPTEMBER 1

SUNLIGHT

We still have bright sunlight throughout the whole month of September, but soon the sunlight will begin to fade. Not so, with the Light of the World – Jesus. We can walk in God's light no matter what the day or night is like.

You may know the hymn **"SUNLIGHT."** Since some of us don't sing the old hymns at church now, we may not have heard it lately. If so, read or sing it as a review. This is a song of our transformation from what we once were to how we live in the sunlight of God's love.

"SUNLIGHT"
by Judson W. Van De Venter (1855-1939)

*I wandered in the shades of night, Till Jesus came to me,
And with the sunlight of His love, Bid all my darkness flee.*

<u>Chorus</u>
Sunlight, sunlight, in my soul today,
Sunlight, sunlight all along the way.
Since the Savior found me, took away my sin,
I have had the Sunlight of His love within.

*Tho' clouds may gather in the sky, And billows round me roll,
However dark the world may be I've sunlight in my soul.*

*While walking in the light of God, I, sweet communion find,
I press with holy vigor on, And leave the world behind.*

*I cross the wide extended field, I journey o'er the plain,
And in the sunlight of His Love, I reap golden grain.*

*Soon I shall Him as He is, The Light that came to me,
Behold the brightness of His face, All through eternity.*

SEPTEMBER 2

FAKE NEWS

We are overrun with lies and bogus news from our newspapers and media stations we depend on to tell us the truth. This is true now and has been common all over the world for ages. Jesus warned us to BEWARE of "false teachers" who may enter our lives.

<u>Matthew 7:15, 16a</u>
Beware of false prophets, which come to you in sheep's clothing, but inwardly they are ravening wolves. Ye shall know them by their fruits.

Even though we suffer from earthly falsehoods; false teachings within our Spiritual lives are even more severe. Jesus knew what was coming and did not want us to be unaware. Let us look at what Jesus warned us about; the dangers of those who lead us astray from His word.

<u>Matthew 16:6, 12</u>
Then Jesus said unto them, Take heed and beware of the leaven of the Pharisees and of the Sadducees. Then understood they how that He bade them not beware of the leaven of bread, but <u>of the doctrine</u> of the Pharisees and of the Sadducees.

<u>Colossians 2:8</u>
Beware lest any man spoil you through philosophy and vain deceit, after the tradition of men, after the rudiments of the world, and not after Christ.

<u>II Peter 3:18</u>
But grow in grace, and in the knowledge of our Lord and Saviour Jesus Christ. To Him be glory both now and for ever. Amen.

SEPTEMBER 3

FOREVER THE SAME

Hebrews 13:8
Jesus Christ the same yesterday, and today, and forever.

Matthew 5: 17 - 18
Think not that I am come to destroy the law, or the prophets: I am not come to destroy, <u>but to fulfil</u>. For verily I say unto you, Till heaven and earth pass, <u>one jot or one tittle</u> shall in no wise pass from the law, <u>till all be fulfilled</u>.

Change, change, change! There are so many changes in every aspect of life. We can hardly keep up with them all. We learn to deal with simple adjustments, but major changes can be so confusing. We can't keep up with all the laws governments place on us. Our only hope is in the Lord. He does not change and is the same forever. His Word (Law) will not change either, so we can believe Him by faith.

Isaiah 45:22, 23
Look unto Me, and be ye saved, all the ends of the earth: for I am God, and <u>there is none else</u>. I have sworn by Myself, the word is gone out of My mouth in righteousness, and shall not return That unto Me every knee shall bow, every tongue shall swear.

Isaiah 55:6 - 8
Seek ye the Lord while He may be found, call ye upon Him while He is near: Let the wicked forsake his way, and the unrighteous man his thoughts: and let him return unto the Lord, and He will have <u>mercy</u> upon him; and to our God, for He will abundantly <u>pardon</u>.
For My thoughts are not your thoughts, neither are your ways My ways, saith the Lord.

SEPTEMBER 4

JESUS' TURN TO ASK QUESTIONS

Jesus asked questions (**?**) of those with whom He had a personal encounter. He opened their eyes of understanding – the way to His kingdom. These are the same questions we must answer for ourselves before Him.

Luke 6:46
And why call ye Me, Lord, Lord, and do not the things which I say?

Mark 8:27b, 29a
*. . . Whom do men say that I am?
But whom say ye that I am? . . . Thou art the Christ.*

Matthew 9:3 - 6
And, behold, certain of the scribes said within themselves, This man blasphemeth. And Jesus knowing their thoughts said, Wherefore think ye evil in your hearts? For whether is easier, to say, Thy sins be forgiven thee; or to say, Arise, and walk? But that ye may know that the Son of man hath power on earth to forgive sins, (then saith He to the sick of the palsy,) Arise, take up thy bed, and go unto thine house.

Matthew 20:22
But Jesus answered and said, Ye know not what ye ask. Are ye able to drink of the cup that I shall drink of, and to be baptized with the baptism that I am baptized with? They say unto Him, We are able.

Matthew 21:28 – 31a
*But what think ye?
A certain man had two sons; and he came to the first, and said, Son, go work today in my vineyard. He answered and said, I will not: but afterward he repented, and went. And he came to the second, and said likewise. And he answered and said, I go, sir: and went not. Whether of them twain did the will of his father?*

SEPTEMBER 5

OUR DEPENDENCY ON GOD

Today, our society depends on many things to meet our needs: education, heritage, knowledge, giant computer systems, modern transportation, spacecraft, eradicating diseases, and the security the government offers. Seemingly necessary at the time, we look back, and see broken promises. As a result of earthly advances, we see new threats we've never dreamed of: the so called 'climate change,' economic chaos, morality swings, angry demonstrations, anarchy, long military involvements, social demands, loss of faith, etc.; and even failed churches. This is brought about, as a whole, by people not wanting to admit our need to turn from our own ways! Through the <u>power of the cross alone</u>, we can receive realistic answers and hope for the future.

<u>II Chronicles 7:14</u>
If <u>My people</u>, which are called by My name, shall humble themselves, and pray, and seek My face, and <u>turn from their wicked ways</u>; then will I hear from heaven, and will forgive their sin, and will heal their land.

<u>II Chronicles 14:11</u>
And Asa cried unto the Lord his God, and said, Lord, it is nothing with Thee to help, whether with many, or with them that have no power: help us, O Lord our God; for we rest on Thee, and in Thy Name we go against this multitude. O Lord, Thou art our God; let not man prevail against Thee.

<u>Psalms 62:7, 8a, c, 12a</u>
In God is my salvation and my glory: the rock of my strength, and my refuge, is in God. Trust in Him at all times; . . . God is a refuge for us. unto thee, O Lord, belongeth mercy.

SEPTEMBER 6

KNOWLEDGE PUFFS UP

It all began in the Garden of Eden -- our desire to have knowledge and be in charge. Eve's bold curiosity reigned supreme until Satan (the serpent) came to deceive her. He knew she could be open and may want to <u>know</u> the differences between good and evil and would defy God's commandment. She ate from the forbidden tree and disobeyed God. Sin (evil) entered into the world through disobeying God's command. Now <u>we</u> are all seeking some kind of <u>knowledge</u> be it good or bad and <u>think we know</u> what's best for us.

<u>Genesis 2:9, 17</u>
And out of the ground made the Lord God to grow every tree that is pleasant to the sight, and good for food; <u>the tree of life</u> also in the midst of the garden, and the tree of knowledge of good and evil. But of <u>the tree of the knowledge of good and evil</u>, thou shalt not eat of it: for in the day that thou eatest thereof thou shalt surely die.

<u>I Samuel 2:3</u>
Talk no more so exceeding proudly; let not arrogancy come out of your mouth: for the Lord is a God of knowledge, and by Him actions are weighed.

<u>I Corinthians 13:4 - 7</u>
Charity suffereth long, and is kind; charity envieth not; charity vaunteth not itself, is not puffed up, Doth not behave itself unseemly, seeketh not her own, is not easily provoked, thinketh no evil; Rejoiceth not in iniquity, but rejoiceth in the truth; Beareth all things, believeth all things, hopeth all things, endureth all things.

<u>Ecclesiastes 1:16b, 17b, 18</u>
I (Solomon) have gotten more wisdom than all they that have been before me in Jerusalem: . . . I perceived that this also is vexation of spirit. For in much wisdom is much grief: and he that increaseth knowledge increaseth sorrow.

SEPTEMBER 7

INSTEAD! INSTEAD OF WHAT?

Isaiah 3 tells of God's great care for Adam. God decided Adam (man) should not be alone and made for him an "help meet." Adam called her "woman." Bone of his bones, and flesh of his flesh because she was made of his rib. Eve and Adam disobeyed God by eating from the Tree of the Knowledge of Good and Evil. Today, misconceptions regarding womanhood have caused much trouble in all the generations thereafter. Not excusing men, but women are rebelling over the fact they were created to be the "help meet". This role is "beneath our dignity" and not the privilege as God intended. We too can believe Satan's lies; giving in to "haughty" (proud) attitudes.

Genesis 2:18, 22 - 24
And the Lord God said, it is not good that the man should be alone; I will make him AN HELP MEET for him. And the rib, which the Lord God had taken from man, made he a WOMAN, and brought her unto the man. And Adam said, This is now bone of my bones, and flesh of my flesh: she shall be called Woman, because she was taken out of Man.

Isaiah 3:16
Moreover the Lord saith, Because the daughters of Zion are haughty, and walk with stretched forth necks and wanton eyes, walking and mincing as they go, and making a tinkling with their feet:

Isaiah 3:18 - 21
In that day the Lord will take away the bravery of their tinkling ornaments about their feet, and their cauls, and their round tires like the moon, The chains, and the bracelets, and the mufflers, The bonnets, and the ornaments of the legs, and the headbands, and the tablets, and the earrings, The rings, and nose jewels,

Isaiah 3:22 - 26
The changeable suits of apparel, and the mantles, and the wimples, and the crisping pins, The glasses, and the fine linen, and the hoods, and the vails. And it shall come to pass, INSTEAD of sweet smell there shall be stink; and INSTEAD of a girdle a rent; and instead of well set hair baldness; and INSTEAD of a stomacher a girding of sackcloth; and burning INSTEAD of beauty. Thy men shall fall by the sword, and thy mighty in the war. And her gates shall lament and mourn; and she being desolate shall sit upon the ground.

What have women become today?

SEPTEMBER 8

KNOW THAT I AM THE LORD

Knowledge might be all well and good, but the most important knowledge is <u>knowing</u> that <u>God is the Lord</u>! As early as in Exodus, God showed His love and mercy to demonstrate that He is the Lord.

Exodus 3:14
And God said unto Moses, <u>I Am that I Am</u>: and He said, Thus shalt thou say unto the children of Israel, <u>I Am</u> hath sent me (Moses) unto you.

From there and beyond, God has shown to all of us (Jews and Gentiles) in His Word and deeds, His power, giving us a view of how He cares and that He is Lord over all. By our faith we believe and accept His love.

Exodus 29:45, 46
And I will dwell among the children of Israel, and will be their God. And they shall know that I am the Lord their God, that brought them forth out of the land of Egypt, that I may dwell among them: I am the Lord their God.

Leviticus 11:44
For I am the Lord your God: ye shall therefore sanctify yourselves, and ye shall be holy; for I am holy: neither shall ye defile yourselves with any manner of creeping thing that creepeth upon the earth.

Psalms 102:12, 25 - 27
But thou, O Lord, shalt endure for ever; and Thy remembrance unto all generations. Of old hast Thou laid the foundation of the earth: and the heavens are the work of Thy hands. They shall perish, but Thou shalt endure: yea, all of them shall wax old like a garment; as a vesture shalt Thou change them, and they shall be changed: But Thou art the same, and Thy years shall have no end.

SEPTEMBER 9

PRACTICE WHAT YOU ALREADY KNOW

There is much we <u>know</u> right now but <u>fail to do</u>. We search for more and more learning, but what is the use, when we ignore what we already know without the "doing"? Even the basic knowledge God loves us and sent His Son to die for us, we push to the back of our minds when we want to go our own way. We often put God on our "back burner" (so to speak), especially when we <u>know</u> what we should do <u>but won't</u>.

<u>Leviticus 20:7, 8</u>
Sanctify yourselves therefore, and be ye holy: for I am the Lord your God. And ye shall keep My statutes, and do them: I am the Lord which sanctify you.

<u>Luke 11:28</u>
But He said, Yea rather, blessed are they that hear the word of God, and keep it.

<u>Romans 12:18, 19</u>
If it be possible, as much as lieth in you, live peaceably with all men. Dearly beloved, avenge not yourselves, but rather give place unto wrath: for it is written, Vengeance is Mine; I will repay, saith the Lord.

<u>Philippians 4:9</u>
Those things, which ye have both learned, and received, and heard, and seen in me, do: and the God of peace shall be with you.

<u>I John 5:18</u>
We know that whosoever is born of God sinneth not; but he that is begotten of God keepeth himself, and that wicked one toucheth him not.

SEPTEMBER 10

VANITY

Vanity and pride are a grave twosome. We can see in the Psalms many descriptions and results for those who harbor and practice this way of life.

<u>Psalms 94:11</u>
The Lord knoweth the thoughts of man, that they are vanity.

Vanity and pride even caused God to banish Satan (Lucifer) from Heaven. He wanted to be like God. We can see the same trait in ourselves. We want to "do" our own way. The consequences can be deadly.

<u>Isaiah 14:12 – 14</u>
How art thou fallen from heaven, O Lucifer, son of the morning! how art thou cut down to the ground, which didst weaken the nations! For thou hast said in thine heart, I will ascend into heaven, I will exalt my throne above the stars of God: I will sit also upon the mount of the congregation, in the sides of the north: I will ascend above the heights of the clouds; I will be like the Most High.

<u>Psalms 4:2</u>
O ye sons of men, how long will ye turn My glory into shame? how long will ye love vanity, and seek after leasing?

<u>Psalms 10:4, 7</u>
The wicked, through the pride of his countenance, will not seek after God: God is not in all his thoughts. His mouth is full of cursing and deceit and fraud: under his tongue is mischief and vanity.

<u>Psalms 12:4</u>
With our tongue will we prevail; our lips are our own: who is lord over us?

<u>Psalms 119: 37</u>
Turn away mine eyes from beholding vanity; and quicken Thou me in Thy way.

SEPTEMBER 11

OUR EVERY NEED

Just look around and see, we are a needy people. This you can't deny.

Revelation 3:17 - 19
Because thou sayest, I am rich, and increased with goods, and have need of nothing; and knowest not that thou art wretched, and miserable, and poor, and blind, and naked: <u>I counsel thee to buy of Me gold tried in the fire,</u> that thou mayest be rich; and white raiment, that thou mayest be clothed, and that the shame of thy nakedness do not appear; and anoint thine eyes with eyesalve, that thou mayest see. As many as I love, I rebuke and chasten: be zealous therefore, and repent.

If we could see the needs in our own lives and the lives of others, we would turn to God and admit He is the only One to "fill our every need" – needs we cannot supply for ourselves. Our needs teach us to depend on Him and let Him be our guide through good and bad times. God knows best and knows what lies ahead. He desires for us to bring Him honor and glory.

Psalms 40:17
*But I am poor and needy; yet the Lord thinketh upon me:
Thou art my help and my deliverer; make no tarrying, O my God.*

Philippians 4:19
But my God shall supply all your need according to his riches in glory by Christ Jesus.

Hebrews 10:36
For ye have need of patience, that, after ye have done the will of God, ye might receive the promise.

SEPTEMBER 12

CONFIDENCE

Confidence in who, what, or where?
Confidence includes boldness, and trust in something or someone. Our U.S. money is imprinted with "In God We Trust." I hope this is your motto today.

Job 31:24, 25, 28
If I have made gold my hope, or have said to the fine gold, thou art my confidence; If I rejoiced because my wealth was great, and because mine hand had gotten much; . . . This also were an iniquity to be punished by the judge: or I should have denied the God that is above.

Psalms 118:8
It is better to trust in the Lord than to put confidence in man.

Proverbs 3:25, 26
Be not afraid of sudden fear, neither of the desolation of the wicked, when it cometh. For the Lord shall be thy confidence, and shall keep thy foot from being taken.

Proverbs 14:26
In the fear of the Lord is strong confidence: and His children shall have a place of refuge.

Ephesians 3:12
In Whom we have boldness and access with confidence by the faith of Him.

Philippians 3:3b
. . . rejoice in Christ Jesus, and have no confidence in the flesh.

Hebrews 3:14
For we are made partakers of Christ, if we hold the beginning of our confidence stedfast unto the end;

SEPTEMBER 13

YOU CALL ME LORD

<u>Revelation 4:11</u>
Thou art worthy, O Lord, to receive glory and honour and power: for thou hast created all things, and for Thy pleasure they are and were created.

In the New Testament, we find instructions and examples of how we fall short, even when we call Jesus Christ our Lord. Sometimes we are fooling ourselves to think we are obeying God; out of ignorance, or just plain stubbornness. The little things in our lives can make us stumble and be unaware of our failings. We need to be cautious to see our true motives every day.

<u>John 6:68, 69</u>
Then Simon Peter answered Him, Lord, to whom shall we go? Thou hast the words of eternal life. And we believe and are sure that Thou art that Christ, the Son of the living God.

<u>Acts 2:21</u>
And it shall come to pass, that whosoever shall call on the name of the Lord shall be saved.

<u>I Corinthians 1:8, 9</u>
Who shall also confirm you unto the end, that ye may be blameless in the day of our Lord Jesus Christ. God is faithful, by Whom ye were called unto the fellowship of His Son Jesus Christ our Lord.

<u>Colossians 1:10 – 13a</u>
That ye might walk worthy of the Lord unto all pleasing, being fruitful in every good work, and increasing in the knowledge of God; Strengthened with all might, according to his glorious power, unto all patience and longsuffering with joyfulness; Giving thanks unto the Father . . .

SEPTEMBER 14

THE DOVE

I have learned the dove belongs to the pigeon family but is often classed with the smaller varieties of birds. Doves are considered "clean," and were used as sacrifices to God in the Old Testament as a representation of gentleness and innocence. Doves are defenseless and are commonly used as a symbol of peace.

<u>Leviticus 14:22</u>
And two turtledoves, or two young pigeons, such as he is able to get; and the one shall be a sin offering, and the other a burnt offering.

In the New Testament, God used the dove as a symbol of the Holy Spirit.
<u>Matthew 3:16, 17</u>
And Jesus, when He was baptized, went up straightway out of the water: and, lo, the heavens were opened unto Him, and He saw the Spirit of God descending <u>like a dove</u>, and lighting upon Him: And lo a voice from heaven, saying, This is My beloved Son, in Whom I am well pleased.

The dove is first referred to in the Bible in Genesis 8:8 – 12, when Noah sent one out to survey the waters of the flood.

Also he (Noah) sent forth a dove from him, to see if the waters were abated from off the face of the ground; But the dove found no rest for the sole of her foot, and she returned unto him into the ark, for the waters were on the face of the whole earth: then he put forth his hand, and took her, and pulled her in unto him into the ark. And he stayed yet other seven days; and again he sent forth the dove out of the ark; And the dove came in to him in the evening; and, lo, in her mouth was an <u>olive leaf</u> pluckt off: so Noah knew that the waters were abated from off the earth. And he stayed yet other seven days; and sent forth the dove; which returned not again unto him anymore.

SEPTEMBER 15

THE CARNAL MIND

Romans 8:6 - 8
For to be carnally minded is death; but to be spiritually minded is life and peace. Because the carnal mind is enmity against God: for it is not subject to the law of God, neither indeed can be. <u>So then they that are in the flesh cannot please God.</u>

Be vigilant! There are consequences in all of life, but when we live carnally in disobedience to the Word of God, we live dangerously. In the end, carnal living will lead to death.

Romans 8:1, 5
There is therefore now no condemnation to them which are in Christ Jesus, who walk not after the flesh (carnal), but after the Spirit. For <u>they that are after the flesh do mind the things of the flesh</u>; but they that are after the Spirit the things of the Spirit.

Colossians 3:2 - 4
Set your affection on things above, not on things on the earth. For ye are dead, and your life is hid with Christ in God. When Christ, who is our life, shall appear, then shall ye also appear with Him in glory.

II Timothy 3:2 – 5
For men shall be lovers of their own selves, covetous, boasters, proud, blasphemers, disobedient to parents, unthankful, unholy, without natural affection, trucebreakers, false accusers, incontinent, fierce, despisers of those that are good, Traitors, heady, high-minded, lovers of pleasures more than lovers of God; Having a form of godliness, but denying the power thereof: from such turn away.

SEPTEMBER 16

"OPEN MY EYES, THAT I MAY SEE"
by Clara H. Scott (1841-1897)

Open my eyes, that I may see
Glimpses of truth Thou hast for me;
Place in my hands the wonderful key
That shall unclasp and set me free.
Silently now I wait for Thee,
Ready, my God, Thy will to see;
Open my <u>eyes</u> – illumine me, Spirit divine!

Open my ears, that I may hear
Voices of truth Thou sendest clear;
And while the wave-notes fall on my ear,
Eve'rything false will disappear.
Silently now I wait for Thee,
Ready, my God, Thy will to see;
Open my <u>ears</u> – illumine me, Spirit divine!

Open my mouth, and let me bear
Gladly the warm truth ev'ry-where;
Open my heart and let me prepare
Love with Thy children thus to share.
Silently now I wait for Thee,
Ready, my God, Thy will to see;
Open my <u>heart</u> – illumine me, Spirit divine!

SEPTEMBER 17

TO PLEASE GOD

Psalms 19:14
Let the words of my mouth, and the meditation of my heart, be acceptable in Thy sight, O Lord, my strength, and my redeemer.

King David was right - let this be our prayer today.
As believers, we desire to love the Lord with all our heart, soul, and strength; but if we are being true to ourselves, we fall short. Therefore, we are called to pray for God's help and guidance throughout our day. We cannot please God without His help and the help of His Holy Spirit.

Psalms 40:8
I delight to do Thy will, O my God: yea, Thy law is within my heart.

Proverbs 12:2
A good man obtaineth favour of the Lord: but a man of wicked devices will He condemn.

Mark 12:33
And to love Him with all the heart, and with all the understanding, and with all the soul, and with all the strength, and to love his neighbour as himself, is more than all whole burnt offerings and sacrifices.

Romans 8:6 - 8
For to be carnally minded is death; <u>but to be spiritually minded is life and peace</u>. Because the carnal mind is enmity against God: for it is not subject to the law of God, neither indeed can be. So then <u>they that are in the flesh cannot please God</u>.

Romans 12:2
And be not conformed to this world: but be ye transformed by the renewing of your mind, that ye may prove what is that good, and acceptable, and perfect, will of God.

SEPTEMBER 18

HUMILITY

There are many positive and negative adjectives and nouns associated with the word HUMILITY. The list touches many areas of our lives where we need to be humble and guard against being proud: awe, beauty, compassion, conceit, conversion, dependence, desires, envy, forgiveness, gentleness, giving, heart, learning, mind, money, patience, pride, righteousness, selfishness, servant, strength, sympathy, understanding, wisdom, etc.

Philippians 2:3
Let nothing be done through strife or vainglory; but in lowliness of mind let each esteem other better than themselves.

Romans 12:16
Be of the same mind one toward another. Mind not high things, but condescend to men of low estate. Be not wise in your own conceits.

1 Peter 3:8
Finally, be ye all of one mind, having compassion one of another, love as brethren, be pitiful, be courteous.

Galatians 5:13
For, brethren, ye have been called unto liberty; only use not liberty for an occasion to the flesh, but by love serve one another.

Ephesians 4:2
With all lowliness and meekness, with longsuffering, forbearing one another in love.

John 3:30
He must increase, but I must decrease.

SEPTEMBER 19

WHEN YOU PRAY

The disciples saw Jesus praying to His Heavenly Father often and then they had enough courage to ask Him to teach them to pray. As He did, we too, as His disciples can learn from this:

<u>Matthew 6:9 - 15</u>
After this manner therefore pray ye: Our Father which art in heaven, Hallowed be Thy name. Thy kingdom come. Thy will be done in earth, as it is in heaven. Give us this day our daily bread. And forgive us our debts, as we forgive our debtors. And lead us not into temptation, but deliver us from evil: For Thine is the kingdom, and the power, and the glory, for ever. Amen. For if ye forgive men their trespasses, your heavenly Father will also forgive you: But if ye forgive not men their trespasses, neither will your Father forgive your trespasses.

Throughout scripture, many specifics and examples of prayers are given to us. Praying is like talking to a dear, dear friend:

<u>John 15:16</u>
Ye have not chosen Me, but I have chosen you, and ordained you, that ye should go and bring forth fruit, and that your fruit should remain: that whatsoever ye shall ask of the Father in My name, He may give it you.

<u>Matthew 6:5</u>
And <u>when thou prayest</u>, thou shalt not be as the hypocrites are: for they love to pray standing in the synagogues and in the corners of the streets, that they may be seen of men. Verily I say unto you, They have their reward.

<u>Matthew 6:6, 7a</u>
But thou, <u>when thou prayest</u>, enter into thy closet, and when thou hast shut thy door, pray to thy Father which is in secret; and thy Father which seeth in secret shall reward thee openly. But when ye pray, use not vain repetitions . . .

SEPTEMBER 20

"JESUS THE VERY THOUGHT OF THEE"
Attributed to Bernard of Clairvaux (1091 – 1153)

JESUS, the very thought of Thee
with sweetness fills my breast;
But sweeter far Thy face to see
and in Thy presence rest.

Nor voice can sing, nor heart can frame,
nor can the mem'ry find
A sweeter sound than Thy blest Name,
O SAVIOR of mankind.

O hope of ev'ry contrite heart,
O joy of all the meek,
To those who fall how kind Thou are!
How good to those who seek!

But what to those who find?
Ah, this Nor tongue nor pen can show –
The love of JESUS, what it is,
None but His loved ones know.

JESUS, our only joy be Thou,
As Thou our prize wilt be;
JESUS, be Thou our glory now
And thru eternity.

SEPTEMBER 21

VOCABULARY

The word "Christian<u>ese</u>" has been coined to explain we should be cautious not to use words others may not be familiar with. I have heard terms in church I did not understand also, but I still wanted to hear and know them so that I would not be ignorant or mis-informed.

All subjects have their own vocabulary to present the concepts contained in each field of study. As a believer, I need to know God's vocabulary to facilitate my understanding of Biblical concepts.

As with any subject, look up any unknown words in the dictionary or in a concordance. The Holy Spirit is always there to guide you into knowledge of the truth.

<u>John 14:26</u>
But the Comforter, which is the Holy Ghost, Whom the Father will send in My Name, He shall teach you all things, and bring all things to your remembrance, whatsoever I have said unto you.

What a beautiful promise from Jesus, before He ascended up to Heaven.

Below is a partial list of "Christian<u>ese</u>" to be familiar with in a handy chart.

"Christian*ese*"

Abomination	Constraineth	Ordained Partaker
Abundant life	Conversation - life style	Quench not the Holy Spirit
Acceptable unto God	Disciple	Perverse
Access to God by faith	Disobedient	Predestinate
Admonitions	Edify	Priesthood, ye are
Adoption – as sons of God	Elect – Election	Propitiation, for our sins
Adversary - the devil	Equal with God	Ransom for us all
Advocate with the Father	Faultless	Recompense
Affliction - endure	Fervent in Spirit	Redeem/Redemption
Age to come	Flesh	Redeemer
Alienated, through ignorance	Foreknown	Reconciliation
Alive for evermore	Fornication	Regeneration
Ambassador for Christ	Foundation	Remission
Anointed – with oil	Godliness	Renew, day by day
Armour - of God	Glorify	Repent
Assurance	Grace, unmerited	Sanctify
Begotten	Grounded	Save to the uttermost
Blameless	Grow in grace	Sheep of His pasture
Bought with a price	Guilty before God	REVELATION of Jesus Christ
Carnal	Harden not your heart	Righteousness
Chasten	Haughty	Shepherd
Christian	Heaven	Sinner, all have sinned
Church of God	Hell	Supplication
Comforter – Holy Ghost	Holiness	Transgression, blotted out
Communion – of Christ	Humility	Trespass
Condemnation	Live in the flesh	Tribulation
Confess our sins	Immortality	Unblameable in holiness
Conform - to His image	Infallible	Undefiled before God
Contrite heart	Iniquity	Ungodly
	Intercession	Unmovable, steadfast
	Justified	Unrighteousness
	Kingdom of God	Unsearchable are His . . .
	Mediator, Jesus Christ	Vengeance
	Mysteries of God	Victory
		Yoke

SEPTEMBER 22

THE CROSS

<u>Galatians 6:14a</u>
But God forbid that I should glory, save in the cross of our Lord Jesus Christ. . .

These words of Paul to the Galatians should be our resolve, too. When we wake up every day, there it is – "the world" - ever changing and ever the more in despair. Yet we are enticed with its pleasures: radio, television, movies, computers, parties, etc. I wear a cross on a chain around my neck, as many of us do, but when thinking back, not one person has asked me what it means to me. I began to ask myself why, and <u>why do I wear it</u>? My cross is a visual reminder to me of what Christ did for me and the whole world. His salvation makes the cross (anywhere) beautiful to me. He is Risen! He dwells . . . in my heart!

<u>Luke 9:23b</u>
If any man will come after Me, let him deny himself, and take up his cross daily, and follow Me.

<u>Colossians 1:18b – 20a</u>
. . . that in all things He might have the preeminence. For it pleased the Father that in Him should all fulness dwell; And, having made peace through the blood of His cross, by Him to reconcile all things unto Himself . . .

<u>Hebrews 12:2 - 4</u>
Looking unto Jesus the Author and Finisher of our faith; Who for the joy that was set before Him <u>endured the cross</u>, <u>despising the shame</u>, and is set down at the right hand of the throne of God. For consider Him that endured such contradiction of sinners against Himself, lest ye be wearied and faint in your minds. Ye have not yet resisted unto blood, striving against sin.

SEPTEMBER 23

OBEDIENCE

We can easily see the difference between anew-born babe and a two-year old. Obedience came easy for us before the age of two. Then came what is commonly called the "terrible twos"; days with tantrums, attitudes, and "NO!" Fortunately, some babies wait a little longer.

We all express our own will and want our own way. God created us with this will to choose. Just like Adam and Eve, we often choose wrong and disobeyed God.

Genesis 2:17
But of the tree of the knowledge of good and evil, thou shalt not eat of it: for in the day that thou eatest thereof thou shalt surely die.

This is a picture of what can happen to us. To remedy this bent, God sent Jesus to **pay** for all our sin, which we could never do for ourselves!

Romans 6:23
For the wages of sin is death; but the gift of God is eternal life through Jesus Christ our Lord.

Acts 5:29
Then Peter and the other apostles answered and said, We ought to obey God rather than men.

Romans 6:12, 16
Let not sin therefore reign in your mortal body, that ye should obey it in the lusts thereof. Know ye not, that to whom ye yield yourselves servants to obey, his servants ye are to whom ye obey; whether of sin unto death, or of obedience unto righteousness?

SEPTEMBER 24

SPEAKING GOD'S WORD

After Jesus' baptism, He was led by the Spirit into the wilderness for forty days and forty nights to prepare for His ministry.

Matthew 4:1 - 4
Then was Jesus led up of the Spirit into the wilderness to be tempted of the devil. And when He had fasted forty days and forty nights, He was afterward an hungred. And when the tempter came to Him, he said, If Thou be the Son of God, command that these stones be made bread. But He (Jesus) answered and said, It is written, (Deuteronomy 8:3) *Man shall not live by bread alone, but by every word that proceedeth out of the mouth of God.*

As He was tempted, Jesus continued to quote Scripture to Satan and stood up to him in the end, saying:

Matthew 4:10, 11:
Then saith Jesus unto him, Get thee hence, Satan: for it is written, (Deuteronomy 6:13) *Thou shalt worship the Lord thy God, and Him only shalt thou serve. Then the devil leaveth Him, and, behold, angels came and ministered unto Him.*

This is an example of how to defeat Satan whenever he tries to tempt us, by calling on God's Holy Spirit to help us in our time of need. Since the whole "Bible" was not written at the time of Jesus, He quoted the Old Testament, which is as important today as it was in His time.

Psalms 91:1 - 3
He that dwelleth in the secret place of the most High shall abide under the shadow of the Almighty. I will say of the Lord, He is my refuge and my fortress: my God; in Him will I trust. Surely He shall deliver thee from the snare of the fowler, and from the noisome pestilence.

SEPTEMBER 25

YOUR IDOL: YOURSELF?

Ask yourself – what is my "idol" (anything we place before God)? God has commanded unconditional loyalty since ancient times in the Old Testament; still true for us today. You may not worship an idol of silver and gold but you might be making an idol of a <u>material goal</u> to attain your own comfort and pleasure. Your idol? <u>Self</u> – what I want!

<u>Deuteronomy 6:5</u>
And thou shalt love the Lord thy God with all thine heart, and with all thy soul, and with all thy might.

<u>Deuteronomy 29:17</u>
And ye have seen their abominations, and their idols, wood and stone, silver and gold, which were among them:

<u>Leviticus 19:4</u>
Turn ye not unto idols, nor make to yourselves molten gods: I am the Lord your God.

<u>I Chronicles 16:25, 26</u>
For great is the Lord, and greatly to be praised: He also is to be feared above all gods. For all the gods of the people are idols: but the Lord made the heavens.

<u>Galatians 5:16, 17</u>
. . . Walk in the Spirit, and ye shall not fulfil the lust of the flesh. For the flesh lusteth against the Spirit, and the Spirit against the flesh: and these are contrary the one to the other: so that ye cannot do the things that ye would.

<u>I John 5:21</u>
<u>*Little children, keep yourselves from idols. Amen.*</u>

SEPTEMBER 26

AS BABES

Sometimes we as adults miss God's attributes of love, grace, power, mercy, etc. So, He revealed many things to "babes" since they are the picture of ones open and willing to follow in the steps of the Jesus. God uses "born again," as a symbol of birth of the "new life" in Him.

John 3:7
Marvel not that I said unto thee, Ye must be born again.

Matthew 11:25
At that time Jesus answered and said, I thank Thee, O Father, Lord of heaven and earth, because Thou hast hid these things from the wise and prudent, and hast revealed them unto babes.

Matthew 21:16
And said unto Him, Hearest Thou what these say? And Jesus saith unto them, Yea; have ye never read (Psalms 8:2), *Out of the mouth of babes and sucklings Thou hast perfected praise?*

Luke 18:16
Verily I say unto you, Whosoever shall not receive the kingdom of God as a little child shall in no wise enter therein.

Luke 10:21
. . . Jesus rejoiced in spirit, and said, I thank Thee, O Father, Lord of heaven and earth, that Thou hast hid these things from the wise and prudent, and hast revealed them unto babes: even so, Father; for so it seemed good in Thy sight.

I Corinthians 3:1 - 3
And I, brethren, could not speak unto you as unto spiritual, but as unto carnal, even as unto babes in Christ. I have fed you with milk, and not with meat: for hitherto ye were not able to bear it, neither yet now are ye able. For ye are yet carnal: for whereas there is among you envying, and strife, and divisions, are ye not carnal, and walk as men?

SEPTEMBER 27

SURELY

While I was thinking and asking for guidance on what to write and search for today, the word "surely" came to my mind from Psalms 23:6. My husband and I tease each other about this word by calling it "Shirley"! Then we add "Goodness", and "Mercy" . . . *shall follow me all the days of my life and I shall dwell in the house of the Lord forever!* What a wonderful promise from God. These three "people" ("Shirley," Goodness, and Mercy) follow us every day by the power of God Himself! Surely = you can be sure of God's love, absolutely!

Genesis 2:17; 3:4
But of the tree of the knowledge of good and evil, thou shalt not eat of it: for in the day that thou eatest thereof thou shalt surely die. And the serpent said unto the woman, Ye shall not surely die:

Psalms 140:13
Surely the righteous shall give thanks unto Thy name: the upright shall dwell in Thy presence.

Isaiah 53:4, 5
Surely He hath borne our griefs, and carried our sorrows: yet we did esteem Him stricken, smitten of God, and afflicted. But He was wounded for our transgressions, He was bruised for our iniquities: the chastisement of our peace was upon Him; and with His stripes we are healed.

John 17:8
For I have given unto them the words which Thou gavest Me; and they have received them, and have known surely that I came out from Thee, and they have believed that Thou didst send Me

Hebrews 6:19a
Which hope we have as <u>an anchor of the soul, both sure and stedfast</u>

SEPTEMBER 28

JESUS, THE MAN

What can I say? The scriptures testify of Jesus Christ, the Son of Man. His words and miracles also testify of Him. Jesus was conceived by the Holy Spirit and born of a virgin. No other person has ever claimed or could claim this. He was born, lived a perfect life, was crucified, resurrected, and ascended to heaven as our **Savior**, **Advocate**, and **Mediator** between God and mankind.

Matthew 1:18
Now the birth of Jesus Christ was on this wise: When as His Mother Mary was espoused to Joseph, before they came together, she was found with child of the Holy Ghost.

Mathew 8:20
And Jesus saith unto him, The foxes have holes, and the birds of the air have nests; but the Son of man hath not where to lay His head.

I Timothy 2:5, 6
For there is One God, and One Mediator between God and men, the man Christ Jesus; Who gave Himself a ransom for all, to be testified in due time.

Isaiah 53:1 - 5
. . . Whom is the arm of the Lord revealed? For He (Jesus) shall grow up before Him (God) as a tender plant, and as a root out of a dry ground: He hath no form nor comeliness; and when we shall see Him, there is no beauty that we should desire Him. <u>He is despised and rejected of men; a man of sorrows, and acquainted with grief:</u> and we hid as it were our faces from Him; He was despised, and we esteemed Him not. Surely He hath borne our griefs, and carried our sorrows: yet we did esteem Him stricken, smitten of God, and afflicted. But He was wounded for <u>our</u> transgressions, He was bruised for <u>our</u> iniquities . . .

SEPTEMBER 29

... in that Day

This phrase is used in both the Old and New Testaments. God not only prophesied of the coming of Christ the Messiah, He also warned us of His judgment when He comes again to set up His Kingdom. His warnings, power and mercy are sprinkled everywhere we read in scripture. Unless we heed these warnings, we cannot accept His mercy and grace. God's first command and warning to mankind, is found in the first few chapters of Genesis. Here we can see the result of mankind's disobedience that affects all of us to this day.

Genesis 2:16, 17
And the Lord God commanded the man, saying, Of every tree of the garden thou mayest freely eat: But of the tree of the knowledge of good and evil, thou shalt not eat of it: for in the day that thou eatest thereof thou shalt surely die.

Isaiah 2:11
The lofty looks of man shall be humbled, and the haughtiness of men shall be bowed down, and the Lord alone shall be exalted in that day

II Timothy 1:18a
The Lord grant unto him that he may find mercy of the Lord in that day:

Matthew 12:36, 37
But I say unto you, That every idle word that men shall speak, they shall give account thereof in the day of judgment. For by thy words thou shalt be justified, and by thy words thou shalt be condemned.

Philippians 1:6
Being confident of this very thing, that He which hath begun a good work in you will perform it until the day of Jesus Christ:

SEPTEMBER 30

THE KING OF LOVE MY SHEPHERD IS
By Henry W. Baker (1821-1877)

Shepherd with sheep has always been the illustration I have understood and cherished since my childhood. The Good Shepherd that laid down His life for the lost sheep – <u>me</u>! He sought me and found me! I do not understand but believe with all my heart. I am His and is mine forever!
Thank you, Dear Lord! I am forever grateful!

"The king of love my Shepherd is"
Whose goodness faileth never;
I nothing lack if I am His
And He is mine forever

Where streams of living water flow
My ransomed soul He leadeth,
And, where the verdant pastures grow,
With food celestial feedeth.

Perverse And foolish oft I strayed,
But yet I love He sought me,
And on His shoulder gently laid,
And home rejoicing brought me.

In death's dark vale I fear no ill
With Thee, dear Lord, beside me;
Thy rod and staff my comfort still,
Thy cross before to guide me.

And so thru all the length of days
Thy goodness faileth never:
Good Shepherd, may I sing Thy praise
Within Thy house forever.

OCTOBER

CHAOS

I Corinthians 14:33
For God is not the author of confusion, but of peace, as in all churches of the saints.

OCTOBER 1

WAIT ON THE LORD

Waiting on the Lord can be so hard! Especially when some say you aren't doing enough to make things happen. But God commands us to wait on Him and promises to give us strength.

<u>Psalms 27:14</u>
Wait on the Lord: be of good courage, and He shall strengthen thine heart: wait, I say, on the Lord.

You see, waiting takes courage, and courage takes faith! Look for all the good the Lord is doing while you are waiting. His word says that He is good unto them that wait and seek Him:

<u>Lamentations 3:25, 26</u>
The Lord is good unto them that wait for Him, to the soul that seeketh Him. It is good that a man should both hope and quietly wait for the salvation of the Lord.

So be encouraged today while you wait on Him – He knows and hears as He is working in the background for your good and putting together His plan for your life.

<u>Psalms 25:5, 21, 22</u>
Lead me in Thy truth, and teach me: for Thou art the God of my salvation; on Thee do I wait all the day. O keep my soul, and deliver me: let me not be ashamed; for I put my trust in Thee. Let integrity and uprightness preserve me; for I wait on Thee.

<u>Isaiah 40:31</u>
But they that wait upon the Lord shall renew their strength; they shall mount up with wings as eagles; they shall run, and not be weary; and they shall walk, and not faint.

<u>Micah 7:7</u>
Therefore I will look unto the Lord; I will wait for the God of my salvation: my God will hear me.

OCTOBER 2

JESUS CALLED

In the Old Testament, we learn God called people audibly to do His work. God can do anything. We don't hear about it often but it can happen. We know Jesus "called" many to do His work in the New Testament. Therefore, we should be careful and available to hear God's still small voice through His Holy Spirit, and do what He wants us to do.

Mark 3:13
And He goeth up into a mountain, and <u>calleth</u> unto Him whom He would: and they came unto Him.

I Samuel 3:4
That the Lord <u>called</u> Samuel: and he answered, Here am I.

Matthew 10:1 - 4
And when He had <u>called</u> unto Him His twelve disciples, He gave them power against unclean spirits, to cast them out, and to heal all manner of sickness and all manner of disease. <u>Now the names of the twelve apostles are these</u>; The first, Simon, who is called Peter, and Andrew his brother; James the son of Zebedee, and John his brother; Philip, and Bartholomew; Thomas, and Matthew the publican; James the son of Alphaeus, and Lebbaeus, whose surname was Thaddaeus; Simon the Canaanite, and Judas Iscariot, who also betrayed Him.

I Timothy 6:12
Fight the good fight of faith, lay hold on eternal life, whereunto thou art also <u>called</u>, and hast professed a good profession before many witnesses.

I Peter 2:21
For even hereunto were ye <u>called</u>: because Christ also suffered for us, leaving us an example, that ye should follow His steps:

OCTOBER 3

"PRECIOUS" THINGS OF GOD

<u>Psalms 139:17, 18</u>
How <u>precious</u> also are Thy thoughts unto me, O God! how great is the sum of them! If I should count them, they are more in number than the sand: when I awake, I am still with Thee.

We are reminded to count our blessings over and over again, but I never thought to count the "PRECIOUS" things of God! The verse above states they are "more in number than the sand." Scripture tells us only some of them since it would be impossible to list them all. Read the small list below and have peace for today; remembering the Lord God is the same yesterday, today and forever.

<u>Psalms 49:8</u>
For the redemption of their soul is <u>precious</u>

<u>Psalms 49:6 - 8</u>
They that trust in their wealth, and boast themselves in the multitude of their riches; None of them can by any means redeem his brother, nor give to God a ransom for him: For the redemption of their soul is <u>precious</u>

<u>I Peter 1:19, 20</u>
But with the <u>precious</u> blood of Christ, as of a lamb without blemish and without spot: Who verily was foreordained before the foundation of the world, but was manifest in these last times for you who through Him are believers in God. . . so that your faith and hope are in God.

<u>II Peter 1:4</u>
Whereby are given unto us exceeding great and <u>precious</u> promises: that by these ye might be partakers of the divine nature, having escaped the corruption that is in the world through lust.

OCTOBER 4

A SWORD FOR THE LORD

We see Gideon took the sword of the Lord with him into battle. This is an example for us to take God's Word with us as we go through life.

Judges 7:20
And the three companies blew the trumpets, . . . and they cried, <u>The sword of the Lord</u>, and of Gideon.

Scripture describes the Bible as being <u>sharper than any</u> *"two edged SWORD."*

Hebrews 4:12
For the Word of God is quick, and powerful, and sharper than any two-edged sword, piercing even to the dividing asunder of soul and spirit, and of the joints and marrow, and is a discerner of the thoughts and intents of the heart.

Since the "sword" is so valuable to our Spiritual safety, why do we leave it at home as we face each day? True, we should know it so well, even by memory so the Holy Spirit can bring it to our mind and guide us in all truth, as needed. But just as Gideon had a physical sword we too can take our physical Bible everywhere we go. We are privileged to search God's Word for wisdom about any problem or question.

John 1:14
And the Word was made flesh, and dwelt among us, (and we beheld His glory, the glory as of the only begotten of the Father), full of grace and truth.

John 16:13
When the Spirit of truth comes, He will <u>guide you into all the truth</u>, for He will not speak on His own authority, but whatever He hears He will speak, and He will declare to you the things that are to come.

John 17:17
Sanctify them through Thy truth: Thy Word is truth.

OCTOBER 5

ALL MEN

God is gracious to "All Men"! Beginning with Adam and Eve He yearned for fellowship with all mankind, desiring that none of us perish. This longing resulted in a way for us (the world – mankind) to come back to Him, as seen in:

<u>John 3:16</u>
For God so loved the world, that He gave His only begotten Son, that whosoever (your name, my name) believeth in Him should not perish, but have everlasting life.

Throughout Scripture God has shown His love and power to bring <u>all</u> of us back to Him. There is a warning of consequence to <u>all</u> that do not heed His Word.

<u>John 5:23, 24</u>
That <u>all men</u> should honour the Son, even as they honour the Father. He that honoureth not the Son honoureth not the Father which hath sent Him. Verily, verily, I say unto you, He that heareth My word, and believeth on Him that sent Me, hath everlasting life, and shall not come into condemnation; but is passed from death unto life.

<u>Acts 1:24</u>
And they prayed, and said, Thou, Lord, which knowest the hearts of <u>all</u> . . .

<u>Romans 5:18, 19</u>
Therefore as by the offence of one (Adam) judgment came upon <u>all men</u> to condemnation; even so by the righteousness of One (Jesus) the free gift came upon <u>all men</u> unto justification of life. For as by one man's disobedience(Adam) many were made sinners, so by the obedience of One (Jesus) shall many be made righteous.

<u>John 1:7</u>
He (John the Baptist) came as a witness, to bear witness about the light, that all might believe through Him.

OCTOBER 6

"HIS EYE IS ON THE SPARROW"

HYMN Public Domaine

Why should I feel discouraged,
Why should the shadows come,
Why should my heart be lonely,
And long for heav'n and home,
When Jesus is my portion?
My constant friend is He:
His eye is on the sparrow,
And I know He watches me;
His eye is on the sparrow,
And I know He watches me.

CHROUS
I sing because I'm happy,
I sing because I'm free,
For His eye is on the sparrow,
And I know He watches me.

Let not your heart be troubled,
His tender word I hear,
And resting on His goodness,
I lose my doubts and fears;
Though by the path He leadeth,
But one step I may see;
His eye is on the sparrow,
And I know He watches me.

Whenever I am tempted,
Whenever clouds arise,
When song gives place to sighing,
When hope within me dies,
I draw the closer to Him,
From care He sets me free;
His eye is on the sparrow,
And I know He watches me;
His eye is on the sparrow,
And I know He watches me.

OCTOBER 7

FOR OUR HOPE
SUSTAINING COMFORT

Psalms 119:49, 50
Remember the word unto Thy servant, upon which Thou hast caused me to hope. This is my comfort in my affliction: for Thy Word hath quickened me.

Who is there that we can turn to in times of fear and loss?

The disciples knew that Jesus was the Christ and there was no one else. Jesus is the Son of the living God on Whom we can trust for all our needs – our hope! Like the disciples, we can believe with all our heart, soul, mind, and strength.

John 6:68, 69
Then Simon Peter answered Him, Lord, to whom shall we go? Thou hast the words of eternal life. And we believe and are sure that Thou art that Christ, the Son of the living God.

Psalms 71:5
For Thou art my hope, O Lord God: Thou art my trust from my youth.

Romans 15:4
For whatsoever things were written aforetime were written for our learning, that we through patience and comfort of the scriptures might have hope.

Romans 5:2
By Whom also we have access by faith into this grace wherein we stand, and rejoice in hope of the glory of God.

II Corinthians 1:3, 4
Blessed be God, even the Father of our Lord Jesus Christ, the Father of mercies, and the God of all comfort; Who comforteth us in all our tribulation, that we may be able to comfort them which are in any trouble

OCTOBER 8

EVEN AS HE WALKED

I John 2:6
He that saith he abideth in Him ought himself also so to <u>walk, even as He walked</u>.

Again, we have a choice to make. It is written in Jeremiah 6, the terrible stubborn choice the people made that cost them dearly. Look it up and see the consequences of their decision - not a pretty picture!

Jeremiah 6:16
Thus saith the Lord, Stand ye in the ways, and see, and ask for the old paths, where is the good way, and <u>walk therein</u>, and ye shall find rest for your souls. But they said, <u>We will not walk therein</u>.

Galatians 2:20
I am crucified with Christ: nevertheless I live; yet not I, but Christ liveth in me: and the life which I now live in the flesh I live by the faith of the Son of God, Who loved me, and gave Himself for me.

Ephesians 2:2, 4, 5
Wherein in time past ye walked according to the course of this world, according to the prince of the power of the air, the spirit that now worketh in the children of disobedience: But God, who is rich in mercy, for His great love wherewith He loved us, Even when we were dead in sins, hath quickened us together with Christ, (by grace ye are saved)

Colossians 3:3 - 5, 8
For ye are dead, and your life is hid with Christ in God. But now ye also put off all these; . . . seeing that ye have put off the old man with his deeds; . . . And have put on the new man.

I Peter 4:2 - 5
That he no longer should live the rest of his time in the flesh to the lusts of men, but to the will of God.

OCTOBER 9

TO AND FRO

II Chronicles 16:9
For the eyes of the Lord <u>run To and FRO</u> throughout the whole earth, to shew Himself strong in the behalf of them whose heart is perfect toward Him. Herein thou hast done foolishly: therefore, from henceforth thou shalt have wars.

Since I have known the first half of this verse existed, I have had the desire, "yes, find me Lord." I truly want my heart to be perfect toward Him and that is only possible through accepting His dear Son as my Savior. So, I am confident He sees and cares for me now and for all eternity. This is my hope for my children, and their children, and their children. See below how others run To and FRO in the scriptures. We are all searching for something.

Job 1:7, 8
And the Lord said unto Satan, Whence comest thou? Then Satan answered the Lord, and said, From going to and fro in the earth, and from walking up and down in it. And the Lord said unto Satan, Hast thou considered my servant Job, that there is none like him in the earth, a perfect and an upright man, one that feareth God, and escheweth evil?

Psalms 107:27
They reel to and fro, and stagger like a drunken man, and are at their wits' end. Then they cry unto the Lord in their trouble, and He bringeth them out of their distresses.

Proverbs 21:6
The getting of treasures by a lying tongue is a vanity tossed to and fro of them that seek death.

Ephesians 4:14
That we henceforth be no more children, tossed TO and FRO, and carried about with every wind of doctrine, by the sleight of men, and cunning craftiness, whereby they lie in wait to deceive;

OCTOBER 10

BE SEPARATE

II Corinthians 6:17, 18
Wherefore come out from among them, and <u>be ye separate</u>, saith the Lord, and touch not the unclean thing; and I will receive you, And will be a Father unto you, and ye shall be My sons and daughters, saith the Lord Almighty.

Looking back many times over the years, I regret that I didn't always remember one of my childhood Sunday School songs, and the true story of Daniel, that encouraged me then. But it can encourage us today to be strong and separate from worldly temptations.

Daniel 1:5, 8, 9
. . . bring certain of the children of Israel, and of the king's seed, and of the princes; Children in whom was no blemish, but well favoured, and skilful in all wisdom, and cunning in knowledge, and understanding science, and such as had ability in them to stand in the king's palace, and whom they might teach the learning and the tongue of the Chaldeans. <u>But Daniel purposed in his heart that he would not defile himself</u> with the portion of the king"s meat, nor with the wine which he drank: therefore he requested of the prince of the eunuchs that he might not defile himself. Now God had brought Daniel into favour and tender love with the prince of the eunuchs.

"DARE TO BE A DANIEL"
by P. P. Bliss (1838-1876)
*Standing by a purpose true,
heeding God's command,
Honor them, the faithful few!
All hail to Daniel's Band!*

Refrain
Dare to be a Daniel,
dare to stand alone!
Dare to have a purpose firm!
Dare to make it known.

OCTOBER 11

CALLED "CHRISTIANS"

ACTS 11:26
And when he (Barnabas) had found him (Paul) he brought him unto Antioch. And it came to pass, that a whole year they assembled themselves with the church, and taught much people. And the disciples were <u>called Christians</u> first in Antioch.

To many, being called a Christian costs them their lives. These we call martyrs. Today our world has gone frantic in doing this deed. It is not new, however, for we learn about **Stephen**, the first Christian **Martyr**, who while preaching the Gospel of Christ, was stoned to death. There have been many millions who followed! Read about some of them that Stephen preached in Jerusalem.

Acts 7:52 - 60
Which of the prophets have not your fathers persecuted? and they have slain them which shewed before of the coming of the Just One; of Whom ye have been now the betrayers and murderers: Who have received the law by the disposition of angels, and have not kept it.

When they heard these things, they were cut to the heart, and they gnashed on him with their teeth. But he (<u>Stephen</u>), being full of the Holy Ghost, looked up stedfastly into heaven, and saw the glory of God, and Jesus standing on the right hand of God, And said, Behold, I see the heavens opened, and the Son of man standing on the right hand of God. Then they cried out with a loud voice, and stopped their ears, and ran upon him with one accord, <u>And cast him out of the city, and stoned him</u>: and the witnesses laid down their clothes at a young man's feet, whose name was Saul. And they stoned Stephen, calling upon God, and saying, Lord Jesus, receive my spirit. And he kneeled down, and cried with a loud voice, Lord, lay not this sin to their charge. And when he had said this, he fell asleep.

OCTOBER 12

MICAH 7:18, 19

Who is a God like unto thee, that pardoneth iniquity, and passeth by the transgression of the remnant of His heritage? He retaineth not His anger for ever, because He delighteth in mercy. He will turn again, He will have compassion upon us; He will subdue our iniquities; and <u>Thou wilt cast all their sins into the depths of the sea</u>.

Oh my! Maybe that is why mankind cannot go down that far into the oceans. Not yet as far as I know! This is another question we can ask God when we see Him. He has told us that when He comes to set up His kingdom there will be no more seas.

<u>Revelation 21:1</u>
And I (John) saw a new heaven and a new earth: for the first heaven and the first earth were passed away; and <u>there was no more sea</u>.

His ways are always higher than our ways even though we love and enjoy the ocean. High prices are paid for even the privilege of living near a beach. This one thing I know, God pardons all our sins – past, present, and future, and remembers them no more. "<u>He delighteth in mercy</u>" His Word says so and He cannot lie!

<u>Psalms 103:12 - 14</u>
As far as the east is from the west, so far hath He removed our transgressions from us. Like as a father pitieth his children, so the Lord pitieth them that fear Him. For He knoweth our frame; He remembereth that we are dust.

<u>Isaiah 43:25</u>
I, even I, am He that blotteth out thy transgressions <u>for Mine own sake</u>, and will not remember thy sins.

<u>Hebrews 10 17</u>
And their sins and iniquities will I remember no more.

OCTOBER 13

<u>PICK – A – VERSE</u> (For Today)

There are stories about people that just open up their Bible at any place for an answer to their problem. I don't believe that is the way it always works. I believe the Holy Spirit leads us to all truth and that one needs to be in the Scripture and seek out what God wants us to know. It is a matter of our will to want to know what God wants to teach us. It may take a while to understand His promptings, that's where the "seek and find" comes in.

<u>Matthew 7:7 - 8</u>
Ask, and it shall be given you; seek, and ye shall find; knock, and it shall be opened unto you: For every one that asketh receiveth; and he that seeketh findeth; and to him that knocketh it shall be opened.

As you read and stop on a verse you can't quite understand, ask the Holy Spirit to help you throughout the day to know how to use it in your life – **a Verse for Today!** Below are a few of my favorites.

<u>Matthew 6:21</u>
For where your treasure is, there will your heart be also.

<u>Matthew 12:35, 36</u>
. . . for out of the abundance of the heart the mouth speaketh. A good man out of the good treasure of the heart bringeth forth good things:

<u>Luke 12:20, 21</u>
But God said unto him, Thou fool, this night thy soul shall be required of thee: then whose shall those things be, which thou hast provided? So is he that layeth up treasure for himself, and is not rich toward God.

<u>II Corinthians 4:7</u>
But we have this treasure in earthen vessels, that the excellency of the power may be of God, and not of us.

OCTOBER 14

O MAN . . .

What doth the Lord require of thee?

Deuteronomy 10:12
And now, Israel, what doth the Lord thy God require of thee, but to fear the Lord thy God, to walk in all His ways, and to love Him, and to serve the Lord thy God with all thy heart and with all thy soul,

Micah 6:8
He hath shewed thee, O man, what is good; and what doth the Lord require of thee, but to do justly, and to love mercy, and to walk humbly with thy God?

We all seem to want a list of rules to follow so we can feel worthy of our redemption. We are worthy through Christ alone! Christ in us provides the desire to follow after Him, not a list of do's or don'ts. However, as we continue to read His Word, we learn what pleases Him and cheerfully obey out of our love for Him.

Joshua 24:14, 15
Now therefore fear the Lord, and serve Him in sincerity and in truth: . . . serve ye the Lord. And if it seem evil unto you to serve the Lord, choose you this day whom ye will serve; whether the gods which your fathers served . . . or the gods of the Amorites, in whose land ye dwell: but as for me and my house, we will serve the Lord.

Psalms 100:2 - 5
Serve the Lord with gladness: come before His presence with singing. Know ye that the Lord He is God: it is He that hath made us, and not we ourselves; we are His people, and the sheep of His pasture. Enter into His gates with thanksgiving, and into His courts with praise: be thankful unto Him, and bless His name. For the Lord is good; His mercy is everlasting; and His truth endureth to all generations.

OCTOBER 15

GOD REVENGETH

Nahum 1:2
God is jealous, and the Lord revengeth; the Lord revengeth, and is furious; the Lord will take vengeance on His adversaries, and He reserveth wrath for His enemies.

Our first reaction to a wrong done to us is to get revenge. This is not God's way because He has taught us that "vengence" is His.

Romans 15:4
For whatsoever things were written aforetime were written for our learning, that we through patience and comfort of the scriptures might have hope.

Romans 12:19
Dearly beloved, avenge not yourselves, but rather give place unto wrath: for it is written, Vengeance is Mine; I will repay, saith the Lord.

This is one of the times we must wait for God's timing and we are called to forgive our enemies. God's timing is always right and we must trust Him to make things right; even if it means to wait for eternity.

Deuteronomy 32:35
To Me belongeth vengeance, and recompence; their foot shall slide in due time: for the day of their calamity is at hand, and the things that shall come upon them make haste.

Psalms 94:1-3
O Lord God, to Whom vengeance belongeth; O God, to Whom vengeance belongeth, shew Thyself. Lift up Thyself, Thou judge of the earth: render a reward to the proud. Lord, how long shall the wicked, how long shall the wicked triumph?

Hebrews 10:30
For we know Him that hath said, Vengeance belongeth unto Me, I will recompense, saith the Lord.

OCTOBER 16

BREAKFAST WITH JESUS

While reading *MORNING and EVENING*, Charles H. Spurgeon's devotional book; he used John 21:12 for his thoughts for the day: *"Come and have breakfast."* This was the third time that Jesus appeared to the apostles after His resurrection. They had fished all night and caught nothing – very interesting. Read about this event for your self - John 21:1 – 14. The thought that entered my mind was instead of doing all the "diets" I have tried over the years, I should dine with Jesus on the food that Jesus so freely prepares for me personally every day. He is the Bread of Life that satisfies our <u>every</u> hunger. Wanting the wrong physical foods will not quell our hunger and most often it is a spiritual hunger for a union with Jesus.

Next time you crave the wrong foods try some Spiritual food from God's Word and accept Jesus' invitation to "**dine**" with Him. "Breakfast" is a good way to start the day both physically and Spiritually.

<u>Luke 12:22, 23</u>
And He said unto His disciples, Therefore I say unto you, Take no thought for your life, what ye shall eat; neither for the body, what ye shall put on. The life is more than meat, and the body is more than raiment.

<u>Luke 22:19</u>
And He took bread, and gave thanks, and brake it, and gave unto them, saying, This is My body which is given for you: this do in remembrance of Me.

<u>John 6:27, 31</u>
Labour not for the meat which perisheth, but for that meat which endureth unto everlasting life, which the Son of man shall give unto you: for Him hath God the Father sealed. Our fathers did eat manna in the desert; as it is written, He gave them bread from heaven to eat.

OCTOBER 17

CHILDREN ARE BLESSINGS FROM GOD
"A full quiver"

Lo, children are an heritage of the Lord: and the fruit of the womb is His reward. As arrows are in the hand of a mighty man; so are children of the youth. Happy is the man that hath <u>his quiver full</u> of them: they shall not be ashamed, but they shall speak with the enemies in the gate (Psalms 127:3 – 5)

Have you seen or heard of the family on TV, with 19 children and counting? Now that's a "full quiver." In today's scheme of things, it has become popular and accepted, not to want any children or at the most, just one. These are two extremes! Which is correct? We are not to judge. All I know from God's Word is that children are gifts from Him; put into our hands to love, cherish, and nurture. Yes, while bringing up children we face trials and heartaches all along the way, that should cause us to remember God is with us and will help us. It is our responsibility to ask Him to come along beside us to the end. Let us count **OUR BLESSINGS** (our dear children).

Psalms 128:1, 3, 4, 6
Blessed is every one that feareth the Lord; that walketh in His ways. Thy wife shall be as a fruitful vine by the sides of thine house: thy children like olive plants round about thy table. Behold, that thus shall the man be blessed that feareth the Lord. Yea, thou shalt see thy children's children,

Proverbs 17:6
Children's children are the crown of old men; and the glory of children are their fathers.

Proverbs 23:24
The father of the righteous shall greatly rejoice: and he that begetteth a wise child shall have joy of him. Thy father and thy mother shall be glad, and she that bare thee shall rejoice.

OCTOBER 18

FEAR HAS COME UPON ME

<u>Psalms 56:3, 4</u>
What time I am afraid, I will <u>trust in Thee</u>. In God I will <u>praise His word</u>, in God I have put my trust; I will not fear

At times when our youngest child became afraid, her father comforted her by reminding her of this verse and to trust and know that God was right there with her. We all have "spells" of fear. They are usually things we imagine that don't even happen that we fear the most. We don't know what to do next and it causes us to fear and doubt, and believe that it is impossible to continue. We just want to quit whatever we are in the middle of. Where do we go? The Lord is there with us too, so let's turn to Him.

<u>Psalms 46:1, 2</u>
God is our refuge and strength, a very present help in trouble. Therefore will not we fear, though the earth be removed, and though the mountains be carried into the midst of the sea;

<u>Romans 8:15</u>
For ye have not received the spirit of bondage again to fear; but ye have received the Spirit of adoption, whereby we cry, Abba, Father.

<u>II Timothy 1:7</u>
For God hath not given us the spirit of fear; but of power, and of love, and of a sound mind.

<u>Hebrews 11:7</u>
By faith Noah, being warned of God of things not seen as yet, moved with fear, prepared an ark to the saving of his house; by the which he condemned the world, and became heir of the righteousness which is by faith.

<u>Hebrews 13:6</u>
So that we may boldly say, The Lord is my helper, and I will not fear what man shall do unto me.

OCTOBER 19

"TELL ME THE OLD, OLD STORY"

We can be reminded of our "first love" for Jesus through the songs and hymns we use to sing. We forget so much over the years, and we need nudges to remember every once and awhile. I hope you know this one and recall how much it meant to you, **"simply, as to a little child."** Read how it describes the wonderful story of Jesus and His love!

"TELL ME THE OLD, OLD STORY"
by A Catherine Hankey (1834-1911)

Tell me the old, old story of unseen things above,
Of Jesus and His glory, Of Jesus and His love.
Tell me the story simply, as to a little child,
For I am weak and weary,
And helpless and defiled

Chorus
Tell me the old, old story,
Tell me the old, old story,
Tell me the old, old story
Of Jesus and His love.

Tell me the story slowly, That I may take it in –
That wonderful redemption, God's remedy for sin.
Tell me the story often, For I forget so soon;
The early dew of morning
Has passed away at noon.

Tell me the story softly, With earnest tones and grave;
Remember, I'm the sinner Whom Jesus came to save.
Tell me the story always, If you would really be,
In any time of trouble,
A comforter to me.

Tell me the same old story When you have cause to fear
That this world's empty glory Is costing me too dear.
Yes, and when that world's glory Is dawning on my soul,
Tell me the old, old story:
'Christ Jesus makes thee whole.'

OCTOBER 20

WHO/WHAT IS YOUR GUIDE

GPS and maps come readily to mind when we think of guidance. We want to get to where we are going as quickly and easily as possible. As we have learned through experience, these systems are not always accurate, but the <u>voice</u> on the GPS sure sounds confident! If we are not alert <u>it</u> can lead us astray. Thankfully, we have the wisdom to know when we are going the wrong direction. So it is with the many voices in the world we hear all around us. We need to be choosy and wise about which ones we will heed. Thank Jesus He did not leave us "Comfortless," and sent His Spirit as our Guide. He keeps us on the right path when we follow His direction through life. Just think of it as a moment by moment map through the twist and turns of our daily journey. Follow Him today.

<u>Psalms 48:14</u>
For this God is our God for ever and ever: He will be our guide even unto death.

<u>Psalms 31:3</u>
For Thou art my rock and my fortress; therefore for Thy name's sake lead me, and guide me.

<u>Psalms 73:24 - 26</u>
Thou shalt guide me with Thy counsel, and afterward receive me to glory. Whom have I in heaven but Thee? and there is none upon earth that I desire beside Thee. My flesh and my heart faileth: but God is the strength of my heart, and my portion for ever.

<u>John 16:13</u>
Howbeit when He, the Spirit of truth, is come, He will guide you into all truth: for He shall not speak of Himself; but whatsoever He shall hear, that shall He speak: and He will shew you things to come.

OCTOBER 21

INSTRUMENTS OF PEACE

The whole world has clamored for peace since Cain killed Able. Now that's a long time. History has recorded periods of peace, but here and now the lack of peace is a problem for all of us. We ask ourselves – what can I do to bring about peace? Is it possible to be an Instrument of peace? Can one person really make a difference? I know the Prince of Peace is coming back again soon, but until He arrives with His judgment on evil, we must be His "Instruments of Peace" wherever we go. As individuals, we can stop <u>our</u> quarrels, envying's, strife's, prejudices, etc.; only through the Holy Spirit's power in our lives. And if or when we fail, we can ask God's forgiveness. Do not be discouraged – one moment at a time. Be aware! Satan is out seeking who he can destroy. But Jesus has called us Blessed! God is glorified through our weakness.

Matthew 5:9
Blessed are the <u>peacemakers</u>: for they shall be called the children of God.!

Romans 6:13
Neither yield ye your members as <u>instruments</u> of unrighteousness unto sin: but yield yourselves unto God, as those that are alive from the dead, and your members as <u>instruments</u> of righteousness unto God.

Psalms 34:14
Depart from evil, and do good; seek <u>peace</u>, and pursue it.

Isaiah 26:3
Thou wilt keep him in perfect <u>peace</u>, whose mind is stayed on Thee: because he trusteth in Thee.

Isaiah 32:17
And the work of <u>righteousness</u> shall be <u>peace</u>; and the effect of <u>righteousness</u> quietness and assurance for ever.

OCTOBER 22

OUR DELIVERER

What are we being delivered from?
Do we really need a Deliverer?
Some people are so confident, they believe they don't need any help. They forget we depend on many people for help (deliverance). We do not all have the same education, skills, health, etc. But the one thing <u>we all need</u> is deliverance from our sinful bent – our affinity to sin! They believe if they live a "good life," all will be okay. Unfortunately, it is to their peril.

<u>II Samuel 22:2, 3</u>
And he said, The Lord is my rock, and my fortress, and my deliverer; The God of my rock; in Him will I trust: He is my shield, and the horn of my salvation, my high tower, and my refuge, my Saviour; Thou savest me from violence.

<u>Psalms 40:17</u>
But I am poor and needy; yet the Lord thinketh upon me: Thou art my help and my Deliverer; make no tarrying, O my God.

<u>Ephesians 1:6, 7</u>
To the praise of the glory of His grace, wherein He hath made us accepted in the Beloved. In Whom we have redemption through His blood, the forgiveness of sins, according to the riches of His grace;

<u>Hebrews 4:16</u>
Let us therefore come boldly unto the throne of grace, that we may obtain mercy, and find grace to help in time of need.

<u>Romans 5:2</u>
*By whom also we have access by faith into this grace wherein we stand, and rejoice in hope of the glory of God. And not only so, but we glory in tribulations also: knowing that
tribulation worketh patience;*

OCTOBER 23

PITY PARTIES

No more "Pity Parties" - Whine no more! Look up in your Bible and read Isaiah 65:19-25. These verses describe the world **then** and **now**, but our hope and redemption has arrived in the shed blood of Jesus Christ on the cross! This is a time to rejoice and be thankful in Him no matter what our circumstance. But we still indulge ourselves in "Pity Parties." We keep wanting our own way, when instead we should keep our eyes on what we have in Christ and think about heaven; **THINK HEAVEN!** When you do, you can't help but **THINK of GOD**.

I can't wait to see my Savior's face!
Heaven is a wonderful place!

I can't even imagine it - when I will see Him face to face. But I believe it with all my heart. Check the list below of facts that we can know about **Heaven**

ON EARTH	IN HEAVEN
Sin	Sin defeated
Broken relationships	Victory (love/respect)
Poverty	Eternally secure (surplus)
Peril	We are in Heaven (safety)
Slander	Drink from the River of Life (no sin)
Famine	Eat from a tree that never withers
Fear	Immortality (forever peace)
Persecution	Blessedness (perfect Acceptance)
Pain	Forever with the Lord (no sorrow or grief)
Distress	In His fullness (perfection)
Death	Life eternal
Sadness	Joy forever more

OCTOBER 24

MERCY

Psalm 51 was written by King David, after Nathan the prophet confronted him about his affair with Bathsheba. This is David's sorrowful plea unto the Lord, after he had sinned, and was asking for God's mercy.

No matter how great or little our sins are, sin is sin, and we too need to confess it and ask for God's mercy and forgiveness. Read it, weep and repent.

Psalms 51:1 - 12
*Have mercy upon me, O God, according to Thy lovingkindness: according unto the multitude of Thy tender mercies blot out my transgressions.
Wash me throughly from mine iniquity, and cleanse me from my sin.
For I acknowledge my transgressions: and my sin is ever before me.
Against Thee, Thee only, have I sinned, and done this evil in Thy sight: that Thou mightest be justified when Thou speakest, and be clear when Thou judgest.
Behold, I was shapen in iniquity; and in sin did my mother conceive me.
Behold, Thou desirest truth in the inward parts: and in the hidden part Thou shalt make me to know wisdom.
Purge me with hyssop, and I shall be clean: wash me, and I shall be whiter than snow.
Make me to hear joy and gladness; that the bones which Thou hast broken may rejoice.
Hide Thy face from my sins, and blot out all mine iniquities.
Create in me a clean heart, O God; and renew a right spirit within me.
Cast me not away from Thy presence; and take not Thy Holy Spirit from me.
Restore unto me the joy of Thy salvation; and uphold me with Thy free spirit.*

OCTOBER 25

DECEPTION IS COMING
(It is here)

Strong deception has long over-run the world. We easily see its negative influence in our country, homes, churches, schools, etc. The scriptures have consistently warned us of this and other falsehoods. The Bible was TRUE then, and is TRUE today! So, be aware and don't be thrown by the world's deception. Accept and know the TRUTH of God and His word.

John 8:42, 44
Jesus said unto them, If God were your Father, ye would love Me: for I proceeded forth and came from God; neither came I of Myself, but He sent Me. . . . Ye are of your father the devil, and the lusts of your father ye will do. He was a murderer from the beginning, and abode not in the truth, because there is no truth in him.

II Peter 2:12 - 14
But these, as natural brute beasts, made to be taken and destroyed, speak evil of the things that they understand not; and shall utterly perish in their own corruption; And shall receive the reward of unrighteousness, as they that count it pleasure to riot in the day time. . . . deceivings while they feast with you; Having eyes full of adultery, and that cannot cease from sin; beguiling unstable souls: an heart they have exercised with covetous practices; cursed children.

Proverbs 8:6, 7
Hear; for I (wisdom) will speak of excellent things; and the opening of my lips shall be right things. For my mouth shall speak truth; and wickedness is an abomination to my lips.

I John 4:6
We are of God: he that knoweth God heareth us; he that is not of God heareth not us. Hereby know we the spirit of truth, and the spirit of error.

OCTOBER 26

"I MUST TELL JESUS"

It's time again to sing another song.
Out of my favorites, I've chosen **"I MUST TELL JESUS."**
The story, stored up in my memory about this hymn brings me to thoughts of my Father. As a new Christian, coming out of the Great Depression, he did have new struggles. This was one of his songs he often requested when the Church song leader asked the audience for a favorite. This was usually done in the Sunday evening services, which we always attended. I can see him singing it as his prayer to God for His help in his new life. **"Jesus can help me, Jesus alone."**

"I MUST TELL JESUS"
by E. A. Hoffman (1839-1929)

I must tell Jesus all of my trials,
I cannot bear these burdens alone;
In my distress He kindly will help me,
He ever loves and cares for His own

Chorus
I must tell Jesus! I must tell Jesus!
I cannot bear my burdens alone;
I must tell Jesus! I must tell Jesus!
Jesus can help me,
Jesus alone.

I must tell Jesus all of my troubles,
He is a kind, compassionate Friend;
If I but ask Him, He will deliver,
Make of my troubles quickly an end.

Tempted and tried, I need a great Savior,
One who can help my burdens to bear;
I must tell Jesus, I must tell Jesus,
He all my cares and sorrows will share.

OCTOBER 27

SO GREAT A SALVATION

There are so many verses showing us the way to Salvation and Eternal Life. By now anyone who has seen a football game on television, has seen John 3:16. In fact we teach this verse to our children at an early age. But there are many more to confirm our most favorite verse:

<u>John 3:16 - 19</u>
For God so loved the world, that He gave His only begotten Son, that whosoever believeth in Him should not perish, but have everlasting life. For God sent not His Son into the world to condemn the world; but that the world through Him might be saved.
He that believeth on Him is not condemned: but he that believeth not is condemned already, because he hath not believed in the Name of the only begotten Son of God. And this is the condemnation, that Light is come into the world, and men loved darkness rather than light, because their deeds were evil.

<u>Acts 4:12</u>
Neither is there salvation in any Other (the only begotten Son of God): for there is none other Name under heaven given among men, whereby we must be saved.

<u>Romans 1:16</u>
For I am not ashamed of the gospel of Christ: for it is the power of God unto salvation to every one that believeth; to the Jew first, and also to the Greek (Gentiles).

<u>Romans 10:9 - 11</u>
That if thou shalt confess with thy mouth the Lord Jesus, and shalt <u>believe</u> in thine heart that God hath raised Him from the dead, thou shalt be saved. For with the heart man believeth unto righteousness; and with the mouth <u>confession</u> is made unto <u>salvation</u>. For the scripture saith, Whosoever believeth on Him shall not be ashamed.

OCTOBER 28

"CYCLE OF SIN"

Have you recognized the "Cycle of Sin" that is taught to us in the Book of James? Simply, every man is tempted, but not of God. We are drawn away by our own lusts, then enticed. When we see something, we are tempted to indulge. We either do it or resist the temptation depending on our obedience to the Word of God. By giving in to our lust demands, sin is born, bringing forth death or terror. But thank God, He has provided a way of escape – repentance!

<u>I Corinthians 10:13</u>
There hath no temptation taken you but such as is common to man: but God is faithful, Who will not suffer you to be tempted above that ye are able; but will with the temptation also make a way to escape, that ye may be able to bear it.

<u>James 1:12 - 15</u>
Blessed is the man that endureth temptation: . . . Let no man say when he is tempted, I am tempted of God: . . . But every man is tempted, when he is drawn away of his own lust, and enticed. Then when lust hath conceived, it bringeth forth sin: and sin, when it is finished, bringeth forth death.

<u>Hebrews 4:15</u>
Seeing then that we have a great High Priest, that is passed into the heavens, Jesus the Son of God, let us hold fast our profession. For we have not an High Priest which cannot be touched with the feeling of our infirmities; but was in all points tempted like as we are, yet without sin. Let us therefore come boldly unto the throne of grace, that we may obtain mercy, and find grace to help in time of need.

<u>Matthew 26:41</u>
Watch and pray, that ye enter not into temptation: the spirit indeed is willing, but the flesh is weak.

OCTOBER 29

A FAITHFUL SAYING

To have a Faithful Saying, it must come from a **Faithful Witness**.

Proverbs 14:5
A _faithful_ witness will not lie: but a false witness will utter lies.

John 12:49, 50
For I (Jesus) have not spoken of Myself; but the Father which sent Me, He gave Me a commandment, what I should say, and what I should speak. And I know that His commandment is life everlasting: whatsoever I speak therefore, even as the Father said unto Me, so I speak.

Jeremiah 42:3,4, 5
That the Lord thy God may shew us the way wherein we may walk, and the thing that we may do. . . . behold, I (Jeremiah) will pray unto the Lord your God according to your words; and it shall come to pass, that whatsoever thing the Lord shall answer you, I will declare it unto you; I will keep nothing back from you. Then they said to Jeremiah, _The Lord be a true and faithful witness_ between us, if we do not even according to all things for the which the Lord Thy God shall send thee to us.

Romans 3:3, 4
For what if some did not believe? shall their unbelief make the faith of God without effect? God forbid: yea, let God be true, but every man a liar; as it is written, That Thou mightest be justified in Thy sayings, and mightest overcome when Thou art judged.

I Timothy 1:15
This is _a faithful saying_, and worthy of all acceptation, that Christ Jesus came into the world to save sinners; of whom I am chief.

Hebrews 10:23
Let us hold fast the profession of our faith without wavering; _(for He is faithful that promised;)_

OCTOBER 30

STAND FAST

As usual, our human trait often demands that we give up on some things we are doing, be it temporal or eternal. But scripture tells us bluntly to "Stand Fast" in our faith. It takes maturity and discipline not to bend with the wind or every doctrine. The best lie contains "little bit of truth," can easily lead us astray. Be aware!

Ephesians 4:14, 15
That we henceforth be no more children, tossed To and FRO, and carried about with every wind of doctrine, by the sleight of men, and cunning craftiness, whereby they lie in wait to deceive; But speaking the truth in love, may grow up into Him in all things, which is the head, even Christ:

Galatians 5:1
Stand fast therefore in the liberty wherewith Christ hath made us free, and be not entangled again with the yoke of bondage.

Psalm 111:8
The works of His hands are verity and judgment; all His commandments are sure. They stand fast for ever and ever, and are done in truth and uprightness.

I Corinthians 16:13
Watch ye, stand fast in the faith, quit you like men, be strong.

Philippians 1:27
Only let your conversation be as it becometh the gospel of Christ: that whether I come and see you, or else be absent, I may hear of your affairs, that ye stand fast in one spirit, with one mind striving together for the faith of the gospel;

Philippians 4:1
Therefore, my brethren dearly beloved and longed for, my joy and crown, so stand fast in the Lord, my dearly beloved.

OCTOBER 31

GOD'S MYSTERIES

Jeremiah 33:3
Call unto me, and I will answer thee, and shew thee great and mighty things, which thou knowest not.

What a promise from God to begin a new day! Do you believe it? How can you not? God cannot lie and those things we "see" that He has shared with us, prove Him to be telling the truth. For me, just looking at the sun's rise and set, tells it all. It happens every day, not by accident. God is Great!

Psalms 78:2, 3
Give ear, O My people, to My law: incline your ears to the words of My mouth. I will open My mouth in a parable: I will utter dark sayings of old: Which we have heard and known, and our fathers have told us.

Daniel 2:28, 47
But there is a God in heaven that revealeth secrets, and maketh known to the king Nebuchadnezzar <u>what shall be in the latter days</u>. Thy dream, and the visions of thy head upon thy bed, are these; The king answered unto Daniel, and said, Of a truth it is, that your God is a God of gods, and a Lord of kings, and a revealer of secrets, seeing thou couldest reveal this secret.

Matthew 13:10, 11
And the disciples came, and said unto him, Why speakest thou unto them in parables? He answered and said unto them, Because it is given unto you to know the mysteries of the Kingdom of Heaven, but to them it is not given.

Colossians 2:2, 3
That their hearts might be comforted, being knit together in love, and unto all riches of the full assurance of understanding, to the acknowledgement of the mystery of God, and of the Father, and of Christ; <u>In Whom are hid all the treasures of wisdom and knowledge.</u>

NOVEMBER

SUNSHINE

Matthew 5:16
Let your light so shine before men, that they may see your good works, and glorify your Father which is in heaven.

NOVEMBER 1

QUOTES OF JESUS

When Jesus speaks, the "hearer" listens. He touches every aspect of life and was even tempted as we are – yet without sin. Hear Him today!

Matthew 3:14, 15
But John forbad Him, saying, I have need to be baptized of Thee, and comest Thou to me? And <u>Jesus answering</u> said unto him, Suffer it to be so now: for thus it becometh us to fulfil all righteousness. Then he suffered Him.

Matthew 4:6, 7
And (Satan) saith unto Him, If Thou be the Son of God, cast Thyself down: for it is written, He shall give His angels charge concerning Thee: and in their hands they shall bear Thee up, lest at any time Thou dash Thy foot against a stone. <u>Jesus said</u> unto him, It is written again, thou shalt not tempt the Lord thy God.

Mark 2:5
When Jesus saw their faith, <u>He said</u> unto the sick of the palsy, Son, thy sins be forgiven thee.

Luke 4:8
And <u>Jesus answered</u> and said unto him, Get thee behind Me, Satan: for it is written, Thou shalt worship the Lord thy God, and Him only shalt thou serve.

Luke 9:57, 58, 62
. . . Lord, I will follow Thee whithersoever Thou goest. And <u>Jesus said</u> unto him, Foxes have holes, and birds of the air have nests; but the Son of man hath not where to lay His head. And <u>Jesus said</u> unto him, No man, having put his hand to the plough, and looking back, is fit for the kingdom of God.

NOVEMBER 2

BREAD OF LIFE

Bread truly is the staff of life. One can hardly go a day without it, unless you are on a special diet. Even then, most diets allow some kind of bread. However, there is the One Bread we must have in our daily life! That bread is Jesus and His Word.

<u>John 6:48</u>
I am that Bread of life.

<u>Matthew 4:4</u>
But He answered and said, It is written, Man shall not live by bread alone, but by every word that proceedeth out of the mouth of God.

<u>Mark 14:22</u>
And as they did eat, Jesus took bread, and blessed, and brake it, and gave to them, and said, Take, eat: this is My body.

<u>John 6:32 - 35</u>
Then Jesus said unto them, Verily, verily, I say unto you, Moses gave you not that bread from heaven; but <u>My Father giveth you the True Bread from heaven</u>. For the Bread of God is He which cometh down from heaven, and giveth life unto the world. Then said they unto Him, Lord, evermore give us this Bread. And Jesus said unto them, <u>I am the bread of life</u>: he that cometh to Me shall never hunger; and he that believeth on Me shall never thirst.

<u>John 6:52, 53 - 56</u>
. . . How can this man give us His flesh to eat? Then Jesus said unto them, Verily, verily, I say unto you, Except ye eat the flesh of the Son of man, and drink His blood, ye have no life in you.

<u>I Corinthians 11:26</u>
For as often as ye eat this bread, and drink this cup, ye do shew the Lord's death till He come.

NOVEMBER 3

HEAVENLY SUNLIGHT

"YOU ARE MY SUNSHINE"
Verse 2

YOU ARE MY SUNSHINE, my only SUNSHINE.
You make me happy when skies are gray.
You'll never know dear; how much I love you.
Please don't take my Sunshine away.

This Song is very special to me because my Mother sang this <u>second verse</u> to me so often when I was a child. It must have been popular during her young married life. When I was visiting her before her 100th Birthday, she reminded me of it and I painted the picture starting out this month of September, for her.

I was thinking about her again today, as I often do; on this her Birthday, and the song. So, I decided to share the words with you. I found it on the Internet and that Johnny Cash made a recording it. So, when I want to hear it again all I have to do is get it on my computer, etc.

This is a, worldly song and comes out so sadly that we cannot compare it with the Sunshine of God – "**HEAVENLY SUNLIGHT.**" He will never leave us nor forsake.

"HEAVENLY SUNLIGHT"
by H. J. Zelley (1859-1942)

Walking in sunlight all of my journey
Over the mountains thru the deep vale:
Jesus has said, I'll never forsake thee –
Promise divine that never can fail.

<u>Chorus</u>
Heavenly sunlight, Heavenly sunlight –
Flooding my soul with glory divine;
Hallelujah! I am rejoicing
Singing His praises - Jesus is mine!

NOVEMBER 4

TOMORROW

Only God knows what will happen tomorrow and what is in His plans. We don't even know if we will be alive to see it. We can make plans, but God directs our steps. Look below and see what we are can learn about "Tomorrow."

Proverbs 27:1
Boast not thyself of to morrow; for thou knowest not what a day may bring forth.

Proverbs 16:9
A man's heart deviseth his way: but the Lord directeth his steps.

Numbers 16:5
And he spake unto Korah and unto all his company, saying, Even tomorrow the Lord will shew who are His, and who is holy; and will cause him to come near unto Him: even him whom He hath chosen will He cause to come near unto Him.

Matthew 6:33, 34
But seek ye first the kingdom of God, and His righteousness; and all these things shall be added unto you. Take therefore no thought for the morrow: for the morrow shall take thought for the things of itself. Sufficient unto the day is the evil thereof.

Luke 12:19- 20
And I will say to my soul, Soul, thou hast much goods laid up for many years; take thine ease, eat, drink, and be merry. But God said unto him, Thou fool, this night thy soul shall be required of thee: then whose shall those things be, which thou hast provided?

Luke 12:29 - 31
. . . neither be ye of doubtful mind. . . your Father knoweth that ye have need of these things. But rather seek ye the kingdom of God; and all these things shall be added unto you.

NOVEMBER 5

SERMON ON THE MOUNT

We find the record of Jesus talking to the multitude in chapters 5, 6, and 7 of Matthew. It has been said that some people try to live by this Sermon alone for their assurance that they are Christians. We realize very quickly we cannot live this way if we are truly honest with ourselves. We are truly "blessed" when we follow after Jesus and not after any impossible attitudes in our earthly bodies. Thank God through Jesus Christ our Savior, He forgives us when we stumble over any one of these points. We will receive this perfection (<u>the law of His Kingdom</u> to come) in heaven through God's dear Son, Jesus Christ.

Please read for yourself these three chapters of Matthew, as here we can <u>only touch on a few</u> of these important things Jesus wants us to know!

<u>Matthew 5</u>

3. Blessed are the poor in spirit: for theirs is the kingdom of heaven. 6. Blessed are they which do hunger and thirst after righteousness: for they shall be filled. 7. Blessed are the merciful: for they shall obtain mercy. 8. Blessed are the pure in heart: for they shall see God. 9. Blessed are the peacemakers: for they shall be called the children of God. 13. Ye are the salt of the earth: but if the salt have lost his savour, wherewith shall it be salted? it is thenceforth good for nothing, but to be cast out, and to be trodden under foot of men. 14. Ye are the light of the world. . . . 15. Neither do men light a candle, and put it under a bushel, but on a candlestick; and it giveth light unto all that are in the house. 16. Let your light so shine before men, that they may see your good works, and glorify your Father which is in heaven. 17. Think not that I am come to destroy the law, or the prophets: I am not come to destroy, but to fulfil. 18. For verily I say unto you, Till heaven and earth pass, one jot or one tittle shall in no wise pass from the law, till all be fulfilled. 27. Ye have heard that it was said by them of old time, Thou shalt not commit adultery: 28. But I say unto you, That whosoever looketh on a woman to lust after her hath committed adultery with her already in his heart.

Matthew 6

6. But thou, when thou prayest, enter into thy closet, and when thou hast shut thy door, pray to thy Father which is in secret; and thy Father which seeth in secret shall reward thee openly. 7. But when ye pray, use not vain repetitions, as the heathen do: for they think that they shall be heard for their much speaking. 8. Be not ye therefore like unto them: for your Father knoweth what things ye have need of, before ye ask Him. 9. After this manner therefore pray ye: Our Father which art in heaven, Hallowed be Thy name. 10. Thy kingdom come. Thy will be done in earth, as it is in heaven. 19. Lay not up for yourselves treasures upon earth, where moth and rust doth corrupt, and where thieves break through and steal: 20. But lay up for yourselves treasures in heaven, where neither moth nor rust doth corrupt, and where thieves do not break through nor steal: 21. For where your treasure is, there your heart will be also. 33. But seek ye first the kingdom of God, and His righteousness; and all these things shall be added unto you. 34. Take therefore no thought for the morrow: for the morrow shall take thought for the things of itself. Sufficient unto the day is the evil thereof.

Matthew 7

12. Therefore all things whatsoever ye would that men should do to you, do ye even so to them: for this is the law and the prophets.

NOVEMBER 6

SWEAR NOT

Mark 6:23, 24
And he sware unto her, Whatsoever thou shalt ask of me, I will give it thee, unto the half of my kingdom. And she went forth, and said unto her mother, What shall I ask? And she said, The head of John the Baptist

There are different kinds of swearing! For something, against something, in anger, or even an oath. But swearing is an affront to God and others, when we casually sound off with a negative explicative. It seems so common in our present day that we try to just brush it off in the name of tolerance. How sad! We may not be offended but God is, and evil is a result of swearing. The examples of "swearing," as an oath, which is not a sin against God, unless it brings about something that brings evil. So, guard what comes out of your mouth even in anger. Let your **yea be yea and your nay be nay**.

Exodus 20:7 and Deuteronomy 5:11 (very important – given twice) **Thou shalt not take the Name of the Lord thy God in vain; for the Lord will not hold him guiltless that taketh His Name in vain.**

Matthew 5:33-37
But I say unto you, <u>Swear not at all</u>; neither by heaven; for it is God's throne: Nor by the earth; for it is His footstool: neither by Jerusalem; for it is the city of the great King. Neither shalt thou swear by thy head, because thou canst not make one hair white or black But let your communication be, <u>Yea, yea; Nay, nay</u>: for whatsoever is <u>more than these cometh of evil.</u>

Mark 6:23, 24
And he <u>sware</u> unto her, Whatsoever thou shalt ask of me, I will give it thee, unto the half of my kingdom. And she went forth, and said unto her mother, What shall I ask?
And she said, The head of John the Baptist.

NOVEMBER 7

"HIGHER GROUND"

This is our prayer: Lord, lift me up and "plant my feet on "Higher Ground."" What does this mean to you? As I read and sing this Hymn, I resolve to live above doubts and fears, and recognize the darts of sin Satan throws at me. I want to have the faith that catches the "joyful sounds" of the saints that live on a "higher plane," as I press on.

"HIGHER GROUND"
by J. Oatman, Jr. (1856-1922)

I'm pressing on the upward way,
New heights I'm gaining every day;
Still <u>praying</u> as I'm onward bound,
"<u>Lord, plant my feet on Higher Ground</u>"

<u>Chorus</u>
Lord, lift me up and let me stand,
By faith, on Heaven's tableland,
A higher plane than I have found;
<u>Lord, plant my feet on **Higher Ground**.</u>

My heart has no desire to stay
Where doubts arise and fears dismay;
Though some may dwell where those abound,
My <u>prayer</u>, my aim, is <u>Higher Ground</u>.

I want to live above the world,
Though Satan's darts at me are hurled;
For faith has caught the joyful sound,
The song of saints on <u>Higher Ground</u>.

I want to scale the utmost height
And catch a gleam of glory bright;
But still I'll <u>pray</u> till heav'n I've found,
"<u>Lord, plant my feet on Higher Ground</u>."

NOVEMBER 8

TREASURES ON EARTH

Even the treasures stored in the "temple"; the Lord's house, are not safe.

<u>I Kings 14:26</u>
And he (the king of Egypt) took away the treasures of the house of the Lord, and the treasures of the king's (the king of Israel) house; he even took away all: and he took away all the shields of gold which Solomon had made.

What and where are your treasures? We all have a different perspective. We have different environments, pressures, life-styles, expectations, desires, etc. These *"treasures"* where *"moths and rust"* can destroy, can also put us into bondage. But the cure is what Jesus has taught us. Ponder the last sentence, that we may often forget.* **"For where your treasure is, there will your heart be also."***

<u>Matthew 6:19 - 21</u>
Lay not up for yourselves treasures upon earth, where moth and rust doth corrupt, and where thieves break through and steal: But lay up for yourselves treasures in heaven, where neither moth nor rust doth corrupt, and where thieves do not break through nor steal: <u>*For where your treasure is, there will your heart be also.*</u> *

<u>Proverbs 15:16</u>
Better is little with the fear of the Lord than great treasure and trouble therewith.

<u>Proverbs 21:20</u>
There is treasure to be desired and oil in the dwelling of the wise; but a foolish man spendeth it up.

<u>Mark 8:36, 37</u>
For what shall it profit a man, if he shall gain the whole world, and lose his own soul? Or what shall a man give in exchange for his soul?

NOVEMBER 9

THE FATHER'S CARE

As humans, it is plainly known that we have many anxieties. They become painfully wearisome at times and become worries which are an affront to God, proving we have lost faith in Him and His Word. A lack of trust in His care. He cares for YOU! How personal is that?

<u>I Peter 5:7</u>
Casting all your care upon Him; for He careth <u>for you</u>.

If we cannot believe He cares for us by providing our basic needs, how can we trust Him for our eternity. He gave His life for us, for the here and now, with the promise of new life – forever.

<u>Matthew 6:24, 25</u>
No man can serve two masters: for either he will hate the one, and love the other; or else he will hold to the one, and despise the other. Ye cannot serve God and mammon. Therefore I say unto you, Take no thought for your life, what ye shall eat, or what ye shall drink; nor yet for your body, what ye shall put on. Is not the life more than meat, and the body than raiment?

<u>Psalms 35:27</u>
Let them shout for joy, and be glad, that favour My righteous cause: yea, let them say continually, Let the Lord be magnified, which hath pleasure in the prosperity of His servant.

<u>Plasms 142:4, 5</u>
I looked on my right hand, and beheld, but there was no man that would know me: refuge failed me; <u>no man cared for my soul</u>. I cried unto Thee, O Lord: I said, Thou art my refuge and my portion in the land of the living

<u>Luke 21:34</u>
And take heed to yourselves, lest at any time your hearts be overcharged with surfeiting, and drunkenness, and cares of this life, and so that day come upon you unawares.

NOVEMBER 10

TWO WAYS

Matthew 7:13, 14
Enter ye in at the <u>strait</u> gate: wide is the gate, <u>broad is the way, that leadeth to destruction</u>, and <u>many</u> there be which go in thereat: Because <u>strait</u> is the gate, and <u>narrow</u> is the way, which leadeth unto life, and <u>few</u> there be that find it.

John 14:4, 6
And whither I go ye know, and <u>the way</u> ye know. Jesus saith unto him, I am the Way, the Truth, and the Life: no man cometh unto the Father, but by Me.

These two passages tell us plainly our two options for life. Either to enter into a relationship with God – by the "narrow" way, which leads to life, or choose the "broad" way that leads to destruction, life without God. We choose one way or the other!

Matthew 7:15
Beware of false prophets, which come to you in sheep's clothing, but inwardly they are ravening wolves.

Luke 1:79
To give light to them that sit in darkness and in the shadow of death, to guide our feet into <u>the way of peace</u>.

John 10:1, 2, 7 - 11
Verily, verily, I say unto you, He that entereth <u>not by the door</u> into the sheepfold, but <u>climbeth up some other way,</u> the same is a thief and a robber. But he that entereth in <u>by the door</u> is the shepherd of the sheep. Then said Jesus unto them again, Verily, verily, I say unto you, I am the door of the sheep. . . . I am the door: by Me if any man enter in, he shall be saved, and shall go in and out, and find pasture. The thief cometh not, but for to steal, and to kill, and to destroy: I am come that they might have life, and that they might have it more abundantly. I am the good shepherd: the Good Shepherd giveth His life for the sheep.

NOVEMBER 11

TWO FOUNDATIONS

Wise man! vs. foolish man!

It is commonly known that our houses should be built on a good foundation – preferably on "rock bottom." This is our temporal dwelling place but we should be more concerned about our eternal home. Take a look at what Jesus has to say about "building" a place. Wise and Foolish.

Matthew 7:24 - 27
Therefore whosoever heareth these sayings of Mine, and <u>doeth them</u>, I will liken him unto a <u>wise</u> man, which built his house upon a rock: And the rain descended, and the floods came, and the winds blew, and beat upon that house; and it fell not: for it was founded upon a rock.

And every one that heareth these sayings of Mine, and <u>doeth them not</u>, shall be likened unto a <u>foolish</u> man, which built his house upon the sand: And the rain descended, and the floods came, and the winds blew, and beat upon that house; and it fell: and great was the fall of it.

"Therefore whosoever heareth these sayings of Mine" - what are these sayings? If we <u>hear</u> them, then must <u>do</u> them to be wise, as we are called for His purposes. Many of us think we are building on "a firm foundation" – the Rock (Jesus), but foolishly we deceive ourselves and go it alone by following our own limited understanding. The foolish man builds his house (life) upon the sand.

Proverbs 10:14
Wise men lay up knowledge: but the mouth of the foolish is near destruction.

Proverbs 13:14, 20
The law of the wise is a fountain of life, to depart from the snares of death. He that walketh with wise men shall be wise: but a companion of fools shall be destroyed.

NOVEMBER 12

O YE OF LITTLE FAITH

O YE OF LITTLE FAITH - Is this true of you? Is this true of me? I think so! For me, a yes.

Sometimes I have doubts and thoughts of why is "this" happening? This cannot be pleasing to the Lord. But God still deals with us with His tender-loving care at these times. He is trying to teach us something He wants us to learn or change in our lives. He is so patient as He needs to work with us our whole life long. As we grow and have more trust, we may not always respond with such little faith to God's prodding.

Luke 9:20
He (Jesus) said unto them, But whom say ye that I am? Peter answering said, The Christ of God.

Matthew 8:25 - 27
*And His disciples came to Him, and awoke Him, saying, Lord, save us: we perish. And He saith unto them, Why are ye fearful, **O ye of little faith**? Then He arose, and rebuked the winds and the sea; and there was a great calm. But the men marvelled, saying, What manner of man is this, that even the winds and the sea obey Him!*

Matthew 16:8 – 9, 11, 12
*Which when Jesus perceived, He said unto them, **O ye of little faith**, why reason ye among yourselves, because ye have brought no bread? Do ye not yet understand, neither remember the five loaves of the five thousand, and how many baskets ye took up? How is it that ye do not understand that I spake it not to you concerning bread, that ye should beware of the leaven of the Pharisees and of the Sadducees? Then understood they how that he bade them not beware of the leaven of bread, but of the doctrine of the Pharisees and of the Sadducees.*

NOVEMBER 13

THE CROSS OF CHRIST

In reading the account of Christ's Cross in the four Gospels (Matthew, Mark, Luke, and John), the gruesome picture of how cruel His crucifixion was, is revealed. Among others, at the foot of the Cross was His mother Mary, and John His disciple. They gazed up into His face and saw His suffering. But God did not leave Him on the Cross – He was buried and rose again. We are promised this victory over death too, for all of eternity with Him.

<u>Job 42:5</u>
*I have heard of Thee by the hearing of the ear:
but now mine eye seeth Thee.*

<u>John 1:29</u>
*The next day John seeth Jesus coming unto him, and saith,
Behold the Lamb of God, which taketh away the sin of the world.*

"NEAR THE CROSS"
by Fanny Crosby (1820 – 1915)

**Jesus, keep me near the cross –
There a precious fountain,
Free to all, a healing stream,
Flows from Cal-v'ry's mountain.**

<u>Chorus</u>
In the cross, in the cross
Be my glory ever,
Till my raptured soul shall find
Rest, beyond the river.

**Near the cross! O Lamb of God,
Bring its scenes before me;
Help me walk from day to day
With its shadows o'er me.**

NOVEMBER 14

THE HARVEST

<u>Proverbs 6:6 - 11</u>
Go to the ant, thou sluggard; consider her ways, and be wise: Which having no guide, overseer, or ruler, Provideth her meat in the summer, and gathereth her food in the <u>harvest</u>. How long wilt thou sleep, O sluggard? when wilt thou arise out of thy sleep? Yet a little sleep, a little slumber, a little folding of the hands to sleep: So shall thy poverty come as one that travelleth, and thy want as an armed man.

Compare below, the Old and New Testaments – how they refer to the harvest. Some refer to the physical harvest, and some refer to the spiritual harvest. Jesus used parables about "seed time and harvest" too, so that with His guidance, we could understand His teachings about His Kingdom of Heaven. Both instructions came from our Father in Heaven.

<u>Genesis 8:22</u>
While the earth remaineth, seedtime and harvest, and cold and heat, and summer and winter, and day and night shall not cease.

<u>Leviticus 25:3 - 5</u>
Six years thou shalt sow thy field, and six years thou shalt prune thy vineyard, and gather in the fruit thereof; But in the seventh year shall be a sabbath of rest unto the land, a sabbath for the Lord: thou shalt neither sow thy field, nor prune thy vineyard. That which groweth of its own accord of thy harvest thou shalt not reap, neither gather the grapes of thy vine undressed: for it is a year of rest unto the land.

<u>Proverbs 10:5</u>
He that gathereth in summer is a wise son: but he that sleepeth in harvest is a son that causeth shame.

NOVEMBER 15

JEREMIAH 29:11 - 13
For I know the thoughts (plans) that I think toward you, saith the Lord, thoughts of peace, and not of evil, to give you an expected end. Then shall ye <u>call upon Me</u>, and ye shall <u>go and pray unto Me</u>, and I will hearken unto you. And ye shall seek Me, and find Me, when ye shall search for Me with all your heart.

What a wonderful promise from God Himself! Can you imagine? He has thoughts (plans) towards us as individuals. Looking back we can see how He has led us. Think on that and desire to follow wherever He leads. So seek Him still with all your heart, and find Him.

<u>Matthew 6:8</u>
Be not ye therefore like unto them: for your Father knoweth what things ye have need of, before ye ask Him.

<u>Matthew 7:7</u>
Ask, and it shall be given you; seek, and ye shall find; knock, and it shall be opened unto you: For every one that asketh receiveth; and he that seeketh findeth; and to him that knocketh it shall be opened unto you.

<u>John 9:31</u>
Now we know that God heareth not sinners: but if any man be a worshipper of God, <u>and doeth His will</u>, him He heareth.

<u>Ephesians 3:20, 21</u>
Now unto Him that is able to do exceeding abundantly above all that we ask or think, according to the power that worketh in us, unto Him be glory in the church by Christ Jesus throughout all ages, world without end. Amen.

<u>James 4:3, 4</u>
Ye ask, and receive not, because ye ask amiss, that ye may consume it upon your lusts. . . . whosoever therefore will be a friend of the world is the enemy of God.

NOVEMBER 16

HEAR MY PRAYER

It seems to me that even the simplest of prayers, God hears and answers. However, there are requirements for Him to hear us: a clean and pure heart, which He has provided through Jesus Christ.

John 14:6
Jesus saith unto him, <u>I am the Way</u>, the Truth, and the Life: no man cometh unto the Father, but by Me.

Romans 10:9, 10
That if thou shalt confess with thy mouth the Lord Jesus, and shalt believe in thine heart that God hath raised Him from the dead, thou shalt be saved. For with the heart man believeth unto righteousness; and with the mouth confession is made unto salvation.

I John 1:9, 10
If we confess our sins, He is faithful and just to forgive us our sins, and to cleanse us from all unrighteousness. If we say that we have not sinned, we make Him a liar, and His word is not in us.

As we accept these terms of the Lord, we have the freedom to come before Him (<u>boldly</u>) to His throne of grace with our requests and petitions, giving Him praise, honor and thanksgiving.

Hebrews 4:16
Let us therefore come <u>boldly</u> unto the throne of grace, that we may obtain mercy, and find grace to help in time of need.

Psalms 66:18
If I regard iniquity in my heart, the Lord will not hear me:

NOVEMBER 17

WORDS of DESTINY
"You are what you think"

Often, I have heard: "you are what you eat!" But that doesn't stop me from over-eating, or eating the wrong things. So, this subject of "<u>words of destiny</u>" has come to my attention again. "You are what you <u>think</u>" I find that the Books of Psalms and Proverbs clearly gives us the pros and cons of what we think and say. Let's learn from our mistakes.

Proverbs 4:4, 5
He taught me also, and said unto me, Let thine heart retain My words: keep My commandments, and live. Get wisdom, get understanding: forget it not; neither decline from the words of My mouth.

Psalms 52:2 - 4
Thy tongue deviseth mischiefs; like a sharp razor, working deceitfully. Thou lovest evil more than good; and lying rather than to speak righteousness. Selah. Thou lovest all devouring words, <u>O thou deceitful tongue</u>.

Proverbs 15:1, 2
A soft answer turneth away wrath: but grievous words stir up anger. The tongue of the wise useth knowledge aright: but the mouth of fools poureth out foolishness.

Proverbs 15:26
The thoughts of the wicked are an abomination to the Lord: but the words of the pure are pleasant words.

Revelation 1:3
Blessed is he that readeth, and they that <u>hear</u> the words of this prophecy, and keep those things which are written therein: for the time is at hand.

NOVEMBER 18

HYPOCRITE

Do you know what a Hypocrite really is? We have our own ideas. For example, when we see someone doing something they condemn others for doing. *Webster's Dictionary* gives us a more accurate meaning: *hypocrisy – the practice of professing beliefs, feelings, or virtues that he/she does not hold (do) or possess.* In other words - *practicing insincerity*. As usual, let's look in the Bible and see what Jesus said.

Job 15:34, 36
For the congregation of hypocrites shall be desolate, and fire shall consume the tabernacles of bribery. They conceive mischief, and bring forth vanity, and their belly prepareth deceit.

Job 36:13. 14
But the hypocrites in heart heap up wrath: they cry not when he bindeth them. They die in youth, and their life is among the unclean.

Matthew 6:2, 3
Therefore when thou doest thine alms, do not sound a trumpet before thee, as the hypocrites do in the synagogues and in the streets, that they may have glory of men. Verily I say unto you, They have their reward. But when thou doest alms, let not thy left hand know what thy right hand doeth:

Matthew 6: 16
Moreover when ye fast, be not, as the hypocrites, of a sad countenance: for they disfigure their faces, that they may appear unto men to fast. Verily I say unto you, They have their reward.

Matthew 15:8, 9
This people draweth nigh unto Me with their mouth, and honoureth Me with their lips; but their heart is far from Me. But in vain they do worship Me, teaching for doctrines the commandments of men.

NOVEMBER 19

MUSTARD SEED

Jesus used the example of the mustard seed when teaching in parables about the Kingdom of Heaven, the one He will be ruler over. The three Gospels, Matthew, Mark, and Luke record this parable along with others that are about the Kingdom of Heaven. We must not confuse these parables with an earthly kingdom. They are specific to the Kingdom of Christ when He comes again to reign.

<u>Matthew 13:31, 32</u>
Another parable put He forth unto them, saying, The kingdom of heaven is like to a grain of mustard seed, which <u>a man</u> took, and sowed in his field: Which indeed is the least of all seeds: but when it is grown, it is the greatest among herbs, and becometh a tree, so that the birds of the air come and lodge in the branches thereof.

<u>Mark 4:26 - 33</u>
And He said, Whereunto shall we liken the Kingdom of God? or with what comparison shall we compare it? It is like a grain of mustard seed, which, when it is sown in the earth, is less than all the seeds that be in the earth: But when it is sown, it groweth up, and becometh greater than all herbs, and shooteth out great branches; so that the fowls of the air may lodge under the shadow of it. And with many such parables spake He the word unto them, as they were able to hear it.

<u>Luke 13:18, 19</u>
Then said He, Unto what is the Kingdom of God like? and whereunto shall I resemble it? It is like a grain of mustard seed, which a man took, and cast into his garden; and it grew, and waxed a great tree; and the fowls of the air lodged in the branches of it.

NOVEMBER 20

EARNESTLY CONTEND FOR THE FAITH

TODAY, read the Book of JUDE. With only one chapter, Jude provides a very important introduction to the Book of Revelation. Jude was the brother of the Lord Jesus, (see) Matthew 13:55 and Mark 6:3. He writes of the apostasy and heresies in the early church, around 68 A.D. As the heretics infiltrate into the Church, he shows vividly how apostasy leads to sinful living which continues today.

Matthew 13:55
Is not this (Jesus) the carpenter's son? is not His mother called Mary? and His brethren, James, and Joses, and Simon, and <u>Judas</u>?

Mark 6:3
Is not this (Jesus) the carpenter, the son of Mary, the brother of James, and Joses, and of <u>Juda</u>, and Simon? and are not His sisters here with us? And they were offended at Him.

Jude 1 - 4
Jude, the servant of Jesus Christ, and brother of James, to them that are sanctified by God the Father, and preserved in Jesus Christ, and called: Mercy unto you, and peace, and love, be multiplied. Beloved, when I gave all diligence to write unto you of the common salvation, it was needful for me to write unto you, and exhort you that ye should <u>earnestly contend for the faith</u> which was once delivered unto the saints. For there are certain <u>men crept in unawares</u>, who were before of old ordained to this condemnation, ungodly men, turning the grace of our God into lasciviousness, and denying the only Lord God, and our Lord Jesus Christ.

Continue on, Jude (verses 5 – 22) ***in your own Bible!***

NOVEMBER 21

PHARISEES

Pharisees are often clumped together with scribes, Sadducees and hypocrites, but there are differences. You see, we can all be hypocrites, but we can't all be Sadducees and Pharisees (of the past). They were also Hypocrites and the Spiritual leaders in Jesus' time, and He was very vocal against them all. He put them in a different class when He condemned them. Therefore, we need to be aware of our Spiritual leaders today. Are they being true to God's Word – the TRUTH? Therefore, if you don't know anything else, KNOW what Jesus taught us while He was here on earth.

Mark 7:5 - 9
Then the Pharisees and scribes asked Him, Why walk not Thy disciples according to the tradition of the elders, but eat bread with unwashen hands? He answered and said unto them, Well hath Esaias prophesied of you hypocrites, as it is written, This people honoureth Me with their lips, but their heart is far from Me. Howbeit in vain do they worship Me, teaching for doctrines the commandments of men. For laying aside the commandment of God, ye hold the tradition of men, as the washing of pots and cups: and many other such like things ye do. And He said unto them, Full well ye reject the commandment of God, that ye may keep your own tradition.

Luke 16:14, 15
And the Pharisees also, who were covetous, heard all these things: and they derided Him. And He said unto them, Ye are they which justify yourselves before men; but God knoweth your hearts: for that which is highly esteemed among men is abomination in the sight of God.

NOVEMBER 22

JESUS LOVES JERUSALEM

Luke 19:41, 42
And when He was come near, He beheld the city, and wept over it. Saying, If thou hadst known, even thou, at least in this thy day, the things which belong unto thy peace! but now they are hid from thine eyes.

O how Jesus loved Jerusalem! Why? How could He? He knew that was where He would be rejected and crucified! He even warned His disciples of this several times. His love for His people, the Jews and all men, that was foretold in Isaiah 53; He would be rejected, and they would not believe on Him (to their doom).

Isaiah 53:2, 3
For He shall grow up before Him as a tender plant, and as a root out of a dry ground: He hath no form nor comeliness; and when we shall see Him, there is no beauty that we should desire Him. He is despised and <u>rejected of men</u>; a man of sorrows, and acquainted with grief: and we hid as it were our faces from Him; He was despised, and we <u>esteemed Him not</u>.

Not only did the Jews reject Him but He was rejected of men (everywhere), especially today. Read the rest of *Isaiah 53*. He bore our sin and wept and died for all.

Isaiah 53:4 - 12
Surely He hath borne our griefs, and carried our sorrows: yet we did esteem Him stricken, smitten of God, and afflicted. But He was wounded for <u>our</u> transgressions, He was bruised for <u>our</u> iniquities: the chastisement of <u>our</u> peace was upon Him; and <u>with His stripes we are healed</u>. All we like sheep have gone astray; we have turned every one to his own way; and <u>the Lord hath laid on Him the iniquity of us all</u>. He was oppressed, and He was afflicted, yet He opened not His mouth: He is brought as a lamb to the slaughter, and as a sheep before her shearers is dumb, so He openeth not His mouth. He was taken from prison and from judgment: and who shall declare His generation? for He was cut off out of the land of the living: for the transgression of My people was He stricken. And He made His grave with the wicked, and with the rich in His death; because He had done no violence, neither was any deceit in his mouth. Yet it pleased the Lord to bruise Him; He hath put Him to grief: when <u>Thou shalt make His soul an offering for sin</u>, He shall see His seed, He shall prolong His days, and the pleasure of the Lord shall prosper in His hand. He shall see of the travail of His soul, and shall be satisfied: by His knowledge shall My righteous servant justify many; for <u>He shall bear their iniquities</u>. Therefore will I divide Him a portion with the great, and He shall divide the spoil with the strong; because <u>He hath poured out His soul unto death</u>: and He was numbered with the transgressors; and <u>He bare the sin of many, and made intercession for the transgressors</u>.

NOVEMBER 23

"THANKS TO GOD!"
An "Old Swedish hymn."

Since my grandparents migrated from Sweden, I must include this hymn for this year's Thanksgiving Season. To experience the real feeling of THANKS, count how many times THANKS was used by the Swedish writer, August Ludvig Storm. You will be blessed as you sing (or read) these words to the Lord and express your gratitude to Him. This Hymn can be found on the Internet so I included some verses that were new to me. Thank You dear God!

"THANKS TO GOD!"
by August Ludvig Storm (1862-1914)

Thanks to God for my Redeemer,
Thanks for all Thou dost provide!
Thanks for times now but a memory,
Thanks for Jesus by my side!
Thanks for pleasant, balmy springtime,
Thanks for dark and stormy fall!
Thanks for tears by now forgotten,
Thanks for peace within my soul!

Thanks to God For boundless mercy
From Thy gracious throne above;
Thanks for ev'ry need provided
From the fullness of Thy love!
Thanks for daily toil and labor
And for rest when shadows fall;
Thanks for love of friend and neighbor
And Thy goodness unto all!

Thanks for prayers that Thou hast answered,
Thanks for what Thou dost deny!
Thanks for storms that I have weathered,
Thanks for all Thou dost supply!
Thanks for pain, and thanks for pleasure,
Thanks for comfort in despair!
Thanks for grace that none can measure,
Thanks for love beyond compare!

NOVEMBER 24

JEWS and GENTILES

The Old Testament does not paint a pretty picture of the Gentiles. But first we have to begin – <u>before</u> the flood. Instead of destroying mankind completely in the flood, God spared only Noah and his family from sure death by placing them in the ark that He told Noah how to build. Noah believed God, and obeyed.

Genesis 6:5 – 8
And God saw that the wickedness of man was great in the earth, and that every imagination of the thoughts of his heart was only evil continually. And it repented the Lord that He had made man on the earth, and it grieved Him at His heart. And the Lord said, I will destroy man . . . for it repenteth Me that I have made them.
But <u>Noah found grace in the eyes of the Lord</u>.

Hebrews 11:7
By faith Noah, being <u>warned of God of things not seen as yet</u>, moved with fear, prepared an ark to the saving of his house; by the which he condemned the world, and became heir of the righteousness which is by faith.

Later God chose <u>Abraham</u> and his descendants to be His chosen people (Jews). Everyone else was a Gentile and were enemies of His people. They were to be separate and not intermingle.

Hebrews 11:8 - 10
By faith Abraham, when he was <u>called to go out</u> into a place which he should after receive for an inheritance, obeyed; and he went out, not knowing whither he went. By faith he sojourned in the land of promise, as in a strange country, dwelling in tabernacles with Isaac and Jacob, the heirs with him of the same promise: For he looked for a city which hath foundations, whose builder and maker is God.

Genesis 10:1, 32
Now these are the generations of the sons of Noah, Shem, Ham, and Japheth: and unto them were sons born after the flood. These are the families of the sons of Noah, after their generations, in their nations (<u>Gentiles</u>): and by these were the nations divided in the earth after the flood.

Things again changed <u>after the coming of Christ</u> and His resurrection. This is where we are today?

Acts 13:46
Then Paul and Barnabas waxed bold, and said, It was necessary that the word of God should <u>first have been spoken to you</u> (<u>Jews</u>): but seeing ye put it from you, and judge yourselves unworthy of everlasting life, <u>lo, we turn to the <u>Gentiles</u>.</u>

Romans 3:23 **and** Romans 5:8
For <u>all have sinned</u> (<u>Jews and Gentiles</u>), and come short of the glory of God; Being justified freely by His grace through the redemption that is in Christ Jesus: But God commendeth His love toward us, in that, while we were yet sinners, Christ died for us.

Romans 11:11
I say then, Have they (<u>Jews</u>) stumbled that they should fall? God forbid: but rather through their fall salvation is come unto the <u>Gentiles</u>, for to provoke them (<u>Jews</u>) to jealousy.

NOVEMBER 25

BE OF GOOD COURAGE

"Be of Good Courage" is found a lot in the Old Testament. As humans (since the fall of man), we need courage to survive. God often told His followers to depend on Him in faith and have courage wherever He leads. In the New Testament, the word "boldness," is used. To be timid is seen as a lack of faith and not realizing that God is with us and will never <u>forsake</u> us. To be forsaken is the beginning of fear, and the end of courage.

<u>Joshua 1:5</u>
There shall not any man be able to stand before thee all the days of thy life: as I was with Moses, so I will be with thee: <u>I will not fail thee, nor forsake thee</u>.

<u>Joshua 1:9</u>
Have not I commanded thee? Be strong and of a good courage; be not afraid, neither be thou dismayed: for the Lord thy God is with thee whithersoever thou goest.

<u>Acts 4:11 - 13</u>
Neither is there salvation in any other: for there is none other name under heaven given among men, whereby we must be saved. Now when they saw the <u>boldness</u> of Peter and John, and perceived that they were unlearned and ignorant men, they marvelled; and they took knowledge of them, that they had been with Jesus.

<u>Psalms 31:24</u>
Be of good courage, and He shall strengthen your heart, all ye that hope in the Lord.

<u>II Corinthians 4:9, 10</u>
Persecuted, but <u>not forsaken</u>; cast down, but not destroyed; Always bearing about in the body the dying of the Lord Jesus, that the life also of Jesus might be made manifest in our body.

NOVEMBER 26

LOVE YOUR ENEMIES

Psalms 143:11,12
Quicken me, O Lord, <u>for Thy name's sake</u>: <u>for Thy righteousness' sake</u> bring my soul out of trouble. And <u>of Thy mercy</u> cut off mine enemies, and destroy all them that afflict my soul: for I am Thy servant.

Who are our enemies? You probably have a few in mind. Perhaps no one had more personal and national enemies than King David in his time. Did God mean for him to love his enemies? What God says is true and man is the liar; so, it must be so. I understand that the way we can love our enemies is to leave them in the hands of the Lord like David did, and ask for "His mercy" to bring us out of trouble. Can we do this? I don't think so on our own, but with God's power He will deliver and help us.

Psalms 38:20 - 22
They also that render evil for good are mine adversaries; because I follow the thing that good is. Forsake me not, O Lord: O my God, be not far from me. Make haste to help me, O Lord my salvation.

Matthew 5:43 – 45
Ye have heard that it hath been said, Thou shalt love thy neighbour, and hate thine enemy. But I say unto you, Love your enemies, bless them that curse you, do good to them that hate you, and pray for them which despitefully use you, and persecute you; That ye may be <u>the children of your Father which is in heaven</u>: for He maketh His sun to rise on the evil and on the good, and sendeth rain on the just and and on the unjust.

Luke 6:27, 28
But I say unto you which hear, Love your enemies, do good to them which hate you, Bless them that curse you, and pray for them which despitefully use you.

NOVEMBER 27

PRACTICE BY DOING

As children, we are told that "Practice makes perfect." I'm sure this is true to some extent but maybe not perfect! As I look back, an example comes to my mind. Around the age of 5 or 6, I was given piano lessons. You see my sister (4 years older) was already a pretty good pianist and it was Mother's hope I would want to play too. Well, after it got harder, the finger numbering vanished, and I had to practice more; I cried and cried and begged Mom to let me quit. It was then after thinking about it, she warned me if I quit, I would be sorry later. Well, I must confess, after years and years had passed Mother was right. I am one of those that have to learn wisdom the hard way.

<u>II Timothy 2:16</u>
<u>Study</u> to shew thyself approved unto God, a workman that needeth not to be ashamed, rightly dividing the word of truth.

"The rest of the story" - thank God, my sister to this day, uses her talent for the Lord, and is still playing the piano for many people at many church functions. So, by "doing," we must practice, practice, practice. Keep on, keeping on!

<u>Proverbs 22:6</u>
Train up a child in the way he should go: and when he is old, he will not depart from it.

<u>Matthew 7:24</u>
Therefore whosoever heareth these sayings of Mine, and doeth them, I will liken him unto a wise man . .

<u>Philippians 4:13</u>
I can do all things through Christ which strengtheneth me.

NOVEMBER 28

JESUS' LAST "WORDS"

While I was searching for the exact "Last Words" Jesus spoke during His crucifixion - I looked them up in the Bible and "Wikipedia" (quite accurate). Maybe you would want to compare them too. I found it very interesting. Tradition uses these "last" seven phrases as His "Last Words," and are especially remembered during the week of Easter when we celebrate (His resurrection). He is not dead but RISEN!

Matthew 28:5, 6
The angel said to the women, "Do not be afraid, for I know that you seek Jesus who was crucified. He is not here, for He has risen, <u>as He said</u>. Come, see the place where He lay."

As "Wikipedia" states: *"Traditionally, these seven sayings are called words of,* 1. Forgiveness, 2. Salvation,
3. Relationship, 4. Abandonment, 5. Distress, 6. Triumph, and 7. Reunion*."*

Luke 23:33, 34   1. **FORGIVNESS**
And when they were come to the place, which is called Calvary, there they crucified Him, and the malefactors, one on the right hand, and the other on the left.
Then said Jesus, "Father, forgive them; for they know not what they do."
And they parted His raiment, and cast lots. garments.

Luke 23:42, 43   2. **SALVATION**
And he said unto Jesus, Lord, remember me when Thou comest into Thy kingdom. And Jesus said unto him, "Verily I say unto thee, Today shalt thou be with Me in paradise."

John 19:26 – 27   3. **RELATIONSHIP**
When Jesus therefore saw His mother, and the disciple standing by, whom He loved, He saith unto His mother, "Woman, behold thy son!"
Then saith He to the disciple, "Behold thy mother!"
And from that hour that disciple took her unto his own home.

Matthew 27:45, 46 - Mark 15:34   4. **ABANDONMENT**
Now from the sixth hour there was darkness over all the land unto the ninth hour. And about the ninth hour Jesus cried with a loud voice, saying,
"Eli, Eli, lama sabachthani?" *that is to say,*
"My God, My God, why hast thou forsaken Me?"

And at the ninth hour Jesus cried with a loud voice, saying,
"Eloi, Eloi, lama sabachthani?" which is, being interpreted,
"My God, My God, why hast thou forsaken Me?"

<u>John 19:28, 29</u>   5. **DISTRESS**
After this, Jesus knowing that all things were now accomplished, that the scripture might be fulfilled, saith, *"I thirst."* Now there was set a vessel full of vinegar: and they filled a spunge with vinegar, and put it upon hyssop, and put it to His mouth.

<u>John 19:30</u>   6. **TRIUMPH**
When Jesus therefore had received the vinegar,
He said, *"It is finished":* and He bowed His head, and gave up the ghost.

<u>Luke 23:46</u>   7. **REUNION**
And when Jesus had cried with a loud voice, He said,
"Father, into Thy hands I commend My spirit":
and having said thus, He gave up the ghost.

NOVEMBER 29

"O HAPPY DAY"

This happy song, is from my childhood memory. It reminds me of my Baptism and many others I have witnessed. The pianist played this hymn every time one was lifted out of the waters of Baptism; as a testimony of their new life in Christ, and that Jesus washed their sins away with His own blood. I can almost see and hear it now.

"O HAPPY DAY"
by Philip Doddridge (1702-1751)

O happy day that fixed my choice
On Thee, my Savior and my God!
Well may this glowing heart rejoice
And tell its raptures all abroad.

<u>Chorus</u>
Happy day, happy day,
When Jesus washed my sins away!
He taught me how to watch and pray
And live rejoicing ev'ry day;
Happy day, happy day,
When Jesus washed my sins away!

O happy bond that seals my vows
To Him Who merits all my love!
Let cheerful anthems fill His house,
While to that sacred shrine I move.

'Tis done, the great transaction's done
I am my Lord's and He is mine;
He drew me, and I followed on,
Charmed to confess the voice divine.

Now rest, my long-divided heart,
Fixed on this blissful center, rest;
Nor ever from my Lord depart,
With Him of ev'ry good possessed.

NOVEMBER 30

DOCTRINE

O be careful of the Doctrine you believe and put your trust into. Even the nations of the world have their own "Doctrine." To make the meaning simple, doctrine is "something that is taught" (both temporal and eternal). Examining what the Bible says about Doctrine, we find Jesus' Doctrine comes from God Himself. This Biblical doctrine should be followed and embraced all of our life and not be deceived by what the world tries to teach us. We can be easily betrayed.

<u>John 7:16, 17</u>
Jesus answered them, and said, My doctrine is not Mine, but His that sent Me. If any man will do His will, he shall know of the doctrine, whether it be of God, or whether I speak of Myself.

<u>Ephesians 4:14</u>
That we henceforth be no more children, tossed to and fro, and carried about with every wind of doctrine, by the sleight of men, and cunning craftiness whereby they lie in wait to deceive

<u>II Timothy 3:16, 17</u>
All scripture is given by inspiration of God, and is profitable for doctrine, for reproof, for correction, for instruction in righteousness: That the man of God may be perfect, thoroughly furnished unto all good works.

<u>II Timothy 4:2</u>
Preach the word; be instant in season, out of season; reprove, rebuke, exhort with all longsuffering and doctrine.

<u>Titus 2:1, 7</u>
But speak thou the things which become sound doctrine: In all things shewing thyself a pattern of good works: in doctrine shewing uncorruptness, gravity, sincerity

DECEMBER

JOYFUL TREES

Psalms 98:4, 8
Make a joyful noise unto the Lord, all the earth: make a loud noise, and rejoice, and sing praise.
Let the floods clap their hands: let the hills be joyful together.

DECEMBER 1

LIFE IS FULL OF TENSIONS

Therefore, I am making this <u>a month of singing</u>, ending with a joyous Christmas and <u>hope</u>!

Today I heard a California Judge made a pronouncement that it is against the law for the Government to put undue tension on criminal illegals that might be deported, even if they are already in jail. This is an over-ruling if I ever heard one. The government can give us "real" tension every year at tax time! Right? Well, most of us do not fall into either of these two categories but there are times we all must deal with the realities of life – facing daily trials and tensions. Sometimes they are the result of <u>our own choices</u>. These are the times one should turn to God in repentance and ask for His forgiveness. But at times troubles are out of our control, caused by others and become so dire that serious tensions abound. God will help us!

<u>Job 1:1</u>
There was a man in the land of Uz, whose name was Job; and that man was perfect and upright,
and one that feared God, and eschewed evil.

<u>Job 1:8 - 10, 12</u>
And the Lord said unto Satan, Hast thou considered My servant Job, that there is none like him in the earth . . . Then Satan answered the Lord, and said, Doth Job fear God for nought? Hast not Thou made an hedge about him, and about his house, and about all that he hath on every side? Thou hast blessed the work of his hands, and his substance is increased in the land.

<u>Job 3:25</u>
For the thing which I greatly feared is come upon me, and that which I was afraid of is come unto me.

DECEMBER 2

ATTITUDE CHANGE

Changing our attitudes never ends – from the negative to the positive or visa-versa. We can have a positive attitude most of the time, but then "whoops," we hit a low spot and turn negative.

There are so many kinds of attitudes that we can't even count them all. Whenever it comes to my mind that I need an "Attitude Change," I know it must start with an attitude of repentance – a turning around. Scripture gives us a way to see and change our feelings into positive attitudes as followers of Jesus Christ.

<u>Matthew 3:8</u>
Bring forth therefore fruits meet for repentance:

<u>Psalms 118:24</u>
This is the day which the Lord hath made; we will rejoice and be glad in it.

<u>Psalms 119:71, 72</u>
It is good for me that I have been afflicted; that I might learn Thy statutes. The law of Thy mouth is better unto me than thousands of gold and silver.

<u>Proverbs 16:18, 19</u>
Pride goeth before destruction, and an haughty spirit before a fall. Better it is to be of an humble spirit with the lowly, than to divide the spoil with the proud

<u>Ephesians 4:31, 32</u>
Let all bitterness, and wrath, and anger, and clamour, and evil speaking, be put away from you, with all malice: And be ye kind one to another, tenderhearted, forgiving one another, even as God for Christ's sake hath forgiven you.

DECEMBER 3

PROMISES OF GOD

When we buy a book that has been compiled with Bible promises, we find it conveniently divided into subjects of concern to us. This is very good for us on the fly when a trial comes up. Even a short phrase can give us help or encouragement, to keep on trusting God's Word. However, do not substitute these books for your own search of promises from God. Study His Word yourself too. Remember He is a personal God – He loves you! He has something special to teach you.

Psalm 77:4 - 6
Thou holdest mine eyes waking: I am so troubled that I cannot speak. I have considered the days of old, the years of ancient times. I call to remembrance my song in the night: I commune with mine own heart: and my spirit made diligent search.

Acts 13:32, 33
And we declare unto you glad tidings, how that the <u>promise</u> which was made unto the fathers, God hath fulfilled the same unto us their children, in that He hath raised up Jesus again; as it is also written in the second Psalm (verse 7), Thou art My Son, this day have I begotten Thee

I Timothy 4:8
For bodily exercise profiteth little: but godliness is profitable unto all things, having <u>promise</u> of the life that now is, and of that which is to come.

Titus 1:2
In hope of eternal life, which God, that cannot lie, <u>promised</u> before the world began;

I John 2:25
And this is the promise that He hath <u>promised</u> us, even eternal life.

DECEMBER 4

OLD

So many of us fear and dread reaching old age. However, I have found our perspective of what old age is, changes as we age. As the years go by, we tend to push it up another 10 years. My Dad thought it was the 70's and he lived to be 90. So now I am aiming for the 90's, God willing, even though Mom lived to see her 100th birthday.

Psalms 90:10
The days of our years are threescore years and ten (70); and if by reason of strength they be fourscore (80) years, yet is their strength labour and sorrow; for it is soon cut off, and we fly away.

Think of this! Society will do anything, not to look, feel, or even think old. Just watch a little TV and you will agree. God gives us so many blessings throughout <u>all</u> our life, so look around, and ahead and recognize what God and is still doing. "***<u>He is ever merciful</u>***" *(*Psalms 37:26).

Job 15:8
With us are both the grayheaded and very aged men, much elder than thy father.

Psalms 37:25, 26
I have been young, and now am old; yet have I not seen the righteous forsaken, nor His seed begging bread. <u>He is ever merciful</u>, and lendeth; and His seed is blessed.

Jeremiah 6:16
Thus saith the Lord, Stand ye in the ways, and see, and ask for the old paths, where is the good way, and walk therein, and ye shall <u>find rest for your souls</u>. But they said, <u>We will not walk therein</u>.

Titus 2:2, 3a
That the aged men be sober, grave, temperate, sound in faith, in charity, in patience. The aged women likewise . .

DECEMBER 5

ETERNITY

Such an important subject! We are all promised an eternity; forever and ever! Our eternity begins the moment we are conceived. However, we will not all <u>receive</u> Eternal <u>Life</u>. The key word is "receive." Beyond being born and babyhood, we must willingly <u>accept</u> or <u>not</u>, determining our outcome of what God offers us by believing on His Dear Son, Jesus Christ, and what He did for us – on the cross - in our place.

Philippians 2:6 - 8
Who, being in the form of God, thought it not robbery to be equal with God: But made Himself of no reputation, and took upon Him the form of a servant, and was made in the likeness of men: And being found in fashion as a man, He humbled Himself, and became obedient unto death, even the death of the cross.

Before we die we must choose – Eternal Life or Eternal Damnation. This may seem harsh from a loving God but He has done everything He willed to do: to save us from sin's penalty of death. **We choose** to believe and trust Him or not determining where we will spend all of Eternity.

Jeremiah 31:3
. . . Yea, I have loved thee with an everlasting love: therefore with lovingkindness have I drawn thee.

Matthew 25:46
And these shall go away into everlasting punishment: but the righteous into life eternal.

Titus 3:5 - 7
Not by works of righteousness which we have done, but according to His mercy He saved us . . .Which He shed on us abundantly through Jesus Christ our Saviour; That being justified by His grace, we should be made heirs . . . to eternal life.

DECEMBER 6

GO

Go is a "little" word but often requires a definite action or response; sometimes easy but more frequently, difficult. Sometimes we have to obey and other times we can say "no." It all depends on who gives the request or command. Even Jesus knew what was to come but He still obeyed the will of God, to "GO" to Jerusalem.

Matthew 20:18, 19
Behold, we go up to Jerusalem; and the Son of man shall be betrayed unto the chief priests and unto the scribes, and they shall condemn Him to death, And shall deliver Him to the Gentiles to mock, and to scourge, and to crucify Him: and the third day He shall rise again.

Psalms 32:8
I will instruct thee and teach thee in the way which thou shalt go: I will guide thee with Mine eye.

Psalms 71:16
I will go in the strength of the Lord God: I will make mention of Thy righteousness, even of Thine only.

Isaiah 6:8
Also I heard the voice of the Lord, saying, Whom shall I send, and who will go for Us? Then said I, Here am I; send me.

Isaiah 30:8
Now go, write it before them in a table, and note it in a book, that it may be for the time to come for ever and ever.

John 15:16
Ye have not chosen Me, but I have chosen you, and ordained you, that ye should go and bring forth fruit . . .

Think about it, we can't even compare ourselves to Job's trials and testings. Read the last Chapter of Job - the rest of <u>his</u> story!

DECEMBER 7

MIDDLE OF THE ROAD

Driving down the middle of the road on a busy highway is rarely a good idea. However, this is a good illustration of a dangerous life style - living in the gray areas of life, the "Middle of the Road." Following the crowd may be more comfortable but, as an individual we choose **what** and **who** we follow. Think of any decision you have made in the past and ask yourself if you have chosen the "Middle of the Road," a compromise or the right road?

<u>Leviticus 26:30</u>
And I (God) will destroy <u>your high places,</u> and cut down your images, and cast your carcases upon the carcases of your idols, and My soul shall abhor you.

<u>I Samuel 8:3</u>
And his (Samuel's) sons walked not in his ways, but turned aside after lucre, and took bribes, and perverted judgment.

<u>I Samuel 15:10, 11a</u>
Then came the word of the Lord unto Samuel, saying, It repenteth Me that I have set up Saul to be king: for he is turned back from following Me, and hath not performed My commandments.

<u>Isaiah 5:20</u>
Woe unto them that call evil good, and good evil; that put darkness for light, and light for darkness; that put bitter for sweet, and sweet for bitter! truth,

<u>Matthew 6:24</u>
No man can serve two masters: for either he will hate the one, and love the other; or else he will hold to the one, and despise the other. Ye cannot serve God and mammon.

DECEMBER 8

"I'LL LIVE for HIM"
by Ralph E. Hudson (1843-1901)

Hymn of <u>Commitment</u>

My life, my love I give to Thee,
Thou Lamb of God Who died for me;
O may I ever faithful be,
My Savior and my God!

<u>Chorus</u>
I'll live for Him who died for me,
How happy then my life shall be!
I'll live for Him Who died for me,
My Savior and my God!

I now believe Thou dost receive,
For Thou hast died that I might live;
And now hence-forth I trust in Thee,
My Savior and my God!

O Thou who died on Calvary
To save my soul and make me free,
I'll consecrate my life to Thee,
My Savior and my God!

That in Heaven He may meet me,
I would be like Jesus;
That His words 'Well done' may greet me,
I would be like Jesus.

<u>Chorus</u>
I'll live for Him who died for me,
How happy then my life shall be!
I'll live for Him Who died for me,
My Savior and my God!

DECEMBER 9

HIDDEN and SECRET THINGS

We like mysteries stories and secrets. When facts are hidden we like to find them out. But with God there are things not known to us until He chooses to <u>reveal</u> them to us.

<u>I Corinthians 2:9, 10</u>
But as it is written, Eye hath not seen, nor ear heard, neither have entered into the heart of man, the things which God hath prepared for them that love Him. But God hath revealed them unto us by His Spirit: for the Spirit searcheth all things, yea, the deep things of God.

<u>Deuteronomy 29:29</u>
The secret things belong unto the Lord our God: but those things which are revealed belong unto us and to our children forever, that we may do all the words of this law.

<u>Daniel 2:22</u>
He revealeth the deep and secret things: He knoweth what is in the darkness, and the light dwelleth with Him.

<u>Mark 13:32, 33</u>
But of that day and that hour knoweth no man, no, not the angels which are in heaven, neither the Son, but the Father. Take ye heed, watch and pray: for ye know not when the time is.

<u>Luke 8:10</u>
And He said, Unto you it is given to know the mysteries of the kingdom of God: but to others in <u>parables</u>; that seeing they might not see, and hearing they might not understand.

<u>Colossians 1:26, 27, 28</u>
Even the mystery which hath been hid from ages and from generations, but now is made manifest to His saints: To whom God would make known what is the riches of the glory of this mystery among the Gentiles; which is Christ in you, the hope of glory. . . warning every man . . .that we may present every man perfect in Christ Jesus:

DECEMBER 10

OBSTACLES

Scripture has many words that represent obstacles: hindrances, cast away, offences, things of men, self-centeredness, my own way, weight of sin, etc. You can think of a few more that influenced your own life. So let's do away with these things that *"so easily beset us."* These may be stumbling blocks hindering the way to salvation of those around us.

Hebrews 12:1
Wherefore seeing we also are compassed about with so great a cloud of witnesses, let us lay aside every weight, and the sin which doth <u>so easily beset us</u>, and let us run with patience the race that is set before us.

Isaiah 57:14
And shall say, Cast ye up, cast ye up, prepare the way, take up the <u>stumbling-block out of the way</u> of My people.

Matthew 16:24, 25
Then said Jesus unto His disciples, If any man will come after Me, let him deny himself, and take up his cross, and follow Me. For whosoever will save his life shall lose it: and whosoever will lose his life for My sake shall find it.

Romans 12:1, 2
I beseech you therefore, brethren, by the mercies of God, that ye present your bodies a living sacrifice, holy, acceptable unto God, which is your reasonable service. And be not conformed to this world: but be ye transformed by the renewing of your mind, that ye may prove what is that good, and acceptable, and perfect, will of God.

Romans 14:13
Let us not therefore judge one another any more: but judge this rather, that no man put a stumblingblock or an occasion to fall in his brother's way.

DECEMBER 11

CRYING

When I was a child I remember I cried a lot, but my memory may be faulty because I had a happy childhood and good parents. So, I believe I cried, either because of my shyness, wanting my own way, or not wanting to do what my parents wanted me to do. Very childlike! Now I cry mostly for something others are going through, or for the wonder of all Christ has done for me. The Bible has mentioned crying many times and recorded that even Jesus cried.

<u>John 11:35</u>
Jesus wept.

<u>Psalms 6:6</u>
I am weary with my groaning; all the night make I my bed to swim; I water my couch with my tears.

<u>Psalms 18:6</u>
In my distress I called upon the Lord, and cried unto my God: He heard my voice out of His temple, and my cry came before Him, even into His ears.

<u>Psalms 34: 17 - 19</u>
The righteous cry, and the Lord heareth, and delivereth them out of all their troubles. The Lord is nigh unto them that are of a broken heart; and saveth such as be of a contrite spirit. Many are the afflictions of the righteous: but the Lord delivereth him out of them all.

<u>Revelation 21:4, 5</u>
And God shall wipe away all tears from their eyes; and there shall be no more death, neither sorrow, nor crying, neither shall there be any more pain: for the former things are passed away. And He that sat upon the throne said, Behold, I make all things new. And He said unto me (John), Write: for these words are true and faithful.

DECEMBER 12

ANSWERS

Have questions, trials and tribulations? We want and need answers so who do we go to? Our first choice should be the Lord as King David did in his time of need. His whole prayer in Psalms 86, gives us great insight into where we can find answers for almost every need.

Psalms 86:7
In the day of my trouble I will call upon Thee: for Thou wilt answer me.

Proverbs 1:23 - 25
If you turn (repent) at My reproof, behold, I will pour out My spirit to you; I will make My words known to you. Because I have called and you refused to listen, have stretched out My hand and no one has heeded, because you have ignored all My counsel and would have none of My reproof

Proverbs 1:28 - 30
Then they will call upon Me, but I will not answer; they will seek Me diligently but will not find Me. Because they hated knowledge and did not choose the fear of the Lord, would have none of My counsel and despised all My reproof.

Isaiah 65:24
And it shall come to pass, that before they (Mine elect) call, I will answer; and while they are yet speaking, I will hear.

Isaiah 66:3, 4
. . . Yea, they have chosen their own ways, and their soul delighteth in their abominations. I also will choose their delusions, and will bring their fears upon them; because when I called, none did answer; when I spake, they did not hear: but they did evil before mine eyes, and chose that in which I delighted not.

DECEMBER 13

A LONGING FOR GOD

In the most important way, mankind has not changed since Adam and Eve had to leave the Garden of Eden. We still have longings for things we do not have any control over. If we did, it wouldn't be a longing. But, our longing for God is the most important one so, He has provided <u>The Way</u> to reach Him through Jesus Christ.

Amos 5:8
Seek Him that maketh the seven stars and Orion, and turneth the shadow of death into the morning, and maketh the day dark with night: that calleth for the waters of the sea, and poureth them out upon the face of the earth: <u>The Lord is His Name</u>:

Psalms 38:9
Lord, all my desire is before Thee; and my groaning is not hid from Thee.

Psalms 107:9
For He satisfieth the longing soul, and filleth the hungry soul with goodness.

Romans 8:22 - 24
For we know that <u>the whole creation</u> groaneth and travaileth in pain together until now. And not only they, but <u>ourselves also</u>, which have the first fruits of the Spirit, <u>even we ourselves groan within ourselves</u>, <u>waiting</u> (longing) for the adoption, to wit, the redemption of our body. For we are saved by hope: but hope that is seen is not hope: for what a man seeth, why doth he yet hope for?

I Timothy 6:10
For the love of money is the root of all evil: which while some coveted after, they have erred from the faith, and pierced themselves through with many sorrows.

DECEMBER 14

JOY FOREVERMORE

Psalms 16:11
Thou wilt shew me the path of life: in Thy presence is fulness of joy; at Thy right hand there are pleasures for evermore.

Not only in this life can we have JOY, but we are promised JOY forevermore! How can we reject so great a God and His love toward us?

I Chronicles 16:34
O give thanks unto the Lord; for He is good; for His mercy endureth for ever.

Psalms 5:11
But let all those that put their trust in Thee rejoice: let them ever shout for joy, because Thou defendest them: let them also that love Thy name be joyful in Thee.

John 15:11
These things have I spoken unto you, that My joy might remain in you, and that your joy might be full.

Acts 2:28
Thou hast made known to me the ways of life; Thou shalt make me full of joy with Thy countenance.

Acts 13:52
And the disciples were filled with joy, and with the Holy Ghost.

Romans 5:10, 11
For if, when we were enemies, we were reconciled to God by the death of his Son, much more, being reconciled, we shall be saved by His life. And not only so, but we also joy in God through our Lord Jesus Christ, by Whom we have now received the atonement.

James 1:2, 3
My brethren, count it all joy when ye fall into divers temptations; Knowing this, that the trying of your faith worketh patience.

DECEMBER 15

IF

IF is a little word implying a question; or an either/or response to an action or thought. An example given in a dictionary is: **"if that's true, what should we do?"** There is an uncertainty connected with IF that calls for a response or conclusion – true or false. Since God cannot lie, the "If's" in the Bible are true.

Genesis 25:22b
. . . *If* it be so, why am I thus? And she went to enquire of the Lord.

Matthew 5:13
Ye are the salt of the earth: but *if* the salt have lost his savour, wherewith shall it be salted? it is thenceforth good for nothing, but to be cast out, and to be trodden under foot of men.

Matthew 6:14, 15
For *if* ye forgive men their trespasses, your heavenly Father will also forgive you: But *if* ye forgive not men their trespasses, neither will your Father forgive your trespasses.

Mark 3:25
And if a house be divided against itself, that house cannot stand.

John 8:24b
. . . for *if* ye believe not that I am He, ye shall die in your sins.

John 15:18
If the world hate you, ye know that it hated Me before it hated you.

Acts 5:39
But *if* it be of God, ye cannot overthrow it; lest haply ye be found even to fight against God.

I Corinthians 15:19
If in this life only we have hope in Christ, we are of all men most miserable.

DECEMBER 16

DELIGHT IN THE LORD

We are God's Delight! Can you believe it?
So, delight in Him also.

Psalms 16:3
But to the saints that are in the earth, and to the excellent, in whom is all My delight.

Proverbs 12:22
Lying lips are abomination to the Lord: but they that deal truly are His delight.

It is hard to believe since we know the conditions we have made for ourselves and live in; He still delights in us even when we wander. It is so because He said so! He still seeks us out and finds us. If and when our children make such a mess, I hope we would be as benevolent.

Job 22:26
For then shalt thou have thy delight in the Almighty, and shalt lift up thy face unto God.

Psalms 1:2
But his delight is in the law of the Lord; and in His law doth he meditate day and night.

Psalms 94:19
In the multitude of my thoughts within me Thy comforts delight my soul.

Proverbs 8:22, 23, 30
The Lord possessed me in the beginning of His way, before His works of old. <u>I was set up from everlasting, from the beginning, or ever the earth was.</u> Then I was by Him, as one brought up with Him: and <u>I was daily His delight,</u> <u>rejoicing always before Him;</u>

Isaiah 58:2a
Yet they seek Me daily, and delight to know My ways . . .

DECEMBER 17

"JESUS LOVES EVEN ME"

How is that? O how wonderful – Jesus loves <u>even me</u>; But the $64,000 question, is do I love Jesus? Do you love Jesus? Loving Jesus is easy for me because He loved me first. I learned this in Sunday School and had this promise all my life! Oh, I hope you have this assurance too!

"JESUS LOVES EVEN ME"
by P. P. Bliss (1838-1876)

I am so glad that our Father in heav'n
Tells of His love in the Book He has giv'n;
Wonderful things in the Bible I see –
This is the dearest, That Jesus loves <u>me</u>.

<u>Chorus</u>
I am so glad that Jesus loves me,
Jesus loves me, Jesus loves me;
I am so glad that Jesus loves me,
<u>Jesus loves even me.</u>

Tho I forget Him and wander away,
Still He doth love me wherever I stray;
Back to His dear loving arms would I flee
When I remember that Jesus loves me.

O if there's only one song I can sing
When in His beauty I see the great King,
This shall my song in eternity be:
O what a wonder that Jesus loves me!

<u>Chorus</u>
I am so glad that Jesus loves me,
Jesus loves me, Jesus loves me;
I am so glad that Jesus loves me,
<u>Jesus loves even me.</u>

DECEMBER 18

THE EYE

Matthew 6:22, 23a
The light of the body is the eye: <u>if</u> therefore thine eye be single, thy whole body shall be full of <u>light</u>. <u>But</u> if thine eye be evil, thy whole body shall be full of <u>darkness</u>.

Romans 3:16 - 18
Destruction and misery are in their ways: And the way of peace have they not known: There is no fear of God before their eyes.

We aren't the only ones who have eyes – God looks down on us and sees the good and evil. So, take care what you see. Our eyes are very precious. Use them wisely and be focused. There is much is written in Scripture about the eyes – both God's and ours.

Proverbs 4:25 - 27
Let thine eyes look right on, and let thine eyelids look straight before thee. Ponder the path of thy feet, and let all thy ways be established. Turn not to the right hand nor to the left: remove thy foot from evil.

Proverbs 6:12 - 14
A naughty person, a wicked man, walketh with a froward mouth. He winketh with his eyes, he speaketh with his feet, he teacheth with his fingers; Frowardness is in his heart, he deviseth mischief continually; he soweth discord.

Proverbs 16:2, 3
All the ways of a man are clean in his own eyes; but the Lord weigheth the spirits. Commit thy works unto the Lord, and thy thoughts shall be established.

Proverbs 23:5, 26
Wilt thou set thine eyes upon that which is not? For riches certainly make themselves wings; they fly away as an eagle toward heaven. My son, give Me thine heart, and let thine eyes observe My ways.

DECEMBER 19

GATE OF HEAVEN

Some of us have a misconception about the "Gate of Heaven." You have even heard jokes about meeting St Peter at the gate of Heaven and how each of us will have to go before God someday - it is not a laughing matter. Only a few will enter in because *narrow is the way*. This is a very serious choice we must make here on earth, before we die. When God is ready to receive us, the Gate (*Jesus said, I am the door*) of Heaven will be opened to those who believe. Oh, glorious day! I'm going to meet my Savior, face to face. Then later, I want to meet St. Peter too.

Matthew 7:13, 14
Enter ye in at the strait gate: for wide is the gate, and broad is the way, that leadeth to destruction, and many there be which go in there at: Because strait is the gate, and <u>narrow is the way</u>, which leadeth unto life, and few there be that find it.

Psalms 118:19 – 21
Open to me the gates of righteousness: will go into them, and I will praise the Lord: This gate of the Lord, into which the righteous shall enter. I will praise Thee: for <u>Thou</u> hast heard me, and <u>art become my salvation</u>.

Luke 13:23 - 25
Then said one unto Him, Lord, are there few that be saved? And He said unto them, Strive to enter in at the strait gate: for many, I say unto you, will seek to enter in, and shall not be able. When once the master of the house is risen up, and hath shut to the door, and ye begin to stand without, and to knock at the door, saying, Lord, Lord, open unto us; and he shall answer and say unto you, I know you not whence ye are.

John 10:7
Then said Jesus unto them again, Verily, verily, I say unto you, I am the door of the sheep.

DECEMBER 20

DEEDS

Titus 3:5
Not by works of righteousness which we have done, but according to His mercy He saved us, by the washing of regeneration, and renewing of the Holy Ghost;

This verse provides the correct view of "Deeds." It is not what we have done for God or others that saves us, but what Christ has done for us. This fact and our love for Him motivates us to do good too, by following His example.

John 3:19 - 21
And this is the condemnation, that light is come into the world, and men loved darkness rather than light, because their deeds were evil. For every one that doeth evil hateth the light, neither cometh to the light, lest his deeds should be reproved. But he that doeth truth cometh to the light, that his deeds may be made manifest, that they are wrought in God.

Colossians 3:8 - 10
But now ye also put off all these; anger, wrath, malice, blasphemy, filthy communication out of your mouth. Lie not one to another, seeing that ye have put off the old man with his deeds; And have put on the new man, which is renewed in knowledge after the image of Him (God) that created Him (Jesus):

Jude 1:14 – 16a
Behold, the Lord cometh with ten thousands of His saints, To execute judgment upon all, and to convince all that are ungodly among them of all their ungodly deeds which they have ungodly committed, and of all their hard speeches which ungodly sinners have spoken against Him. These are murmurers, complainers, walking after their own lusts; and their mouth speaketh great swelling words . .

.

DECEMBER 21

DRAW CLOSER

It is our privilege and responsibility to desire to draw closer to God as much as He guides and allows us to be. Our will is so strong we often forget and go about the day doing just what we want to do. The hymn below gives us good reasons to draw closer.

"NEAR TO THE HEART OF GOD"
by Cleland. B. McAfee (1866-1944)

There is a place of quiet rest,
Near to the heart of God,
A place where sin cannot molest,
Near to the heart of God.

Chorus
O Jesus, blest Redeemer,
Sent from the heart of God,
Hold us who wait before Thee
Near to the heart of God.

There is a place of comfort sweet,
Near to the heart of God,
A place where we our Savior meet,
Near to the heart of God.

Chorus
O Jesus, blest Redeemer,
Sent from the heart of God,
Hold us who wait before Thee
Near to the heart of God.

There is a place of full release,
Near to the heart of God,
A place where all is joy and peace,
Near to the heart of God.

DECEMBER 22

BE STILL

Psalms 46:10a
Be still, and know that I am God:

Over the sink in our kitchen, this verse reminds me to keep calm and go at a slower-pace than whatever it is around me preventing me from knowing, "*He is God*"! Every day I see it, so I want to include it again this month, at the close of the year. For me, living a hectic lifestyle can shut out the voice of the Holy Spirit and makes me go my own way. We get so wrapped up with worldly demands, we can often forget God.

Job 3:25
For the thing which I greatly feared is come upon me, and that which I was afraid of is come unto me.

Job 37:14 - 18
Hearken unto this, O Job: stand still, and consider the wondrous works of God. Dost thou know when God disposed them, and caused the light of His cloud to shine? Dost thou know the balancings of the clouds, the wondrous works of Him which is perfect in knowledge? How thy garments are warm, when He quieteth the earth by the south wind? Hast thou with Him spread out the sky, which is strong, and as a molten looking glass?

Psalms 4:4
Stand in awe, and sin not: commune with your own heart upon your bed, and be still. Selah.

Isaiah 57:20, 21
But the wicked are like the troubled sea, when it cannot rest, whose waters cast up mire and dirt. There is no peace, saith my God, to the wicked.

DECEMBER 23

AVOID EVIL

The History of evil (sin) began way back to the Garden of Eden. God gave a great warning against it. The Psalms, Proverbs and Ecclesiastes, have much to teach us about what evil is. Some we know and still do, and some we need to open our eyes to, and be aware of. Notice even in Genesis, we want to throw the blame on someone else for our disobedience to God (Sin).

Genesis 2:16, 17
The Lord God commanded the man (Adam), saying, Of every tree of the garden thou mayest freely eat: But of <u>the tree of the knowledge of good and evil</u>, thou shalt not eat of it: for in the day that thou eatest thereof thou shalt surely die.

Genesis 3:12, 13
And the man said, <u>The woman</u> whom Thou gavest to be with me, she gave me of the tree, and I did eat. And the Lord God said unto the woman, What is this that thou hast done? And the woman said, <u>The serpent beguiled me</u>, and I did eat.

Ecclesiastes 5:2
Be not rash with thy mouth, and let not thine heart be hasty to utter anything before God: for God is in heaven, and thou upon earth: therefore let thy words be few.

Mark 7:20 - 23
And He (Jesus) said, That which cometh out of the man, that defileth the man. For from within, out of the heart of men, proceed evil thoughts, adulteries, fornications, murders, Thefts, covetousness, wickedness, deceit, lasciviousness, an evil eye, blasphemy, pride, foolishness: All these evil things come from within, and defile the man.

Proverbs 8:13
The fear of the Lord is to hate evil: pride, and arrogancy, and the evil way, and the froward mouth, do I hate.

DECEMBER 24

CHRISTMAS EVE!

Let us not forget the reason for the season. All our gifts are under the tree, and anticipation is everywhere. But, if all the trimmings are missing for one reason or another, we should still rejoice and be thankful for the greatest gift of all - the gift of love from God who sent His Son Jesus to give us hope and promise of new and everlasting life. To fully recall what a miracle Jesus' birth was, **read** Luke 2:1 - 21. To God be the Glory!

> *And it came to pass in those days, that there went out a decree from Caesar Augustus, that all the world should be taxed. (And this taxing was first made when Cyrenius was governor of Syria.) And all went to be taxed, every one into his own city. And Joseph also went up from Galilee, out of the city of Nazareth, into Judaea, unto the city of David, which is called Bethlehem; (because he was of the house and lineage of David:) To be taxed with Mary his espoused wife, being great with child. And so it was, that, while they were there, the days were accomplished that she should be delivered. And she brought forth her firstborn son, and wrapped Him in swaddling clothes, and laid Him in a manger; because there was no room for them in the inn. And there were in the same country shepherds abiding in the field, keeping watch over their flock by night. And, lo, the angel of the Lord came upon them, and the glory of the Lord shone round about them: and they were sore afraid. And the angel said unto them, Fear not: for, behold, I bring you good tidings of great joy, which shall be to all people. For unto you is born this day in the city of David a Saviour, which is Christ the Lord. And this shall be a sign unto you; Ye shall find the Babe wrapped in swaddling clothes, lying in a manger. And suddenly there was with the angel a multitude of the heavenly host praising God, and saying,*
>
> *Glory to God in the highest,*
> *and on earth peace, good will toward men.*

And it came to pass, as the angels were gone away from them into heaven, the shepherds said one to another, Let us now go even unto Bethlehem, and see this thing which is come to pass, which the Lord hath made known unto us. And they came with haste, and found Mary, and Joseph, and the Babe lying in a manger. And when they had seen it, they made known abroad the saying which was told them concerning this Child. And all they that heard it wondered at those things which were told them by the shepherds. But Mary kept all these things, and pondered them in her heart. And the shepherds returned, glorifying and praising God for all the things that they had heard and seen, as it was told unto them. And when eight days were accomplished for the circumcising of the Child, His name was called <u>Jesus</u>, which was so named of the angel before He was conceived in the womb.

DECEMBER 25

"JOY TO THE WORLD"
By Isaac Watts (1674-1748)

We can only imagine what the shepherds saw and heard that night, when the angels announced the birth of Jesus Christ to them in the sky. We do know however, they left all they had, and found where He laid. It had to be very exciting, and they must have been taught early in their life time, to look for the Messiah. Why else would they be so excited and look for Him?

JOY TO THE WORLD, the Lord is come!
Let earth receive her King:
Let every heart prepare Him room,
And Heaven and nature sing,
And Heaven and nature sing,
And Heaven, and Heaven And nature sing.

JOY TO THE WORLD, the Savior reigns!
Let all their songs employ;
While fields and floods, rocks, hills, and plains
Repeat the sounding joy,
Repeat the sounding joy,
Repeat, repeat, the sounding joy.

No more let sins and sorrows grow,
Nor thorns infest the ground;
He comes to make His blessings flow
Far as the curse is found,
Far as the curse is found,
Far as, far as, the curse is found.

He rules the world with truth and grace,
And makes the nations prove
The glories of His righteousness,
And wonders of His love, And wonders of His love,
And wonders, and wonders of His love.

DECEMBER 26

"AWAY IN A MANGER"

We celebrate Christmas because we want to honor the birth of Jesus Christ. Although we do not know on what date He was born, the whole world knows what CHRISTMAS means. Jesus Christ was born! So, let us remember: <u>The Reason for The Season!</u>

"AWAY IN A MANGER"
Source unknown, maybe by Martin Luther

Away in a manger, *no crib for a bed,*
The little Lord Jesus laid down His sweet head;
The stars in the sky looked down where He lay,
The little Lord Jesus, asleep on the hay.

The cattle are lowing, the Baby awakes,
But little Lord Jesus, no crying He makes;
I love Thee, Lord Jesus! Look down from the sky,
And stay by my cradle till morning is nigh.

Be near me, Lord Jesus, I ask Thee to stay
Close by me forever, and love me, I pray;
Bless all the dear children in Thy tender care,
And fit us for heaven, to live with Thee there.

DECEMBER 27

OUR ONLY HOPE
Our Redeemer, Savior

When I opened up my dictionary to the word redeemer, I was surprised to read the second listed meaning was just one word, **Christ**. Then under the word Redemption, Christ was also referred to as *"the salvation from sin through His sacrifice."* So true! Christ delivered us with His payment of death for our ransom: the payment for our sin. When you "redeem" something, you pay the required price.

Job 19:25 – 27
For I know that my Redeemer liveth, and that He shall stand at the latter day upon the earth: And though after my skin worms destroy this body, yet in my flesh shall I see God: Whom I shall see for myself, and mine eyes shall behold and not another; though my reins be consumed within me.

Psalms 24:5
He shall receive the blessing from the Lord, and righteousness from the God of his Salvation.

Luke 1:47
And my spirit hath rejoiced in God my Saviour.

Luke 2:11
For unto you is born this day in the city of David a Saviour, which is Christ the Lord.

II Timothy 1:10
But is now made manifest by the appearing of our Saviour Jesus Christ, Who hath abolished death, and hath brought life and immortality to light through the gospel:

I John 4:14
And we have seen and do testify that the Father sent the Son to be the Saviour of the world.

DECEMBER 28

AN OPENED BIBLE

The Bible is still the best seller, according to Brandon Gaille. He also stated on the Internet, "only one in three Bible owners know Jesus delivered the Sermon on the Mount. Billy Graham is the more popular answer than the correct answer." Additionally, a Gallup survey found less than 50% of Americans can name the first book of the Bible." If you have come this far this year, we have had "An Opened Bible" daily. If you are anything like me, we have developed a love for God's Word, and have learned many things.

Ephesians 2:1 – 5
And you hath He quickened (made alive), who were dead in trespasses and sins; Wherein in time past ye walked according to the course of this world, according to the prince of the power of the air, the spirit that now worketh in the children of disobedience: Among whom also we all had our conversation in times past in the lusts of our flesh, fulfilling the desires of the flesh and of the mind; and were by nature the children of wrath, even as others. But God, who is rich in mercy, for His great love wherewith He loved us, Even when we were dead in sins, hath quickened us together with Christ, (by grace ye are saved;)

Hebrews 4:12
For the Word of God is quick, and powerful, and sharper than any two-edged sword, piercing even to the dividing asunder of soul and spirit, and of the joints and marrow, and is a discerner of the thoughts and intents of the heart.

Psalms 119:11, 12, 89
Thy Word have I hid in mine heart, that I might not sin against Thee. Blessed art Thou, O Lord: teach me Thy statutes. For ever, O Lord, Thy Word is settled in heaven.

DECEMBER 29

"CHRIST RETURNETH!"
Our Blessed Hope!

<u>Titus 2:11 - 15</u>
For the grace of God that bringeth salvation hath appeared to all men, Teaching us that, denying ungodliness and worldly lusts, we should live soberly, righteously, and godly, in this present world; Looking for that <u>blessed hope</u>, and the <u>glorious appearing</u> of the great God and our Saviour Jesus Christ; Who gave Himself for us, that He might redeem us from all iniquity, and purify unto Himself a peculiar people, zealous of good works. These things speak, and exhort, and rebuke with all authority. Let no man despise thee.

"CHRIST RETURNETH!"
by H. L. Turner (19th century)

*It may be at morn, when the day is awaking,
When sunlight thru darkness and shadow is breaking,
That Jesus will come in the fullness of glory
To receive from the world His own.*

Chorus
*O Lord Jesus, how long, how long
Ere we shout the glad song —
Christ returneth! Hallelujah!
Halelujah! Amen, Hallelujah! Amen,*

*It may be at midday, it may be at twilight,
I may be, perchance, that the blackness of midnight
Will burst into light in the blaze of His glory,
When Jesus receives His own.*

*While hosts cry Hosanna, from heaven desending,
With glorified saints and the angels attending,
With grace on His brow,
Like a halo of glory,
Will Jesus receive His own*

*O joy! O delight! Should we go without dying,
No sickness, no sadness, no dread and no crying,
Caught up thru the clouds with our Lord into glory
When Jesus receives His own.*

DECEMBER 30

"FACE TO FACE"

Many times, I have wondered what it will be like to see Jesus someday. It is something we can't really imagine; but C. E. Breck (1855 – 1934) tried to put it into words with insight, helping us visualize it while we are still here on earth.

"FACE TO FACE"
by Carrie E. Breck (1855-1934)

Face to face with Christ, my Savior,
Face to face – what will it be?
When with rapture I behold Him,
Jesus Christ who died for me.

Chorus
Face to face I shall behold Him,
Far beyond the starry sky;
Face to face, in all His glory,
I shall see Him by and by!

Only faintly now I see Him,
With the darkling veil between;
But a blessed day is coming,
When His glory shall be seen.

What rejoicing in His presence,
When are banished grief and pain.
When the crooked ways are straightened,
And the dark things shall be plain.

Face to face – O blissful moment!
Face to face – to see and know;
Face to face with my Redeemer,
Jesus Christ who loves me so!

I Corinthians 13:12a
For now we see through a glass, darkly; but then <u>face to face</u>:

DECEMBER 31

WE SHALL SEE HIM

We will see Jesus some day and it may be sooner than we think! O be ready!
The words of this hymn, **WHEN WE ALL GET TO HEAVEN,** will put our minds at ease as we think about Christ's coming for His own. Look up and anticipate it. Watch and wait for that glorious day!

"WHEN WE ALL GET TO HEAVEN"
Eliza E. Hewitt (1851-1920)

Sing the wondrous love of Jesus,
Sing His mercy and His grace;
In the mansions, bright and blessed
He'll prepare for us a place

<u>Chorus</u>
When we all get to heaven,
What a day of rejoicing that will be!
When we all see Jesus,
We'll sing and shout the victory.

While we walk the pilgrim pathway
Clouds will over-spread the sky;
But when trav-'ling days are over
Not a shadow, not a sigh.

Let us then be true and faithful,
Trusting, serving ev'ry day;
Just one glimpse of Him in glory
Will the toils of life repay.

Onward to the prize before us!
Soon His beauty we'll behold;
Soon the pearly gates will open –
We shall tread the streets of gold.

THE GOSPEL
OUR CONCLUSION and HOPE

I John 3:1 - 3
Behold, what manner of love the Father hath bestowed upon us, that we should be called the sons of God: therefore the world knoweth us not, because it knew Him not. Beloved, now are we the sons of God, and it doth not yet appear what we shall be: but we know that, when He (Jesus Christ) shall appear, we shall be like Him; for we shall see Him as He is. And every man that hath this <u>hope</u> in him purifieth himself, even as He is pure.

Revelation 1:7, 8
Behold, He cometh with clouds; and every eye shall see Him, and they also which pierced Him: and all kindreds of the earth shall wail because of Him. Even so, Amen.
I am Alpha and Omega, the beginning and the ending, saith the Lord, which is, and which was, and which is to come, the Almighty.

www.ingramcontent.com/pod-product-compliance
Lightning Source LLC
Chambersburg PA
CBHW071554080526
44588CB00010B/904